'Everyone talks about being custon... ... ...
Customer Copernicus explains why, based on real-world examples. It has
practical guidance on how to do better. If you're saying you want to
be a customer-led success, read this. It will help.'

Peter Duffy, CEO Moneysupermarket Group

'Business leaders often say "we are customer focused" and the words
sound good. But how often are they true? Like the great astrono-
mer Copernicus, The Customer Copernicus is a different way of looking
at the world showing what "customer focus" really means. Fact-
based, opinionated, challenging and ultimately inspiring, Dawson
and Meehan explain how "outside-in" beliefs can transform an ailing
business into a financial success and an innovator making life better
for its customers. If you have time for only one business book this
year, this would be the one.'

Gavin Esler, award winning television and radio
broadcaster, novelist and journalist

'Charlie Dawson and Seán Meehan explain very vividly what it takes
to transform an organisation towards a customer centricity and how
to avoid falling back into old habits. The different case studies are
brilliant examples of how companies can achieve a sustainable shift
towards an outside-in customer-led organisation and that all starts
with a strong belief to do the right thing for its customers. Especially
in today's time, this book is a great reminder and a demonstration
that organisations will only deliver superior business results in the
long term if they put the customer needs at the centre of their marketing activities.'

Rolf Fallegger, Member of Group Management and Head of
Marketing, Lindt & Sprüngli

'The most inspiring and impressive entrepreneurs and founders I
know believe unconditionally in putting customers and the frontline
first. The Customer Copernicus is really refreshing and hugely important,
especially today – it ought to be on the desk of every CEO!'

Kim Fausing, President and CEO, Danfoss

'Customer-centric systems and behaviours are the key to success. But if it's that obvious why is it so hard to do ... and harder yet to sustain? Dawson and Meehan take this puzzling conundrum and propose well thought out and actionable solutions. A must read for business leaders navigating today's markets.'

Dan Futter, *Chief Commercial Officer,*
The Dow Chemical Company

'Outside-in thinking with the customer at the centre, sustained by many Moments of Belief, has been critical to DBS' evolution. *The Customer Copernicus* will put you on this path.'

Piyush Gupta, CEO DBS

'CEOs never fail to say that the customer is the heart of their business – and some might even believe it – but they seldom do what it takes to make it a reality. This book lifts the veil. It shows what customer focus actually means, how companies put it into practice, and how they keep it alive amid all the vicissitudes of business life. This book helps companies to survive.'

Anthony Hilton, *author, broadcaster*
and award winning journalist

'The definitive book on how to build, nurture, and *sustain* a customer-led organisation. Dawson and Meehan show how firms through shared beliefs, systems, processes, and engrained customer obsession make it "how things are *always* done around here."'

Bernie Jaworski, *Peter F. Drucker Chair in Management and the*
Liberal Arts, Drucker School of Management

'At Tesco in thirty years we went from a 10% to a 30% market share. We did it by becoming more and more customer focused. Seán and Charlie have worked hard to find out how it was done by Tesco and many other businesses besides. Lots to learn here.'

Tim Mason, *CEO, Eagle Eye and former*
Deputy CEO, Tesco

'For those who want to turn the prevailing "inside-out" view in companies to "outside-in" and ensure long-term success.'

Paul Polman, *co-founder, Imagine*
and former CEO, Unilever

'Putting customers first is simple to say but hard to do. Using real-world stories, *The Customer Copernicus* shows why and what it takes to succeed. These ideas would be useful to anyone looking to run a more successful, more sustainable business.'

David Potts, *CEO, Morrisons*

'Customers are the lifeblood of any healthy business. *The Customer Copernicus* explains how and why they need to be at the centre of our thinking and why this is much more difficult than it may seem.'

Woods Staton, *Executive Chairman, Arcos Dorados*

'*The Customer Copernicus* produces the answer to a pertinent question – if the customer at the centre of business thinking is such simple common sense, why do most organisations find it so difficult?'

Sir John Timpson, *Chairman, Timpson*

THE CUSTOMER COPERNICUS

Some companies are great for customers – not only do they care but they change whole markets to work better for the customers they serve. Think of Amazon, easyJet and Sky. They make things easier and improve what really matters – obvious, surely? They have also enjoyed huge business success, growing and making plenty of money.

The Customer Copernicus answers the question that follows – if it's obvious and attractive why is it so rare? And then it answers a second question, because Tesco, O2 and Wells Fargo were like this once. Why, having mastered it, would you ever stop? Because all three did, and two ended up in court.

The Customer Copernicus explains how to become and how to stay customer-led. It directly addresses the customer-led reality gap – the profusion of claims to put customers first versus the paucity of real examples.

The crucial element explaining it all is belief – people's shared beliefs about what matters inside an organisation. Natural beliefs are inside-out, company first. Customer-led beliefs are outside-in and not natural at all. The ONLY way to become and stay outside-in is through Moments of Belief – bold, costly and risky customer-led actions.

You can learn from leaders of some of the most customer-led organisations in the world, now and in the past, from successes and failures. These include Tesco, easyJet, DBS, Sky, Handelsbanken, Pepsico and O2 with 18 different businesses from around the world across many sectors covered with substance. You will get insight into what really matters and why – people's shared beliefs about success – and how to change those beliefs to become truly customer-led and successful.

The book is practical, colourful and down to earth while answering a crucial question for our age. It is essential reading for leaders and teams who want their organisations to stay competitive by developing a more purposeful and innovative culture.

Charlie Dawson is the founder of The Foundation, a London-based consultancy that helps organisations create customer-led success.

Seán Meehan is the Martin Hilti Professor of Marketing and Change Management at IMD Business School, Lausanne, Switzerland.

THE CUSTOMER COPERNICUS

How to be Customer-Led

*Charlie Dawson
and Seán Meehan*

Routledge
Taylor & Francis Group

LONDON AND NEW YORK

First published 2021
by Routledge
2 Park Square, Milton Park, Abingdon, Oxon OX14 4RN

and by Routledge
605 Third Avenue, New York, NY 10158

Routledge is an imprint of the Taylor & Francis Group, an informa business

British Library Cataloguing-in-Publication Data
A catalogue record for this book is available from the British Library

Library of Congress Cataloging-in-Publication Data
Names: Dawson, Charlie, 1966-author. | Meehan, Seán, author.
Title: The customer copernicus: how to be customer led/Charlie Dawson
    and Seán Meehan.
Description: Abingdon, Oxon; New York, NY: Routledge, 2021. | Includes
    bibliographical references and index.
Identifiers: LCCN 2020050954 (print) | LCCN 2020050955 (ebook) |
    ISBN 9780367539191 (hardback) | ISBN 9780367564636 (paperback) |
    ISBN 9781003097877 (ebook)
Subjects: LCSH: Customer relations. | Corporate culture.
Classification: LCC HF5415.5 .D386 2021 (print) | LCC HF5415.5 (ebook) |
    DDC 658.8/12–dc23
LC record available at https://lccn.loc.gov/2020050954
LC ebook record available at https://lccn.loc.gov/2020050955

ISBN: 978-0-367-53919-1 (hbk)
ISBN: 978-0-367-56463-6 (pbk)
ISBN: 978-1-003-09787-7 (ebk)

Typeset in Joanna MT Std
by Deanta Global Publishing Services, Chennai, India

To Nicola — Charlie

To Gill — Seán

CONTENTS

About the authors   xiii
Acknowledgements   xv

Introduction: Why should I believe you?   1

1   Why customer-led beliefs matter   16
Tesco: Propelled and derailed by its beliefs   16
From trader to retailer to leader   20
A confident leader comes crashing back to earth   26
Sustaining an outside-in orbit over time   29
Conclusion and recap   32

2   What being customer-led looks like   36
Walkers: The characteristics of a customer-led organisation   36
Using all the elements for success   42
Six activities fuelled by the outside-in leadership approach   48
Customer-led leadership   56
Conclusion and recap   63

3   What being customer-led feels like   66
Sky: Believe in better   66
Shared beliefs: The way we do things around here   70
Specific belief systems: Inside-out and outside-in   74

From a wing and a prayer to Sky's the limit   76
The lesson: Believe in better   85
The contrast of an inside-out belief system   88
The unnatural outside-in success of Zalando   92
Tell-tale signs of outside-in versus inside-out
    belief systems   96
Conclusion and recap   98

4   Creating customer-led beliefs   **104**
easyJet: The airline that moved from inside-out to outside-in   104
Moving from inside-out to outside-in in four stages   107
The remarkable turnaround of easyJet   110
Exploring burningness at DBS   120
Exploring Moments of Belief at AO   123
Exploring systematic ways of working outside-in at Deliveroo   127
Conclusion and recap   131

5   Losing customer-led beliefs   **136**
O2: From outside-in to inside-out   136
The inevitability of falling from outside-in to inside-out   137
From remarkable customer leadership to conventional
    utility at O2   140
The challenge of internal forces at Virgin Atlantic   150
The challenge of external forces at Market Basket   157
The challenge of a competing rule changer at Nokia   162
Conclusion and recap   167

6   Protecting customer-led beliefs   **172**
Handelsbanken: Sustaining outside-in beliefs   172
How to sustain an outside-in belief system:
    Three critical elements   179
Knowing a belief system really matters at John Lewis
    Partnership and W.L. Gore   185
A continual flow of Moments of Belief at Hilti   193
Being boldest when challenged most: LEGO   197
Conclusion and recap   201

Conclusion: Believe in better   **206**

Index   213

ABOUT THE AUTHORS

Charlie Dawson is the founder of The Foundation (www.the-foundation
.com), a consultancy set up in 1999 to help organisations be more successful by being customer, not financially led, creating value for customers as
the first priority but also for the business, so commercial success is decisive
and sustained.

The growth of The Foundation has been a journey of learning, working
out what it takes to put customer-led ideas into practice in the real world –
something that sounds obvious but is elusively difficult.

At its simplest, organisations find being customer-led hard because people naturally see the world from the inside-out. The Foundation's approach
helps teams see, experience and believe in success that is inherently outside-in. In this way clients are helped to solve their trickiest growth challenges. To achieve this has meant bringing together skills usually found
separately, in particular customer and business understanding. It has also
meant translating intent into action, motivating change and inspiring high
performance using similar human insight within a business to that used to
understand customers externally.

Charlie was originally inspired by working on a new car company launch
that did this by happy accident to great effect, and it was in discussing the
story with the MBA class at London Business School that Charlie and Seán
first met – Seán was doing his PhD there at the time.

The Foundation has long relationships with HSBC, Visa, M&S and the Volkswagen Group, and recent projects include helping Jaguar Land Rover keep more customers, helping Morrisons find ways to differentiate and compete strongly in future including developing a strong and authentic purpose, helping eBay get better at creating trust and helping John Lewis find a future in Home Services as a customer-led business.

He previously worked in advertising and has a First Class degree in Manufacturing Engineering from Cambridge.

Seán Meehan is the Martin Hilti Professor of Marketing and Change Management at IMD, Lausanne, Switzerland. Upon completing his PhD at London Business School in 1997 he joined IMD where he has designed and led executive development programmes focused on developing 'outside-in' leaders, and has held several leadership positions. He commenced his career with Arthur Andersen & Co. serving clients in Oil and Gas, Media, Retail and Financial Services. He is a Certified Public Accountant and was a Director of Marketing at Deloitte.

He is a board member of CEEMAN (the Central and Eastern European Management Schools Association) and advises a number of CEOs on strategy, transformation, customer-centricity and succession.

His passion is customer centricity and it follows that his research interests encompass the nature and effectiveness of customer value creation and change management practices. In addition to developing case materials, he has published his work in, among other publications, *Harvard Business Review, MIT Sloan Management Review, Business Strategy Review, strategy+business, Marketing Research, Marketing Science Institute Reports*, the *Financial Times* and the *Wall Street Journal*. He has received many awards for his research including the Marketing Science Institute's Alden G. Clayton award, The Academy of Marketing's Houghton Mifflin award, the CEEMAN Research Champion award and scholarships from the Economic & Social Research Council and London Business School. He is co-author of *Simply Better: Winning and Keeping Customers by Delivering What Matters Most* (Harvard Business School Press, 2005) which was named 'Marketing Book of the Year' by the American Marketing Association. This was followed by *Beyond the Familiar: Long Term Growth through Customer Focus and Innovation* (Jossey Bass, 2011).

ACKNOWLEDGEMENTS

Writing this book has been a long old journey. A labour of love, to different degrees at different times across the seven years it took to write it, which would never have been possible without inspiration, encouragement and help from many friends and colleagues. We can only mention a few here.

The Customer Copernicus stands on the shoulders of many progressive contributors to the field of management practice in relation to the customer. These include George Day, Peter Drucker, Roger Martin, Chris Zook and James Allen.

We were fortunate we could explore and test our ideas with a range of people at seminars, forums, roundtables and meetings. We are grateful to those who shared their experiences and learning as they lived with the challenges and rewards of becoming and staying customer-led. These included: Mark Attan, Gill Barr, John Browett, Andy Brown, Andy Caddy, Gordon Campbell-Gray, Deborah Corless, Filip Dames, Peter Duffy, Joe Ferry, Vernon Everitt, Richard Gillies, Martin Glenn, Nick Green, Lewis Grundy, Elaine Grix, Guoy Hamilton-Fisher, Patrick Lewis, Dame Carolyn McCall, Lisa McDowell, Lord (Ian) MacLaurin, Graham McWilliam, James Millet, Alan Penlington, Jørgen Gylling Poulsen, John Roberts, Stephen Robertson, David Robey, Pernille Sahl Taylor, Mikael Sørensen and Sir John Timpson. Helping us to explore further and make sense of our data along the way have been many insightful researchers from the IMD Information Centre, as well as Karine Avagyan and Alice Meehan.

The Foundation advisory board members Anthony Hilton, Cath Keers, Tim Mason, Sigurd Reinton and Richard Rivers provided robust challenge and great insight as we began to formulate our ideas. As they developed, we discussed them with, and got additional input from, Patrick Barwise, Goutam Challagalla, Gill Ereaut, Charles Handy, Tim Mason (again, in a lot of depth), Anand Narasimhan, Robin Pharoah, Frazer Smith (who shared with us the idea of 'burningness') and Peter Yorke.

We owe special thanks to Simon Caulkin who read an early draft and put us back on track, to Elen Lewis who wrestled with our ideas and helped us get them down and express them clearly, as well as to Bernie Jaworski, Gareth Jones, Adam Morgan, Chris Styles and Ramiro Villagra who provided critical review of our later work.

Our colleagues at IMD, Dominique Turpin, Jean-Francois Manzoni, Delia Fischer, Lucy Jay-Kennedy, Beverley Lennox, Lindsay McTeague, Vincenzo Palatella and Sally Peck, and The Foundation Partners past and present, particularly Anna Miley, John Sills and Charlie Sim currently and James Alexander, Terry Corby, Nick Cross and Tim Sefton from the past: they have all supported this project and helped shape our story using, among other tools, encouragement, patience and good humour.

Thanks to Rebecca Marsh, Senior Editor at Routledge for her belief in our project, and to Sophie Peoples, Editorial Assistant, as well as Tom Bedford and Catherine Scarratt for their expert support. We have been accompanied on the final lap by the talented Elizabeth Baldwin, helping us see how to take the ideas in the book out into the world.

On the home front, with yet more patience and yet more encouragement plus tolerance of weekend working and much besides, partners and children who grew up in the time this took to get written: Charlie's wife Nicola plus Gina, Josh and Millie, and Seán's wife Gill along with Alice and Emma.

If you got this far then we should also thank you. You are, after all, the customer (quite a committed one in fact given the length of what's above). As we go on to say at great length, without you this would be a pointless exercise.

INTRODUCTION

WHY SHOULD I BELIEVE YOU?

There are many ways to center a business. You can be competitor focused, you can be product focused, you can be technology focused, you can be business model focused, and there are more. But in my view, obsessive customer focus is by far the most protective of Day 1 vitality.

Jeff Bezos, CEO, Amazon
Letter to Shareholders, April 2017[1]

Earning lifelong relationships, one customer at a time, is fundamental to achieving our vision.

John Stumpf, Chairman and CEO, Wells Fargo
Letter to Shareholders, February 2016[2]

While the words sound the same, the realities are very different. In his April 2017 letter to shareholders, Bezos conveys a vivid picture of what being customer-led looks like and what it takes. Stumpf, in his 2016 letter, also says all the right things: 'We are on our customer's side.' And, for a casual observer at the time, this might have suggested Wells Fargo was as customer-led as Amazon.

Yet eight months later, in October 2016, Stumpf was forced to resign in the wake of a scandal revealing the bank had opened as many as 2 million accounts without the knowledge or approval of its customers, unfairly taking advantage of customer relationships to meet sales targets. Whatever he said or thought, the reality on the ground was the antithesis of being on the customer's side.

What leaders say (and perhaps think) their company does and what it *actually* does can often be at odds. There is a saying/doing gap. We shouldn't take customer-first exaltations at face value. They are common. But true customer-led success is not.

To understand what we mean, we need to get beyond soundbites and into reality. Timpson, a family-owned UK retail business that has experienced significant ups and downs since its launch in 1865, has become a shining example of customer-led success in the last two decades.

Crucially, Timpson is also a commercial success, growing from 300 branches, 970 colleagues, £40 million in sales and £3.3 million in profit in 1998 to 2,120 branches, 5,800 colleagues, £330 million in sales and £30 million in profit by 2018.

The work Timpson employees do is far from glamorous. Timpson's core offer is in shoe repairs and key cutting. They also mend locks. And the group has grown into dry cleaning and photographic printing, not industries others are rushing into.

Timpson's breakthrough into customer-led thinking followed a tough spell in the 1970s and '80s when the business, having been sold to a plc, was led based on targets. If a target was missed one week, then it was adjusted the next, usually by putting up prices a little to make the number appear possible while all else remained the same. Most times, this meant the situation got worse. In John Timpson's (now chairman) view, it was missing the point of the business. So, in 1983, he with the backing of Candover, a venture capitalist, bought back the shoe sales and repair businesses – the original core of the family business. They were tough times. He thought he might lose it all and be the family member who failed to keep Timpson afloat after over 120 years of trading. Facing falling sales, he sold the shoe shop business and was left with just shoe repairs. Shoe repairing was a declining market and competition was intense – anyone could fix shoes from a small space on the high street.

Gradually a way of running the company came together, built by paying attention to one shop at a time, looking at what worked and encouraging it to spread. Cutting keys emerged as a strong complementary offer – when they put keys in the window, stores sold more.

But the key to the business's exceptional customer-led growth was less literal – it was John Timpson's realisation that success depended on the way they served their customers. The people working at the front-of-house counter and the relationships they built fed the shoe repair and key-cutting business.

The next realisation was that Timpson could make this customer service exceptional. In 1998, the business made a decisive change and introduced 'upside-down management,' which it borrowed from Nordstrom. This meant the business had to do three things:

1. Find exceptional, friendly people to work in its stores.
2. Give them complete freedom to do what they feel is right for customers.
3. Support them in every possible way so they can be at their best.

These words are easy to say but acting on them goes against all sorts of conventional business wisdom. How did Timpson make such an unlikely recipe work so well across a national business?

The critical component in being customer-led is a shared, explicit, unambiguous belief that creating customer value in new and better ways is the guiding principle that defines 'the way we do things around here.' This is what we call an outside-in belief system – one that takes a perspective that starts outside the business – with customers – and looks back in to work out how the business might respond. As Zook and Allen explain in *The Founder's Mentality*, this is not uncommon among early stage companies. Incredibly focused, they behave as insurgents, leading the charge on an industry on behalf of customers, minimising bureaucracy, obsessing about customers and making sure the front line has every possible support to serve them in new and better ways.[3]

The corollary is inside-out, starting with you and what matters to your business then pushing it onto the outside world. Inside-out perspectives are common; outside-in perspectives and beliefs are, unsurprisingly, rare. 'Unsurprisingly' because it is clear the dominant paradigm has been that of the 'shareholder first.' Ever since Jensen and Meckling's much cited rebuke of managerial capitalism and promotion of shareholder value capitalism, the latter has, with rare exceptions, driven managerial decision-making and shareholder short-termism.[4]

The Business Roundtable (which represents 181 CEOs of some of the largest companies in the US) had been a prominent and explicit advocate of the shareholder-first approach. However, in 2019, in calling for a more inclusive approach, it acknowledged the negative societal impact of shareholder-first thinking and to considerable fanfare advocated a multistakeholder approach: deliver value to customers, invest in employees, deal fairly and ethically with suppliers, support the community and generate long-term value for shareholders.

> Each of our stakeholders is essential. We commit to delivering value for them, for the future success of our companies, our communities and our country.[5]

While all stakeholders are self-evidently essential and committing to delivering value for all of them is laudable, this is rather ambiguous and, therefore, problematic guidance. Being customer-led is about putting customers first – not first among equals. It's not a new idea – Drucker argued for it in 1954. Roger Martin similarly pointed out the futility of seeking multiple objectives simultaneously and argued persuasively for the primacy of customers among other stakeholders. His elegant recommendation:

> ... companies should seek to maximize customer satisfaction while ensuring that shareholders earn an acceptable risk-adjusted return on their equity.[6]

Notwithstanding the prominent and credible advocacy of the Business Roundtable, its collective belief in a multi-stakeholder approach is likely to take time to become the norm, if indeed it gains traction at all. Drucker and Martin's ideas have had plenty of time – since 1954 in Drucker's case – so greater advocacy and something to trigger a breakthrough are likely to be needed for such beliefs to become mainstream. Everyday horror stories of poor customer experiences, as well as too many examples of some managers' downright unacceptable means of prioritising shareholder returns over delivering on customer commitments, means they have yet to catch on.

Whereas today we take the solar system as a given, Nicolaus Copernicus' thesis that the Earth and the other planets orbited the Sun rather than it all being centred on the Earth was met with incredulity. It went against not just popular belief but also the Church. Such was the scale of this issue that he diplomatically dedicated the book he had written to set out his ideas – *De revolutionibus orbium coelestium* – to Pope Paul III, and he also added a note that acknowledged the book's theory was unusual and proposed that if it helped astronomers with their calculations, then it perhaps did not matter whether the theory behind it was really true.

When and whether a customer-led, outside-in belief system will ever decisively replace the prevailing inside-out shareholder-first set of beliefs is impossible to know. Our aim though in publishing *The Customer Copernicus* is to support this movement, embracing this Copernican shift and taking the conversation up another step. We want to show how to create a truly customer-led business, a business that sees the customer as central and itself on the periphery from the customer's perspective. We explain why this is a good perspective to hold, what the pitfalls are with adopting it and how to avoid them.

Creating and maintaining outside-in beliefs is a significant challenge because the default is the opposite – to be guided by what we call inside-out beliefs. Inside-out beliefs mean putting the classic metrics like sales growth, market share and profitability of the business first, prioritising hitting sales targets and obsessing over short-term profitability as the driving motivation.

We have learned that the ONLY thing that changes a business from being inside-out to outside-in is a succession of what we call 'Moments of Belief.' These are specific, bold, customer-led initiatives or decisions that on the surface look costly and risky. The expenditure needed is clear, the value to the customer is clear, but the immediate benefit to the business is not. In many conventional businesses to press ahead would appear naively optimistic. It turns out, however, that when the initiative is taken, it benefits the business significantly too. It signals to the organisation that this kind of action can work well commercially, well enough to sustain a healthy business, and that 'this is the way we do things around here,' this is what we believe, this is crucially what customer-led success looks like.

Timpson has just such a succession of Moments of Belief – tangible ways of doing things that challenge conventional wisdom and yet work very well, both for customers and the business. For example, the price list is only treated as a guide and branch colleagues are encouraged to give discounts if they think it is the right thing to do. There is no national direction on what is promoted and how it is displayed. These are up to each local Timpson team. Gouy Hamilton-Fisher, Timpson's director for colleagues and support, described a recent store visit led by a temporary 'mobile manager' as the store manager was on holiday. A customer came in with a locket to be engraved. The £30 estimate was more than she could pay, so she thanked the man and turned to walk out. Gouy stopped her and asked her what she wanted to pay. '£10–£15,' she said. He looked to the manager, who offered to engrave her locket for £12.50, much to the customer's delight. Everyone in store has the power to make choices in areas that most businesses simply wouldn't allow.

Chairman John Timpson and chief executive James Timpson (his son) try to visit at least 15 stores every week, and such visits are part of the routine of all management colleagues. Gouy revealed that a recent store visit didn't feel right, so they asked the area manager an open question to find out what was going on. It turned out the local store manager was going through a divorce. 'I'll get up there,' said the area manager. Gouy reckons more than half of Timpson's job is social work, offering interest-free loans if colleagues get in trouble with money, time off to sort things out at home, or the chance to apply for a fund to realise a long-held dream.

We interpret the steady flow of Moments of Belief in Timpson's as a testament to how well outside-in beliefs are embedded. To be customer-led, care needs to be given to the people and their beliefs as well as the systems and processes that are more visible.

Darren Brown, an area manager at Timpson, told us how deeply the beliefs are embedded. 'The beliefs are strongly held – if you have the right people as colleagues, great at customer care and they feel fully supported and are given freedom, then it all works.' Another area manager, Kyle Ballard, helped us appreciate why this is so critical. 'We work hard to recruit the right people. In photographic developing, it can be hard to say 'the customer is always right' – sometimes they make mistakes. But our job even then is to make them feel like they are right. So, we recruit for personality.'[7]

And beyond such Moments of Belief, there are unusual and tangible ways Timpson operates, an important part of the system that shows everyone 'this is how we do things around here.' For example:

- Timpson's unusual recruitment policy does not rely on formal tests, panels and CVs. Applicants need only supply a name and phone number. Then it's about getting a sense of the applicants – the look in their eyes, the readiness of their smiles, whether they are driven and ambitious in some way so they have energy. People rated as a 9/10 or 10/10 will be offered a position. It's an informal scale that measures friendliness, positivity and warmth. The belief is that Timpson lives or dies by having truly Timpson people who can (and must) be given full freedom and authority.
- There are just two rules for people working in stores: look the part and be 100% honest. Everything else is flexible. Timpson name badges are designed to encourage everyone to talk regardless of hierarchy. They bear the person's first name, when they joined and an outside interest or hobby.
- Every store colleague has a £500 allowance to spend on their own initiative to settle a complaint. Requests by nervous area managers to be consulted before a pay-out is made are firmly discouraged as undermining the potential for providing memorable service.
- The only formal review process is the April Happy Index. One sheet of paper is given to everyone in the business. They are asked to rate the support from their area manager on a scale of 1 to 10. Most areas get close to a 100% feedback from stores, with ratings for every area manager. Many get 10/10 from everyone they work with, but this process can also spell the end of some area managers' careers with Timpson.
- Since there are no conventional sales targets for keys cut or shoes repaired, people are rewarded for a job well done in a customer-centric rather than sales-centric way with a simple weekly bonus shared between the people in the store. The weekly target is 4.5 times the wages paid out in that shop during that particular week. Colleagues share 15% of all sales above the target. This gives everyone involved immediate feedback on how they are doing.

According to area manager Sid Hubbard:

> Too good to be true? Sounds like it, but it is true. Timpson knows that how the front line takes care of customers every day is what matters, so they go beyond the normal in supporting the team and giving them freedom.[8]

Getting to this point has been a relentless battle. John Timpson describes a 'strong rubber band pulling us to be like everyone else. People joining from the outside don't understand that we give total freedom to the people who serve the customers and that they are not allowed to issue orders. They have to work out how to look after the team to help them be the best they can.' According to Janet Leighton who has the uncommon title of director of happiness and whose role is to 'push the culture,' this is now the established and well-shared belief and practice.[9]

We will return to all these themes later, but our overall aim is to explain why this is all so much harder than it looks.

In fact, *The Customer Copernicus* sets out to answer two connected questions:

1. Given that customer-led success can be extremely rewarding AND tends to look obvious in case studies, why is it so rarely achieved?
2. And once a company does manage this unusual feat, why doesn't the success last forever?

This is an area where it is easy to talk at cross-purposes. When we say 'customer-led' we don't mean just asking customers what they want and then doing it. That's not what Timpson does. Or Amazon. We mean understanding what customers value – the problems they are really trying to solve or the outcomes they want – and then finding new and better ways to create this value, solve their problems or achieve the results they want. It looks like leading in a market, not following, like inventing, not benchmarking, and it creates tremendous value in all sorts of ways.

When companies do this well, their customers do well – they, or we, get a better quality of life, better solutions, lower costs of all kinds – financial but also effort, time, emotional pain, attention and so on. Think Deliveroo versus a traditional takeaway or Sky against a handful of broadcast channels. It's not just the customers that benefit; the companies do well too – reaping significant and lucrative rewards. Customer-led success can be extreme, e.g. catapulting O2 from laggard to market leadership in telecoms, tripling easyJet's profits in the competitive airline business, taking Tesco from third in the UK retail supermarket league to third in the world.

So, it's obvious, it's valuable, it's talked about by everyone and yet ...

We have been working in this field, wrestling with this question, for more than 20 years. But in the process of writing this book, we realised that what goes on in organisations that's visible is not the full story, just as symptoms do not always easily reveal their cause. When we are in a social environment like a workplace, we are guided by an invisible hand – the shared beliefs of the group, or the *discourse*, to give it its anthropologically more accurate name. What do people believe success looks like? How do people believe success is achieved? Two questions that are answered not by asking but by observing, i.e. finding clues in how people speak, what gets their time, how offices are arranged, what earns a pat on the back and what gets ignored. This all resides in the organisational subconscious and yet, as anyone who has worked in an organisation for any time realises, we all feel the forces at work, we formulate beliefs about what is valued, and critically, we find ways to fit in. We recognise and live the shared beliefs of the organisation. Then, on top of this recognition, we saw two competing belief systems that are pivotal to answering our questions about the rarity and fleetingness of success – inside-out beliefs and outside-in beliefs.

Looking inside-out is natural – you sit every day inside the organisation with your colleagues close, customers distant, and you make assumptions about the way things are done that don't get challenged. This is not customer-led.

Looking outside-in is not natural. In fact, it's downright odd. It means finding ways to stand in the shoes of customers, seeing the bigger picture of their problems and all of the solutions – not just competing ranges of supermarket ready meals, but alternatives including going out to eat or ordering a takeaway or having a snack and using the money to go to the cinema. And then it means being utterly determined to find new and better solutions, unlimited by preconceptions of a defined market and the obvious competition.

It's unnatural for other reasons too, reasons we will explore in depth. But before we explain, let us share some evidence we have gathered to show what's being described here is real.

We asked over 400 CEOs and executive team members of large companies how they viewed the drivers of performance in their companies.[10] We first asked them to name the top three contributors to performance from a list of 12 factors that were suggested to us during in-depth interviews with 50 executives.[11] Four were mentioned significantly more than the others – customer understanding and response, people, operational excellence and innovation (see Figure I.1).

Further, the most common combination of three priorities were customer understanding and response, operational excellence and people (47 respondents reported this combination).

However, our survey suggests that while people say being customer-led is important, few make it happen. In practice, customers lose out to other more influential stakeholder groups and other priorities. While 62% of businesses claim being customer-led is one of the main drivers of their success, our data suggests only 24% behave in accordance with this belief and as a result enjoy superior results. Many who claim they are acting in a customer-led way are, in reality, making different choices and doing different things. There is a saying/doing gap. The bottom line is that executives

Importance of factors contributing to competitive performance

Figure I.1 Performance drivers: Espoused beliefs. (Source: Charlie Dawson, Seán Meehan & Karine Avagyan. 2017. *The Belief Trade-Off: Customers or Efficiency First?* Lausanne: IMD Business School.) https://www.imd.org/contentassets/ e60e4c757a6e49ddbf86daa6302f9348/imd_article_thebelieftradeoff_ v2.pdf

frequently say (and often believe) they are customer-led when in fact they are not.

With further modelling[12] it became clear that executives pursue one of two overall approaches, or sets of beliefs, in their quest for competitive superiority – an efficiency approach or a customer value approach.

The analysis also showed that only the customer-value approach is positively associated with superior competitive performance. So, this reinforces the need to understand what's going on – being customer-led seems to make things better for businesses, not just for the customers they serve.

These models also showed ways in which customer-led companies are different. They have an employee focus on customer-value creation, have a shared understanding of their key customers, make an effort to satisfy clearly identified customer segments, are good at bringing customer propositions to the market, and they have a high level of employee engagement. Crucially, and maybe less intuitively, they are also 'focused on the numbers.'

The group believing in the efficiency route to success, while still declaring customers to be one of their top three priorities, did not experience superior business performance.

Being customer-led is rewarding, it delivers results for all kinds of companies from all kinds of industries – from retail to telecoms, financial services and media – and because it is far from commonplace, it represents an opportunity. It is interesting because it runs against the natural order of things, and it is truly challenging to implement and – as Zook and Allen explain – sustain against the inevitable pressures that come with success. The erosion of the insurgent beliefs – Zook and Allen's equivalent of our outside-in beliefs – is what usually follows.[13]

To help management teams understand the challenge of becoming customer-led and to help them take concrete steps to transform their businesses, The Customer Copernicus is organised around insights derived from our decades of practice and research in this area.

Chapter 1 explains why being customer-led *matters* by telling a story about the whole customer-led journey through the example of Tesco, from being inside-out to achieving rare success by becoming resolutely customer-led and outside-in through a series of Moments of Belief. It shows how this leads to growth in a core market, broadens to new markets, then eventually to a natural weakening of customer-led resolve and the loss of outside-in conviction as other stakeholders become more influential. There is a painful return to the more common inside-out belief system alongside a decline in business and customer success. We then outline our proposition and introduce our framework.

Chapter 2 reviews what good looks like – the visible, crucial activities and leadership style of a customer-led business. There are six activities that especially matter – making clear choices about which customers to serve and which needs to meet, developing guiding insights that give the business an edge, creating innovative propositions, empowering colleagues, using approaches that encourage rapid learning, and having a customer-planning process. The leadership style that works has three components: being genuinely outward-looking, being clearly committed to the customer internally and being assertive externally and, therefore, prepared to lead in the market. Although this kind of formula is well established, leadership teams generally struggle to embrace the complete set.

In Chapter 3, we describe what good feels like. The importance and power of the prevailing shared beliefs is recognised and the way they guide everyday behaviour and critical decision-making, providing a lens through which colleagues in a business make sense of the world around them. Recognised in anthropology, the study of group human behaviour – and, as already mentioned, more formally labelled discourse – includes not only the language but also the range of other observable manifestations of deeper, unspoken, shared assumptions about the way the world works, what success is and how success is achieved.

Having highlighted the pivotal role of shared beliefs, we explore how organisations create these beliefs in the first place in Chapter 4. We show how they can be changed from the conventional inside-out to the remarkable outside-in. We argue that having an outside-in belief system is rare because it is unnatural and very hard to create. This would explain why so many who profess to be or intend to be customer-led never achieve it. We observe that efforts are frustrated if they don't break free from the strong gravitational forces relentlessly pulling mature organisations back to the more natural inside-out belief system. They are missing an essential ingredient, a kind of rocket fuel providing thrust and momentum – Moments of Belief, which are customer-led actions or initiatives that are good for customers but risky for the business. When they work, they show people across the organisation, for real, that customer-led success can be achieved. When people *en masse* see the results in their own organisations, they start to believe that being customer-led 'might just work around here.' Repeated Moments of Belief solidify the belief that this is what we are all about, this is what we must do more of to really succeed. Simple, but not easy ...

In Chapter 5, we explore the inevitability of *losing* customer-led beliefs. Why, even when a business has transitioned into a customer-led success, it remains unnatural and therefore difficult to sustain over the long term. We show how time extracts a price by diminishing the strength of belief in the group of individuals who first established it, and how the people who joined in the formative years come to take it for granted. We also show how growth brings increasing complexity, scale and distance from the world outside. These forces, akin to a kind of organisational gravity, continually pull the belief system back down to earth. Without a special kind of defence, the business eventually reverts to the more natural inside-out way of working. Often this descent is painful — a crash landing rather than a gentle touchdown. Only deliberate action to nurture shared outside-in beliefs will keep you aloft, something even more unusual than the actions that fostered the outside-in-ness in the first place.

In Chapter 6, we show how you can *protect* these customer-led beliefs. What's needed are three things. First, paying attention to your belief system, an unusual activity in most organisations where it is mostly unspoken; second, ensuring Moments of Belief flow continually to show everyone what matters around here is just as unusual as it's always been; and third, being boldest when challenged most, protecting the trailblazing customer-led ethos, not the business model that expressed it but which is now challenged. In these ways, despite being unnatural, the North Star of the customer stays front and centre, and the business continues creating customer value in new and better ways to attract, retain and grow the value of its customer relationships.

In our Conclusion, we provide more insight into why this is so difficult, and why so few organisations sustain a successful customer-led approach in the long run. The problem is that inconvenient actions, like challenging your own business model because a better alternative is emerging, are painful. To become customer-led in the first place, to take action that is outside-in and therefore risky, requires a pre-condition, one we call 'burningness.' This emerges from one of three things —

pain, fear or ambition. The first is unarguable because something is going wrong now (the burning platform). The second is less effective as a stimulus because the temptation is to wait and see (maybe the worst won't happen). The third is least common because it requires having so much ambition that you're prepared to risk the current, perfectly adequate status quo to pursue it. Once you have become a customer-led success, you're not in pain. You have to summon up from within yourself the ambition, or maybe amplify a distant fear, to the degree needed to continue to pull up trees on behalf of the customer. Tough.

In summary, this book explains why so much hot air is wasted eulogising customers to so little effect. It seeks to demystify 'customer-centricity.' It illustrates why so many companies have not backed up their words with effective action in their pursuit of customer-led success. It describes what it takes to become a genuine customer champion and how to sustain it.

Above all it challenges you to ask, 'what do I truly believe success is, and how do I believe that success can be achieved?' The question everyone else will rightly ask, why should we believe you?

Notes

1   www.sec.gov/Archives/edgar/data/1018724/000119312517120198/d37336
    8dex991.htm

2   www08.wellsfargomedia.com/assets/pdf/about/investor-relations/annual
    -reports/2015-annual-report.pdf

3   Zook, Chris & James Allen. 2016. *The Founder's Mentality: How to Overcome the Predictable Crises of Growth*. Boston, MA: Harvard Business Review Press.

4   Jensen, Michael C. & William H. Meckling. 1976. 'The Theory of the Firm: Managerial Behavior, Agency Costs and Ownership Structure.' *Journal of Financial Economics*, 3 (4): 305–360.

5   Business Roundtable. 19 August 2019. 'Business Roundtable Redefines the Purpose of a Corporation to Promote "An Economy That Serves All Americans"' Business Roundtable. Retrieved from www.businessrou ndtable.org/business-roundtable-redefines-the-purpose-of-a-corporation -to-promote-an-economy-that-serves-all-americans

6   Martin, Roger. 2010. 'The Age of Customer Capitalism.' *Harvard Business Review*, 88 (1): 58–65.

7   Interview with authors, 9 and 12 December 2019.

8   Interview with authors, 9 December 2019.

9   Interview with authors, 10 December 2019.

10 The survey was sent to 8,000 IMD alumni and other executives from over 4,500 companies in 134 countries in late 2016. The 454 respondents (a response rate of 5.7%) comprise CEOs (41%) and executives with responsibility for business development (11.5%), marketing (10.5%), finance (8.5%), HR (5%), production (4.5%) and 'other' (19%).

11 We conducted in-depth interviews with a convenience sample of 50 senior executives exploring how customers are treated as stakeholders in their companies.

12 We examined more closely whether and how beliefs drive business performance, using structural equation models (SEM). The best-fitting model included two latent variables (we labelled them as Efficiency Lever and Customer Value Lever), which were negatively correlated. Only the Customer Value Lever had direct positive effect on Performance.

13 Zook, Chris & James Allen. 2016. *The Founder's Mentality.*

1

WHY CUSTOMER-LED BELIEFS MATTER

The purpose of business is to create a customer.

Peter Drucker

Tesco: Propelled and derailed by its beliefs

The remarkable rise of a British retailer, which began life as a market stall in East London and went on to become a bank, a mobile phone network, the recipient of £1 for every £7 spent on the British high street and the third largest retailer in the world, is a story of why customer-led beliefs matter. Tesco's growth story takes us on two decades of expansion, from the 1980s to the 2000s, powered by courage and a belief that doing the right thing for customers was also the right thing for the business. And like all the best stories, there is a narrative arc, a struggle and a stumble as Tesco falls from its dizzying heights.

A significant step in Tesco's journey happened in 1992, when the retailer faced a crisis of confidence. In a drooping economy and under fierce competition from new discounters Aldi and Lidl, the supermarket was struggling to fulfil a long-held ambition to overtake Sainsbury's.

Terry Leahy, Tesco's first marketing director and subsequently chief executive from 1997–2011, went on the offensive. He declared that they were not being bold enough:

> Successful companies do not just focus on what customers want but put the customer at the centre of all they do. The customer should drive the entire business. We ... were not thinking as customers.[1]

On the back of the biggest piece of consumer research in its history, Tesco learned that supermarket customers were broadly happy with products and prices, but they didn't care much for the experience of shopping. If Tesco could do something about the shopping experience, it would finally be in a position to take the initiative over its rivals. Customers were telling Tesco how to overtake Sainsbury's.

Leahy launched a package of measures, the so-called 'bricks in the wall,' to address 200 issues that customers had told researchers they had with the supermarket experience. The bricks were swiftly assembled. The first was Tesco's Value Lines range, a couple of hundred Tesco-branded products that were cheaper than Aldi. In stores, a programme of 'new look refits' addressed a whole collection of bricks in one makeover, all improving aspects of the customer's shopping experience. One of the biggest, and something customers disliked most, was queuing. A new approach was developed that became the 'One-in-Front' initiative, eventually introduced in 1994. Tesco's promise was that if any line had more than two customers waiting, an extra checkout would be opened. They would keep on opening checkouts until the queues subsided or until every till was manned. The costs would be significant – an estimated £60 million in a year when Tesco reported pre-tax profits of £528 million.[2] But what about the benefits? Would customers come more often, spend more per visit, or just smile and do exactly as they had before, providing no return on the investment? For a while the senior management team hesitated, unable to agree whether this was a good decision.

While the debate was still being had, the board learned that Sainsbury's was also poised for a big launch. Faced with the prospect of being trumped by its arch-rival, and gnawed by the burning desire to win, the board's insistence on a better business case evaporated. Within a week, Tesco committed the funds, bought the media and publicly announced the One-in-Front initiative for the following Sunday.

One-in-Front was what we call a Moment of Belief – a commitment to a customer-led innovation that unmistakably signalled to the organisation the leadership's belief that being customer-led results in business success. Illustrating to the organisation what it meant to 'think as a customer,' it was a turning point. Tesco was leading, not following.

Like most customer-led initiatives, One-in-Front put customers first, even though it might be costly for the business, at least in the short term. Yes, it was clear that customers didn't like queuing. It was also clear that it would cost the business £60 million a year to fund. What was not clear in advance was precisely what customers would do in response. It took a degree of conviction, of belief, to incur the cost of a customer-led initiative such as One-in-Front because there was no guarantee of a financial return.

Belief determines whether a customer-led action gets taken – belief in it being the right thing for the business to do, and belief that over time it will deliver a measurable return on investment for the business as a result.

Tesco came to embody what it means to be customer-led – understanding what customers value and finding new and better ways to create it, looking from the outside-in, not from the inside-out. Building on the success of One-in-Front, Tesco's subsequent customer-led moves propelled it from a poorly placed number three in UK food retailing in 1982 with a 12% market share to the undisputed leader with a 33% UK share and third in the world in 2012. By then, Tesco was a grocer, a general merchandiser, a mobile phone network, a bank and more. It operated in 13 countries and generated profits of £3.8 billion on revenues of £72 billion. It was all the more shocking, then, when after more than 30 years of uninterrupted growth, the Tesco success story abruptly ended.

In 2014, Tesco reported its first profit decline in 20 years, an unprecedented 3.7% reverse in like-for-like sales in the first quarter, two profit warnings, an admission that it had overstated half-year profits by £250 million, and later that it had suspended four senior UK executives. The loss that year amounted to £6.4 billion pre-tax, one of the largest in UK corporate history.

Tesco's rise and fall illuminates what's at the heart of our story – by creating customer value and allowing business value to follow, a company can achieve exceptional and sustained profitable growth. But this way of operating is harder to sustain than it is to achieve in the first place.

The burning desire that leads a business to become customer-led, to take the first risky steps through the early Moments of Belief, is hard to maintain after a decade or more of success. When a competitor arrives from an unexpected angle, creating value for customers in new and better ways, are the incumbent leaders still curious enough, hungry enough, and brave enough to challenge what works? If they listen more to other stakeholders – easy to do when you're now a hero – it is terribly difficult to spot cracks emerging in your business's competitive edge. This is like a gradual and imperceptible force pulling an organisation back to earth, back to being inside-out and, like gravity, it is irresistible in the absence of countermeasures.

As a result, despite seeming obvious, and despite being valuable for customers and businesses alike, this outside-in way of working is unnatural.

What it means to be customer-led and why it matters

A customer-led organisation is one that **understands what customers value** – the problems they are really looking to solve or the outcomes they want, not necessarily the product or service they are buying – **and creates this value in new and better ways** – they innovate based on what matters to customers, not just what's established as the competitive battleground in the market.

It matters because we are describing an organisation that succeeds by doing a fundamentally better job for customers. It means the enterprise takes its lead from customers and then trailblazes on their behalf. As a result, more customers are attracted, more return, and over time each one on average buys more. It matters because it's good for business.

Yet, as we saw with Wells Fargo, there is often a disconnect between the degree to which businesses believe they are in touch with customers and their customers' experiences in reality. A study from IBM and Econsultancy revealed that while the majority of leaders 'strongly agree' they are providing a superior customer experience offline, online and on mobile, only one in three customers believe their favourite brands understand them.[3]

The 'customer first' literature has influenced the climate for what is said. But it has not penetrated far into what is done. This disconnect is exacerbated by the tension faced by many business leaders in their desire to listen to all stakeholders. Executives are acutely aware that their performance is judged by a range of audiences – shareholders, customers, employees, suppliers, regulators, local communities and society. These stakeholders comprise the ecosystem within which a corporate strategy is implemented and in different ways they legitimise the activities of the corporation. Executives go to great lengths to ensure all are aware of their efforts to address each of their interests – but there is no doubt that over time shareholders have become the dominant stakeholder.[4,5] To keep shareholders happy on a quarter-by-quarter basis, the natural way of thinking has to be inside-out – targets to hit and a push to hit them repeatedly.

We also believe that some stakeholders are more important than others. But our position is in line with Peter Drucker who argued that success starts with and is led by the customer. The broad thrust of Drucker's argument is that all value in a business ultimately flows from attracting and retaining customers, so customer-value creation should be central to all activities.[6]

This sounds dull and familiar. But our position, in a crowded field of executives claiming the same thing is that very few do it – very few companies are truly customer-led.

From trader to retailer to leader

Tesco's unlikely origin was as a market stall selling war-surplus groceries like golden syrup and fish stock in London's East End at the end of the First World War. It opened its first store in 1931, went public in 1947, then over the next three decades enjoyed success driven by the opportunism and entrepreneurial flair of founder Jack Cohen and his handpicked team of hard-driving store managers. The business reflected this – it was a highly successful, decentralised retailer with a motley collection of 800 stores.

Ian MacLaurin, Tesco's first external CEO, was ambitious and began whipping the company into a shape where it could measure itself against 'real' retailers such as Marks & Spencer and Sainsbury's, the choice of the middle classes. At that time, they were in a different league to the scrappy upstart.

Tesco made a lot of progress through the late 1970s and 1980s by benchmarking Sainsbury's, closing the gap between the two. Operation Checkout in 1977 was an almost overnight refit and rebranding of the Tesco estate, improving products, reducing prices and exercising control. It was financed by scrapping Green Shield Stamps, a loyalty scheme dear to Cohen's heart, but by that time, less valued by customers. A huge success, Operation

Checkout laid the groundwork for a series of mutually reinforcing reforms, anchored in the recruitment of a cadre of bright young executives, among them Terry Leahy and Tim Mason, who, as 'the class of '82,' would embody the ambitions of the new upwardly mobile Tesco. Half the existing stores were judged sub-standard and closed. MacLaurin instituted weekly store visits for the board, followed by discussing what had been seen and tweaking strategy accordingly.

The rule of thumb for decisions became 'better, simpler, cheaper' – shorthand for better for customers, simpler for staff, or cheaper for Tesco – and it always had to be at least one of the first two, never just 'cheaper for Tesco.' From 1987 to 1990, Tesco's turnover rose 50%, profitability doubled, the operating margin touched 6% and floor space grew by 10% a year.

Tesco's Moments of Belief fuel growth

Clubcard and Tesco.com were particularly important Moments of Belief for Tesco, the former paving the way for entry into financial services. Conceived as a way of thanking existing customers for their loyalty, Clubcard encouraged them to spend more and brought in a flood of new shoppers (no fewer than 20 million in 2001 alone). The payoff from the hefty upfront investment of £100 million, though, came not from the promotional incentives, but indirectly from the customer insights that the card data yielded. The value was clear from the very first pilot, when dunnhumby's Clive Humby walked the Tesco board through 16 different shopping baskets showing the 16 segments of Tesco shoppers identified in their data. At the end of the presentation, there was a deathly hush until MacLaurin broke the silence with words that have gone down in the company's history:

> I've learned more about my customers in the last 30 minutes than I have in the last 30 years.[7]

The customer insights drawn from Clubcard gave rise to a stream of further innovations and Moments of Belief, including a new approach to segmentation with Tesco's Finest launched to sit alongside its standard and Value own brands. It was clear from the data that there was a significant group of existing customers that visited Waitrose and M&S for special treats and were prepared to pay more for premium products. Tesco's Finest brand was introduced in 1998 and by 2009 it was bigger than Coca-Cola in terms of UK sales.[8]

Another Moment of Belief came with Tesco's ethnic food range, World Foods. Its launch emerged through an analysis of Clubcard data from a store in a British town with a large proportion of ethnic minorities, which showed many shoppers weren't buying the expected staples from Tesco; instead, they were purchasing large sacks of rice and loose bunches of herbs from local markets. Tesco built a superstore in the area in 2005, which offered 800 different products designed to appeal to specific minority ethnic groups, up from 150 in the previous store. It had a halal butcher and newspapers in Arabic, Urdu, Punjabi and Bengali. Subsequent analysis revealed that not only had the target group's share of spend increased, but also the upscale white shoppers accounted for a quarter of the store's World Food sales.[9] By creating something of value for its ethnic shoppers, Tesco had also created value for other customers and for the business.

Clubcard created a more systematic way to be customer-led, ensuring the retailer stayed rooted to the idea of creating value for customers first. Other Moments of Belief and innovations flowing from Clubcard's insights included 24-hour opening, the Healthy Living range, Organics and 'Free-From' – a range free from allergens such as gluten and wheat. When 'Free-From' first launched with high expectations in 2003, initial sales were disappointing. However, an analysis of Clubcard customer data revealed that the pioneering range was attracting new shoppers into Tesco and that they bought a great deal more than just the Free-From range. The business case was not product-led – predicated on just the sales of the Free-From products – it was customer-led based on the benefits of attracting more customers and their spend across all categories.

As this demonstrates, being customer-led isn't simply about being nice to customers – it's about making the business tangibly better for customers. This is why being customer-led matters. As CEO Sir Terry Leahy put it:

> What creates loyalty is how much we understand your life and what we do about it that helps your life. You could just use the data to make customers do what you want them to do, and use it as a tool to sell more things to them. We never wanted to do that. Our competitors had all the details of what their customers bought too, but if you don't have the vision as a retailer that you are doing this to understand customers better, and deepen that relationship, you're always going to wonder why you're making the effort.[10]

The 1996 launch of Tesco.com, the group's online shopping service, was another important Moment of Belief. Obvious as it seems now, at that time, computers were bulky, slow and expensive and only a minority of UK households possessed one. But Tesco went for it in a big way, choosing to distribute from stores with staff picking products from the same shelves as customers rather than building dedicated and more efficient internet shopping warehouses. Tesco.com became another giant success, the group's online presence sealing its surge to industry leadership. Leahy and Mason, at launch deputy chief executive and marketing director respectively, had no doubts from the start:

> The idea was utterly compelling to us ... we had no choice but to do all we could to make it possible, to overcome the well-known obstacles and make a profitable business. [It would] make life easier for customers.[11]

Tesco.com wasn't just a way for customers to shop online. It was a way to pay £5 to save hours each week driving to a store, walking around the physical shop, selecting each item, putting it in a trolley, unloading it at the checkout, re-packing it, paying and driving home. Thanks to Clubcard, even the very first time a Tesco shopper used the online service it had their weekly shopping list, making it swift to get what was needed. Such a dramatic benefit meant it was an excellent way for Tesco to secure an even greater share of these shoppers' spend.

Tesco moved fast because it saw these benefits and felt a burning desire to be first. Its approach – picking from stores – meant it could expand to cover the country at pace.

By the late 1990s, Leahy and Mason had graduated to the C-suite, with MacLaurin as chairman, and together they set about deepening, broadening and internationalising the business and the outside-in culture that had led to its success.

To succeed, the leadership would have to find ways to spread true customer-led belief. Beyond the signals of Moments of Belief, they went about this by explicitly and repeatedly articulating the business's values, which were unusually expressed as short sentences – 'No one tries harder for customers,' and 'Treat people as you want to be treated.' This was done in workshops, presentations and frequently in conversations of all kinds throughout the 14 years of Leahy's tenure as CEO.

Tesco also developed its own version of Kaplan and Norton's balanced scorecard as an organisation-wide 'steering wheel' to ensure that the customer remained first among equals in terms of management priorities, with a dedicated customer plan and customer key performance indicators (KPIs), such as whether customers could get what they want or how long they had to queue, with performance tracked and reviewed accordingly. Further, to ensure managers experienced the implications of their decisions on the shop floor, every year 3,000 of them spent a week at the front end, serving customers, filling shelves, working in the store's back office and manning customer-service desks.

Top management knew that what makes all the difference to the outlook of 'head office' people is first-hand human experience – 'immersion' in the outside world, standing in customers' shoes, looking back in. When business leaders speak directly to customers and learn viscerally what they really think and feel, they 'get it' – they are decisively reminded what really matters to their customers and why. They see with fresh eyes where their firm, products and services come in the complex hierarchy of the customer's life (low down!).

With culture and management systems aligned behind the customer, Tesco was confident it could apply the same principles to domains beyond food. Financial services would be a natural starting point. The company could apply useful insights from Clubcard and offer a credit card that provided many of the same benefits but taken further. Tesco Personal Finance, complete with the Tesco credit card, was launched in 1997, initially as a joint venture with the Royal Bank of Scotland.

Tesco subsequently secured a banking licence in its own right; by 2020 Tesco Bank had 5.3 million customer accounts with over £7.7 billion in savings accounts.[12] Another notable success has been Tesco Mobile run in partnership with O2, a telco that has its own customer-led story to tell, one that we'll be exploring further in Chapter 5.

The outside-in perspective is an uncommon way to see the world

What we are describing through Tesco's story is an uncommon way to see the world. Being customer-led is about outside-in beliefs, and these beliefs are not natural. The typical perspective is shaped by colleagues who are distant from customers, limited by assumptions that what's sold is what customers want, constrained because these views are hardly ever challenged. This is an inside-out perspective, and it is the prevalent view. It stands in contrast to being customer-led.

At an individual level, it can be difficult to think outside-in, but it's not because the information isn't available – there is usually far more customer insight, market analysis, trend forecasting and the like than anyone in an organisation can deal with. The problem is that the information doesn't have the impact it needs to prompt uncomfortable or inconvenient decisions.

At an organisational level, it is harder still. Shared inside-out beliefs are often 'obvious.' You want to sell more? Set higher sales targets, reward people generously for hitting them, shout at them if they don't (or worse, as in the infamous case of Wells Fargo). The thing is it works ... for a while. Until the pushing from the business starts to lose alignment with customer demand. That's where scandals come from; mis-selling, misleading, high pressure sales and, taken to extremes, the destruction of business trust and collapse.

Outside-in beliefs on the other hand are unnatural and uncommon in business. Outside-in ideas are clearly valuable to the customer, but while the costs to the business are certain, the benefits are not, and the costs tend to be immediate with the business benefits coming further down the line.

As we've already shown, while many companies believe they are customer-led, their actions say otherwise. What people believe collectively about the nature of business success and the way it is achieved is the nub of the issue. The shared but unspoken beliefs across a group determine how they act at every level from top to bottom, from the vastness of international supply chains to how salespeople interact with customers and everyday conversations over a cup of coffee.

There are also visible cultural cues, but an organisation's overt character and purpose, why it says it exists and how it says it behaves, its stated purpose, values, vision, brand promises and the like, are often not what tells you what is truly believed.

The shared beliefs of the organisation, its discourse, are the truest reflection of 'what really matters around here.' Moments of Belief like Tesco's One-in-Front demonstrate for real that an outside-in approach to business is being taken and works.

A confident leader comes crashing back to earth

Tesco's growth was also international, and for a long while, this seemed destined to be the biggest success of all. By 2008, Tesco was trading successfully in 12 countries, stretching from central Europe to Asia (including China), using the Tesco values and customer-led approach as the basis for the businesses, whatever its customer-facing brand. At its peak, International was contributing 19% of group revenues and accounting for half of all sales and profit growth. However, the US, graveyard of so many UK retail expansions, was slow to warm to Tesco's approach and the timing was not good for the launch of its Fresh & Easy US brand. Fortunes were changing.

Tesco thought hard about the US. The top team was aware of the scale of the challenge. But they felt there was an opportunity to apply skills learned in the heat of the ultra-competitive UK market, especially in making fresh food widely available and accessibly priced. Tesco's Fresh & Easy launched in November 2007, and the firm invested rapidly in growing store numbers because the model used off-site fresh food preparation facilities that only worked if they ran at scale. This commitment to early growth before real-world testing was unusual for Tesco. When Tim Mason, after a hectic first month overseeing the launch, was due to discuss it on prime-time TV, Morgan Stanley announced a $3 billion loss. The TV slot was taken away as the business found itself dealing with the consequences of the global financial crisis. With losses mounting, unnerved shareholders demanded more focus on Tesco's core but weakening UK business.

In the UK, Tesco was being challenged by Aldi and Lidl, the same discounters who had given them cause for concern in the early 1990s. When you have 33% market share, any significant new competitive growth is going to hurt. Would Tesco see it early and respond with something that was better for customers? That would be the customer-led way, but by this point, the senior team was not in touch with the day-to-day reality of customers and had a great deal else on its plate.

As the clouds gathered, and after a skiing accident that took a toll on his health, Leahy (now Sir Terry) stood down as CEO in 2011, saying that he had achieved his two big ambitions: to make Tesco the UK's largest supermarket chain and to take the business overseas. He declared himself satisfied that the firm's purpose and values had become 'a firm reality' that would '... sustain Tesco through its challenges and encourage and grow future leaders.'[13]

The markets were not convinced. On the day of the announcement, the company lost 2.4% of its market value. Tesco had become a large, complex organisation that was heavily reliant on its home market to finance its franchise development. In the face of the ferocious price competition, like-for-like domestic sales were on a downward trend, slowed only by increasingly generous, targeted Clubcard offers and funding from suppliers. To begin with, these actions closed a small gap between expectations and actual performance, but what started as small became bigger each quarter, and before long the business was pushing like hell to make the numbers. That's the characteristic of an inside-out business.

In pursuit of fresh momentum, Philip Clarke, Leahy's successor as CEO, announced a £1 billion UK store makeover in October 2012, coupled with the training and deployment of extra staff. But these investments coincided with difficulties in the international business. Group profits dropped by 12%. Within a year, the group had lost more than 50% of its market capitalisation in the most turbulent period in Tesco's history. From Leahy's departure to the end of 2013, as Clarke asserted his control, the business lost seven of its nine executive board directors with a total of more than 150 years of Tesco experience (and a great deal of shared belief in the way the business succeeded). As part of this swathe of cuts, Fresh & Easy filed for Chapter 11 bankruptcy in the US in October 2013, and Tesco abandoned its efforts to extend its out-of-town hypermarket estate in the UK.

By July 2014, as trading worsened, Tesco was losing 1 million customer visits a week. After a second profit warning and with his turnaround plan in tatters, Clarke's own 40-year career at Tesco came to an abrupt end.

Commentators blamed Leahy's overconfidence and Clarke's slowness to react. They argued that problems overseas, especially in the US and China, demanded a faster and more decisive response. In the same way, the challenge to the UK core business represented by Aldi and Lidl should have been more effectively addressed.[14] Perhaps most damning was the observation that Tesco's purpose and values had been abandoned. One journalist reported:

> It became a bit arrogant about its position, lost its customer focus
> and stopped innovating ... the company became too focused on profit

and stopped investing in stores and customer service. This lack of investment became all too obvious on the shop floor.[15]

As well as culminating in the largest ever loss by a UK publicly traded company, Tesco, over the course of its fall, lost two-thirds of its market capitalisation.

However, by September 2018, after a period of significantly restructuring its core business – UK grocery – Tesco had stabilised, remaining as market leader, albeit with a reduced 27.4% market share, compared to Sainsbury's 15.4% and Asda's 15.3%,[16] and reporting positive sales and profit growth arising from strengthening shopper preference. So, what happened? Was Tesco's crash inevitable? What if anything could have kept the business on track, true to its beliefs, leading in its markets on behalf of its customers?

The lesson is that if the customer-led rise is tough, avoiding the fall is tougher. To characterise Tesco's fall as attributable to managerial hubris is flawed, or at least simplistic. Tesco's rise and fall shows that even when outside-in beliefs are well-established, they are never secure.

What made Tesco a disproportionate success was its transformation from being run in an inside-out way, like most businesses, to growing the shared belief that it could achieve what it really wanted by thinking and working outside-in. Tesco created new and better ways of solving customers' problems and giving them what they wanted through spotting opportunities and understanding what customers valued.

With success, maintaining these unusual, shared outside-in beliefs becomes increasingly difficult, even more difficult than it was to create them in the first place. There are so many more people, so much dilution of the original team that learned first-hand, so many distractions that draw attention away from what matters outside to focus on what's closer to hand.

Just as Moments of Belief gave Tesco's people the boldness to put customer value ahead of the existing business model in ways that were difficult to justify, so we observe a gravitational force gradually pulling people back to hitting the numbers over leading for customers, relying on rather than challenging the existing business model. The alarming thing is that this is totally natural.

In a company's early days entrepreneurs and their customers are usually well-aligned. They look at the world and the market from the perspective of their customers; in these early days, outside-in Copernican beliefs, thoughts and actions are a natural consequence of this immersion. Founders typically split the bulk of their time and energy between product development and marketing. They are close to their customers and acutely aware of their needs and wants, what alternatives exist and how to develop something where every detail matters.

With success and time, senior executives can find it increasingly difficult to stay on course. They gradually move from insurgent to incumbent, from nothing to lose to having much to protect.[17,18]

Like gravity being stronger on a large planet such as the earth compared to a small entity like the moon, the increasing size of the successful company draws management more strongly inwards, towards the centre and away from the everyday concerns of serving customers. This is the natural arc of a company – being pulled back down to earth after achieving extraordinary success – and we will explore it further in Chapter 5 when we analyse the fortunes of O2, Nokia, Market Basket and Virgin Atlantic.

Sustaining an outside-in orbit over time

Like an athlete in top form or an artist 'in the flow,' for a company, being customer-led is intensely rewarding. But it is very unusual. Some companies get to be customer-led for a while (as we shall see from Handelsbanken in Chapter 6); some never get there at all.[19] Tesco maintained its outside-in orbit for three decades – a remarkable feat. Yet, it eventually succumbed to the pull of inside-out gravity; under competing pressures, the clarity of the outside-in vision was compromised and blurred. Shareholders' interests usurped those of customers and normality reasserted itself. Short-term, self-referenced urgency won out over customer focus. Tesco eventually lost its resistance to the gravitational forces all businesses must contend with, the forces that customer-led businesses escape and then resist week in, week out, unless or until they can do so no longer.

As GE's former CEO, the late Jack Welch, memorably put it, 'Hierarchy in most organisations means everyone has their face toward the CEO and their ass toward the customer.'[20]

As we illustrate in Figure 1.1, very few leadership teams break out from this gravitational pull. If they are to manage to develop the shared

An analogy is useful in understanding this unequal struggle. Imagine the business is a planet and customers are floating in space, free to make choices between alternative offers from different planets or businesses. The people who serve customers are on the surface of the planet, in touch with customers, but the leaders are buried right at the core. They literally look at the world from the inside outwards, with the customer view obscured by layers of people, departments, issues and the like.

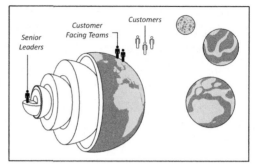

Then add the idea of gravity – the bigger the organisation gets the stronger gravity pulls leaders in, keeping them anchored to their internal perspectives.

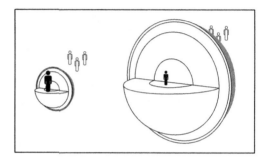

Escaping from the company's pull, lifting off from the planet is hard. It needs rocket fuel and a multi-stage rocket – successive Moments of Belief – to get to escape velocity and up into an outside-in orbit.

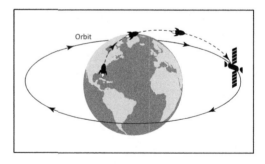

Figure 1.1 The battle to escape the gravity of inside-out beliefs

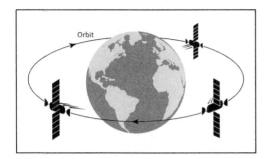

And having got there, staying there, maintaining orbit, is just as hard. The gravitational pull continues, relentlessly pulling the leaders down, and unless they actively resist – more rocket bursts, more Moments of Belief – then they will lose momentum ...

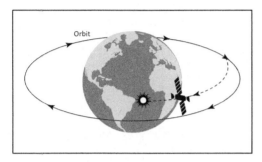

... start to fall from orbit and eventually crash back down to earth. They become inside-out again, often with a bump. This is the natural arc of a customer-led company.

Figure 1.1 Continued

beliefs that the world works the other way around, starting from where their customers stand, from the outside in, then they need exceptional circumstances:

- **Burningness** – an unusual word we use to describe the sense that something is burning, be it feelings of pain, fear or ambition (in descending order of effectiveness). Whichever it is it needs to be strong enough to make continuing with business as usual simply unacceptable. An example is Tesco's visceral, uncompromising ambition, their urge to catch up with and overtake Sainsbury's.
- **An outside-in instinct** to look beyond the market to customers to see what needs fixing on their behalf, finding inspiration in what is usually seen as impossible. For example, Tesco's customer research that revealed 200 issues customers had with their shopping experience.
- **A first Moment of Belief** to turn burningness into a bold step forward, a market-leading offer that creates value for customers in new and better ways, and that in time is shown to bring reward back to the business as well – customer-led actions tend to have costs now and benefits

later. For example, Tesco's Moment of Belief, the One-in-Front queuing initiative.

- **A succession of Moments of Belief** that follow the first success with a second and a third, until the stream of successful customer-led actions coalesces into a shared conviction that the organisation exists for customers first and succeeds by putting customers first. The pattern is established.

- **Making outside-in activities systematic**, establishing organisation-wide mechanisms for reinforcing the shared beliefs by constantly showing colleagues what matters to customers, where there are gaps and opportunities, how to go after them and then making it easy to respond in a distributed, widespread way.

When this has worked, when the business has escaped gravity and achieved an outside-in orbit, the pull of normality remains, unrelenting, trying to draw the organisation back to earth. Like a planet, the larger a business becomes – a natural corollary of success – the stronger the gravitational pull inwards. Eventually, over many years, it overwhelms resistance at least in most cases, and the outside-in belief system comes crashing back down. The battle to stay aloft is sometimes longer and sometimes shorter. And there are cases where after several decades it is still being won, with Handelsbanken and W.L. Gore being two examples that we will explore in detail later in the book. But they remain exceptions to the rule and they fight continually to protect their shared outside-in beliefs.

Conclusion and recap

Terry Leahy didn't change his view on the importance of shoppers and improving their lives; rather, he and those around him lost touch with their realities, both the way customers saw the world and the alternatives they were being offered. The discourse changed. Decision-making remained assertive and committed, but he and his successor made calls in the latter years that ultimately destroyed shopper and shareholder value. In earlier times, Leahy learned that being assertive and committed were what made Tesco's ideas fly – new formats, Clubcard, internet shopping and more. Now these habits led to mistakes and blindness to feedback from colleagues who were closer to the customer truth.

At Tesco, the actions and decisions remained those of an assertive and committed leadership, but their effectiveness diminished because the leaders' focus had gradually changed from outside to inside. Like a satellite that achieves escape velocity to go into orbit around a planet, a business can propel itself into taking an outside-in perspective. But as the years go by, momentum fades and gravity brings the satellite, or the company's belief system, right back down to earth.

Customer-led businesses always start with the customer. It means they take an unnatural, outside-in perspective and their beliefs are fuelled by a series of trailblazing Moments of Belief, which eventually become a shared belief in 'the way things are done around here.' Ultimately, this growth and perspective is impossible to maintain as demands placed on leadership become more complex, urgent and inside-out. Customer-led, outside-in companies can stay on track for longer by paying attention to their outside-in belief systems, maintaining a flow of Moments of Belief to fuel their outside-in convictions and addressing threats and opportunities in customer-led ways.

The Customer Copernicus explores the ways great things can be achieved, for customers and for those associated with the business, when organisations work wholeheartedly on behalf of their customers' needs. And it shows that, without realising it and without conscious resistance, many of these extraordinary and great companies become detached from their outside-in beliefs. Momentum fades and the shared conviction that 'we are working for customers first' becomes diluted; they lose customer focus and often lose business momentum in ways that result in a crash.

In the rest of the book, we'll be exploring the thorny issues surrounding this arc. If something as simple as understanding what customers value and finding new ways to create it can create significant business success, why don't more companies operate this way? And why don't more sustain it when they get there? We'll be analysing the success behind companies including Sky, O2, easyJet, Handelsbanken, W.L. Gore and DBS Bank to understand how Moments of Belief can establish a customer-led trajectory for a company and reinforce outside-in ways of working. Our next chapter examines what customer-led organisations look like through the Walkers business at PepsiCo, which created huge growth through a relentless focus on creating value for crisp customers in new and better ways.

Notes

1   Leahy, Terry. 2012. *Management in 10 Words*. London: Random House Business, p. 18.

2   Ryle, Sarah. 2013. *The Making of Tesco: A Story of British Shopping*. London: Bantam Press, p. 213.

3   Tornquist, Stefan. n.d. 'The Consumer Conversation: The Experience Void between Brands and their Customers.' Econsultancy in association with IBM. Retrieved from ftp://ftp.software.ibm.com/software/be/pdf/Great_experience_divide.pdf

4   Martin attributes Meckling and Jensen's rebuke of managerial capitalism in 1976 as the impetus for the current era of 'maximising shareholder value'.

5   Martin, Roger. 2010. 'The Age of Customer Capitalism.' *Harvard Business Review*, 88 (1): 58–65.

6   This proposition was tested by an extensive multi-year research project sponsored by the Marketing Science Institute, which provides ample evidence of the effect of prioritising customer-value creation ahead of other pressing and legitimate concerns. The weight of subsequent scholarly evidence clearly supports the 'customer first' argument.

7   Leahy, Terry. 2012. *Management in 10 Words*, p. 65.

8   Hayward, Martin. 2009. *Any Colour You Like as Long as It's Any Colour You Like*. London: dunnhumby, p. 26.

9   Hayward, Martin. 2009. *Any Colour You Like*, p. 28.

10 Hayward, Martin. 2009. *Any Colour You Like*, p. 23.

11 Tim Mason, interview with authors, 8 September 2014.

12 Tesco Bank website as at February 2021 https://bank.tescoplc.com/about-us/key-facts/

13 Wood, Zoe & Julia Finch. 8 June 2010. 'Tesco's Terry Leahy to step down after 14 years.' *The Guardian*. Retrieved from www.theguardian.com/business/2010/jun/08/tesco-sir-terry-leahy-steps-down

14 Felsted, Andrea & Andrew Hill. 23 July 2014. 'The inside story of how Clarke's tenure at Tesco came to an end.' *Financial Times*. Retrieved from www.ft.com/content/c04ebdaa-1254-11e4-a581-00144feabdco/

    Wright, Tricia & Sudip Kar-Gupta. 22 September 2014. 'UK's FTSE falls as Tesco tumbles.' *Reuters*. Retrieved from www.reuters.com/article/markets-stocks-ftse/uks-ftse-falls-as-tesco-tumbles-idUKL6N0RN36L20140922/

Chester, G. A. 14 April 2014. 'The shares that analysts hate: Tesco PLC and Wm Morrison Supermarkets plc.' *Motley Fool*. Retrieved from www .fool.co.uk/investing/2014/04/14/the-shares-that-analysts-hate-tesco-plc -and-wm-morrison-supermarkets-plc/

Simms, Andrew. 22 September 2014. 'Tesco: Why did it all go so wrong?' *The Guardian*. Retrieved from www.theguardian.com/commentisf ree/2014/sep/22/tesco-pursuit-of-profit-britains-biggest-supermarket/

Barford, Vanessa. 20 April 2012. 'Five things Tesco got wrong.' *BBC News Magazine*. Retrieved from www.bbc.com/news/magazine-17767565

15 Thomas, Helen. 22 September 2014. 'Tesco can't even account for its problems.' *Wall Street Journal*. Retrieved from www.wsj.com/articles/u-k-s -tesco-cant-even-account-for-its-problems-1411398685/

16 Butler, Sarah. 27 September 2018. 'Sainsbury's and Asda may have to offload 460 stores to seal merger.' *The Guardian*. Retrieved from www.t heguardian.com/business/2018/sep/27/sainsburys-and-asda-could-close -400-stores-to-complete-merger

17 Greiner, Larry E. 1972. 'Evolution and Revolution as Organisations Grow.' *Harvard Business Review*, 50 (4): 37–46.

18 Greiner points out the challenges that success and growth bring. He describes five phases of evolution experienced as a company matures – creativity, direction, delegation, co-ordination and collaboration. Transition from one phase to the next presents an existential threat. He refers to these as the crises of leadership, autonomy, control and red tape. They are threatening because they draw the attention of management inwards, diluting the power of the original outside-in perspective.

19 John Petter, former CEO of BT's Consumer Division, interview with authors 10 March 2018. Petter described to us the battle as being between optimis-ers and re-inventors. Optimisers start with finance and see the business within a framework and look to improve margin continually. Re-inventors start with customers and push to make competitive leaps. The optimisers often, over time, gain the upper hand and that means an inside-out view prevails.

20 Jack Welch, email correspondence, October 2019.

2

WHAT BEING CUSTOMER-LED LOOKS LIKE

If you're not trying to make things better, why are you here?

Seth Godin

Walkers: The characteristics of a customer-led organisation

Walkers is a business worth studying. Between 1992 and 2004, its customer-led approach to growth catapulted the crisps business from revenues of £280 million to over £600 million. Not only that – in a grocery market known for the relentless rise in the share of retailers' own labels, Walkers grew in share terms, reducing supermarkets' own brands to a minority position.

The story starts in the early '90s when PepsiCo was well on its way to establishing Walkers as a megabrand. A packet of Walkers crisps was a staple in 69% of British lunchboxes,[1] and the future looked bright. Some companies might have rested on their laurels at this point, but Walkers' leadership team wanted to explore new avenues of value creation, outside the confines of the existing business.

There were clues to new and better ways of creating customer value emerging beyond the world of salt and vinegar crisps in a packed lunch.

Walkers noticed that in America, corn tortilla chips were booming; Frito-Lay, also owned by PepsiCo, had launched Doritos in 1964 as a pioneering brand and had seen it become a billion-dollar sales market leader.[2] Then, prompted and encouraged by Phileas Fogg, an aspiring UK niche player that was gaining traction with its upmarket tortilla chips, Walkers challenged itself to replicate the US success of Doritos in its home market.

In the UK, research showed that evenings represented the single biggest snacking occasion, accounting for 24% of consumption compared to 16% at lunch.[3] Traditionally, the crisp brand was not associated with being eaten in the evening, but rather than assuming this was impossible to change, Walkers looked to move into the lucrative evening snacking market, so far dominated by sweet, indulgent treats.

Here was an organisation that was not prepared to be complacent about its current success. As Walkers' boss at the time, Martin Glenn, said:

> Always look for new benchmarks. Find out where you under-perform and define your market differently. If you've made it to the top of the tree, it's time to start on the forest.[4]

As a result of this mentality, Walkers created two successful customer-led brand extensions – Doritos, corn tortilla chips, and Sensations, premium crisps for adults. They were both hard-won – ideas that initially looked impossible, asking difficult questions that took determination to answer, and then requiring courage to invest when returns were not guaranteed.

Indeed, in the case of the Doritos' launch in 1994, Walkers' owner, PepsiCo, had to rally even more confidence because an earlier attempt to launch corn tortilla chips in the UK failed. It had also experienced a tough time with two previous UK launches of US successes – a corn curl called Cheetos and a ridged crisp called Ruffles. The work on the Doritos' launch that followed was about learning and adjusting until everything clicked into place. As Glenn recalled:

> It was a big call ... Yes, it was well thought through and there was a good consumer case. But you never quite know when you're investing £15–£20 million based on a lot of people changing regular buying habits ...[5]

Meanwhile, Walkers' foray into premium big bags of crisps through Sensations came from the insight that although adults were starting to enjoy savoury snacks in the evening, this was a very different proposition from lunchtime, where Walkers' products dominated. By launching 'Posh crisps from Walkers' with grown-up flavours like Thai Sweet Chilli, premium packaging with food values, and large sizes suitable for sharing and distribution in alcohol outlets, Sensations extended the business's footprint beyond the packed lunch into evening snacking, opening up a new customer-led opportunity. Instead of being preoccupied with battling over market share against own-label competitors, Walkers led the establishment of a whole new category in the UK. After only 12 weeks, Walkers Sensations had established itself as the third biggest brand in what was defined, inside-out, as the crisp market, behind Walkers' standard crisps and Pringles, with a share of nearly 4%.[6]

Both brand extensions reflect an outside-in leadership mentality – a desire to build long-term customer value rather than competing within an established market, something that will inevitably, eventually lead to commoditisation. And it is this assertiveness, commitment and ability to look outside the confines of the organisation that defines Walkers' customer-led leadership, which we'll be exploring in this chapter.

As we noted, Walkers' customer-led moves created an extraordinary growth trajectory. Even more remarkably, and contrary to the relentless trend, Walkers had consolidated its hold on the category so much that by 2004, it was taking a whopping 70% of the crisp market by volume against private label's 18%, compared to 46% and 35% respectively in 1995, according to IRI.[7] This shows the value being added by Walkers in the eyes of customers as it fought back against 'the same for less' own-label proposition.

The Walkers' story, as with the Tesco story in the previous chapter, is about a leadership team having the ability to stand in customers' shoes and finding the confidence to follow through on insights and innovation leading to commercial breakthroughs. We're especially interested here in identifying the characteristics that define a customer-led organisation like Walkers.

What does being customer-led look like? What leadership style encourages a common thread of actions among companies that reflect an outside-in mentality? What actions did Walkers' leadership take to propel growth during this period? And how did these actions reflect an outside-in mentality? What is it in the activities and the visible leadership style of a customer-led business that seems to mark it out as special? This is about describing the systematic, repeatable and scalable aspects of a customer-led organisation.

What good looks like

Because being customer-led is unnatural, customer-led organisations stand out. They take action that differs from their peers and competitors, action that reflects an outside-in mentality. They understand what customers value beyond what's being sold to them today – the problems they're trying to solve or the outcomes they really want. They are also skilled at creating this value in new and better ways, improving on the set of solutions currently on offer.

Their performance reflects their skill as they grow new markets or gain market share. And if market share is the measure, it is crucial that the market is defined in broad outside-in ways that recognise the problem the players are solving for customers, and therefore the true competitive set. For example, there is a big difference between a supermarket ready meal (a product category) and nice food fast (an outcome achieved in many different ways from Pret A Manger, the freshly-made-sandwich chain, to Deliveroo or Uber Eats, the restaurant meal delivery services).

It is relatively easy to be customer-led as a start-up because the few people involved can all see their customers and the role they play in giving them what they want, and they can also see how successful they are immediately and in ways that have impact. If they aren't creating value for customers in some way that is new and better than before, at least locally, then they are unlikely to last for long.

But taking the approach to a bigger, broader audience requires a different way of operating, and the first customer-led challenge is delivering your current solution while ensuring that you keep asking whether this creates value for customers in ways that stay or get further ahead of the continually evolving alternatives.

As an example, while Walkers' customer-led growth was driven by two impressive brand extensions – Doritos and Sensations – underlying all of this was the company's constant quest for quality. It was on a journey of continuous improvement where Walkers developed a 'Gold Standard' crisp created from the very best potatoes and fried in the very best conditions. This was the ideal of the perfect crisp it strived to put into every pack, every day of the year. No mean feat when you're dealing with 350,000 tonnes of potatoes a year. During the '90s, Walkers invested in a series of costly innovations to boost quality, including first replacing plastic bags with foil and the air in the bags with pure nitrogen to improve freshness further. As Martin Glenn said:

> Most companies test quality against both their own current products and their competitors' products. This can be a useful exercise, but it can also produce an attitude in which a business is satisfied with products that are 'good enough.' The result of this is an inevitable downward drift in quality as products get benchmarked against a declining standard.[8]

This quest for the perfect crisp underpinned everything at Walkers. Glenn pays tribute to Zweifel crisps in Switzerland for fuelling his belief that quality pays in this industry. The Swiss potato chip manufacturer is obsessed with quality and has a 70% share in its home market[9] where consumption per capita is high and crisps are not viewed automatically as junk food. As with many other customer-led leaders, Glenn's outside-in beliefs are reinforced by learning from examples of other businesses succeeding in new and different ways elsewhere. Here, Zweifel's focus on quality and its subsequent success in Switzerland supported Glenn's confidence that a similar approach could work in the UK. We'll see more examples of customer-led leaders looking to other markets and industries for inspiration throughout the book. They help people see, and even more importantly believe, that there are new and better ways to create customer value in their own organisations.

So, Glenn's relentless focus on quality happened for a reason. Walkers' leadership team believed that investing in higher quality with all of the associated costs would eventually bring a return, even though the costs were immediate and definite, and the returns not guaranteed and in the future. Glenn said, 'If you have a high-quality product, it will sell faster, it has higher margins and you can reinvest in growing demand.'[10]

This is an example of an outside-in belief. Each time an investment was made in foil or nitrogen to improve the freshness of the product, Walkers was doing things that no customer would ever directly ask for. They were also activities that it would be easy for Walkers to avoid, in the process saving money and boosting short-term profits. Yet each time the investments flowed through into evidence that customers noticed the quality, valued the difference and increasingly preferred Walkers over the alternatives. As a result, the shared outside-in beliefs of the whole team involved were reinforced each time – Moments of Belief, in other words.

What happened with Walkers happens with other companies too. Over the years, we have identified six activities we believe are disproportionately important in creating customer-led success. These are: making clear customer choices; using guiding insight; developing innovative propositions; empowering people; rapidly learning; and creating a business-wide customer plan. Three aspects of a visible leadership style also play a crucial role: being assertive in the market; being committed internally; and being externally focused. We'll be examining these later in the chapter, but before then, it's useful to know what they are.

While some of these activities may appear familiar and reflect what matters to many organisations, the disproportionate value comes when a customer-led company with an outside-in belief system follows this approach completely. Indeed, our research suggests that this is how exceptional customer-led success is created. We'll be highlighting the differences between more common inside-out companies and unusual outside-in companies throughout the book.

To give an example, while 'making clear customer choices' about which customer needs to address might suggest drawing conclusions from focus groups for many organisations, it means much more in an outside-in environment where it is akin to reframing a market. Think Henry Ford and faster horses versus new cars. Outside-in companies want to make an accepted industry work fundamentally better: while a focus group on quick and easy ready meals might suggest new recipes from another country or redesigning the packaging to better showcase the ingredients, an outside-in approach would reframe the entire market to make it better for consumers – to bring restaurant food home with Deliveroo, for example.

Before we get into more detail, let us describe more fully what customer-led success looks like through the Walkers story.

Using all the elements for success

Walkers crisps had an unlikely beginning. In 1948, unreliable post war supplies forced Henry Walker, a Leicester butcher, to diversify into potato chips. They were peeled and chopped by hand, cooked in dripping in a rusty old fryer, sprinkled with salt and sold in a packet with the slogan, 'Potato Crisps by Walkers: Guaranteed Absolutely Pure.'

Walkers remained a mainly regional brand until it was bought by PepsiCo in 1988. The new owner brought in a fresh sense of professionalism, a burst of energy and fantastic resources.

In the early 1990s, PepsiCo was well on its way to establishing Walkers as a megabrand, but it wanted to explore new avenues of value creation, rather than fall into commoditisation and the risk of creeping own-label dominance. Conscious of the need to be proactive if it was to succeed, the management team made three customer-related choices about the way it would manage the company:

- Keep the business simple and focused on a few big moves, keeping complexity at bay and giving focus and cut-through to relationships with retailers and consumers.
- Add margin, looking for ways to add value for consumers in ways they would be happy to pay for, and that retailers would, therefore, support.
- Consider which customers and which needs would be the priority.

Walkers aimed to look at the world through customers' eyes. This became a crucial way of reframing the whole market. While a product-led, inside-out business would concentrate on inventing new flavours and different shapes, Walkers' fresh perspective unveiled a whole new set of growth opportunities through different snacking occasions. Instead of slightly tweaking what customers were already buying, Walkers investigated what customers really valued, the problems they wanted to solve or the outcomes they wanted.

One of the reasons Walkers had made itself into the UK's biggest crisp brand was its success in smuggling itself into the nation's lunchboxes. One of the downsides that followed was that people wanted something different when they got home from work. But as evenings represented the single biggest snacking occasion – 24% of all snack consumption[11] – Walkers could see an opportunity, albeit not one that was easy to capture. In time, this would lead to not one, but two highly successful brand extensions – Doritos and Sensations. According to Glenn:

> We're a restless bunch ... We like to challenge ourselves – and we like to take bold steps. Life's too short to make small changes to small things all the time. Make small changes to big things, make big changes to bigger things.[12]

The next challenge was to think about this growing occasion with insight, trying to understand the current range of solutions in the market and where there might be opportunities to provide what customers valued in new and better ways. While market research showed that Walkers couldn't stretch into anything sweet, like cakes, the brand could work on anything savoury.

The Walkers team came upon a useful way of looking at the world that opened up opportunities. Rather than thinking in terms of markets and market share, they looked at calories. Over time people's calorie consumption has remained broadly flat, but opportunities had emerged from making calories healthier, more enjoyable or more rewarding in other ways. Glenn explained:

> As a manager of a business in the category, it is important to see where your share of calories will come from, ensuring it is from other sectors who won't be looking at you as a competitor ...[13]

Making the choice to focus on the evening 'snack with alcohol' occasion, the question became about understanding the calories currently being consumed and what value they were currently bringing to the experience, not just as food but as part of the social interaction too. This definition of value, the enjoyment of a social occasion of which food is a central part, is what could then be enhanced in new and better ways with innovation.

Walkers found two sources of inspiration – looking first internationally at this 'with alcohol' occasion and secondly looking at niches in the UK for clues that it could build on at greater scale. Looking internationally highlighted the popularity of corn tortilla chips in the US, and studying a niche product in the UK made by Kettles suggested the potential for a premium big bag of crisps.

It wasn't the first time the Walkers' team had dabbled with corn tortillas, but without the insight and big picture choices, previous efforts had lacked conviction; discouraged by early failures, the team had called a halt to the project. Managers had viewed the first attempt as just a product launch, not a bigger idea that would take many elements to be woven together to make it work.

The first iteration of Doritos was as a fully formed product idea that would either work or not. The initial failure was interpreted as evidence that it was a bad idea. The second Doritos iteration started with the belief that there was an opportunity in the area of adult snacking and an acceptance that initially the proposition would not be 100% perfect. The work that followed was about learning and adjusting until it clicked, or until it was clear there really was something more fundamental they would need to address to make it click.

The team moved fast to put a business case together and then assemble a cross-functional team to import the necessary machinery, build a new factory and develop training to sell the new proposition in ways that would make the most of its difference. By working harder on the details of flavour, packaging and distribution, the new team eventually found a breakthrough formula that firmly established tortilla chips, and the Doritos brand, in the UK. As Glenn recalled:

> It was a powerful experience ... People knew that the Doritos project for Walkers would be a step change. We would have pulled off something remarkable that would become a source of pride. The factory was built in record time and in three months we'd tripled the size of market.[14]

In 2002, Glenn and his team repeated the feat with the launch of Sensations. They took the niche premium idea of crisps that could be enjoyed as an evening snack and brought it to the masses. Glenn explained:

> We were always looking for gaps, there was a restlessness. How could we build a bigger proposition for people in the evening? What was the branded proposition for evening snacks? We'd already tried big bags of Walkers crisps, but consumers didn't want cheese and onion crisps in the evening because they'd already had them with their lunchtime sandwich ... We wanted to help consumers see that there was a difference ...[15]

The inspiration came from Kettle Foods' big bags of hand-fried crisps, packaged and positioned as a specialist product with authenticity and food values. Based in Norfolk (although US owned) to be as close to its potato growers as possible, Kettles offered new flavours like sea salt and balsamic vinegar and blue stilton and port. This was the inspiration for Walkers to create the Sensations range of premium big-bag crisps, produced to be genuinely high quality.

But inspiration from Kettle's product was just one part of the story. Walkers also used scale to build the other insights into ways to add value to the consumption occasion – using sophisticated packaging design with adult food cues and ensuring availability in off-licenses (UK retailers of beers, wine and liquor for consumption off premises) as much for positioning as for sales. Similarly, in supermarkets, Walkers argued for the creation of an adult snack category, not just a display of 'big bags versus small bags' as a product-led approach would have suggested.

In technical terms, Sensations is a proposition rather than a product. It is a better outside-in solution to a customer problem, or to providing an outcome that customers want. If it had just been conceived as an inside-out product extension, it would likely have failed. But by reflecting the world as seen through the eyes of customers, it became a rounded offer and a resounding success. The success of Sensations took even Walkers by surprise with sales exceeding the target by 200% inside the first year.[16]

Acting on these insights and propositions in the UK was only possible because PepsiCo gave the UK leadership team the space and freedom to devise its own direction. But it also created opportunities to find an edge and creative inspiration from the global resources of a corporation, making learning easy and adding to the local insights of the team. The freedom to respond to what local customers value contrasts with the more common command-and-control approach of many international businesses.

Turning the propositions into success on the ground took another kind of empowerment. Unless retailers are convinced by a new idea, consumers won't ever get to see them. So, sales teams' relationships with the stores they sell through are critical. To make this work they were given confidence and freedom rather than instructions and control, with a simple story to tell and a clear rationale for what they were doing. They defined the brand platform with the disarmingly honest and memorable line: Posh crisps from Walkers. Walkers also created a regular rhythm of news, so the story could be re-told in ways that were natural not pushy, such as the launch of new flavours or a new celebrity starring in the ads. By understanding and believing in the direction, then having a common framework for describing it, the sales team found they could be collectively effective in ways that suited all involved.

Learning from many sources and having a curious mindset was central to success. The speed of learning was increased by deliberately setting out to make learning, not just sales performance, central to the way success was defined. This turned judgements from 'good versus bad' into a quest to understand what worked well and why, alongside what could work better and how.

As the learning came together and a view of the opportunity sharpened up for both Sensations and Doritos, it was translated into a customer-led plan. This meant setting objectives for what had to be achieved that started with customer outcomes, helping everyone involved keep an outside-in perspective. For example, the quality of the distribution achieved mattered more than the quantity – it was crucial to create a premium adult snacking category in supermarkets and to appear in off-licenses not corner shops. Walkers was not choosing off-licenses to sell large quantities of crisps in year one. The customer outcomes determined the success of the business, so a customer plan came ahead of the financials.

The Walkers story demonstrates how an outside-in organisation acts in different ways across the entire company. This is not simply about a marketing department creating a new bag of crisps, but a whole new well-rounded offer. Hence, Walkers reframed distribution by persuading retailers to redefine an entire category. This was a mammoth achievement – the many different elements came together so that Walkers created customer value in new and better ways.

Back to Martin Glenn:

> Having great ideas is one thing but turning those ideas into vehicles for growth is something quite different. The ideas that succeed in the market are not necessarily the most brilliant ones, but the ones that are driven by companies that know how to put a total business strategy behind them and how to follow it through with a ruthless attention to detail.[17]

The Walkers team over time grew a deeply held belief that starting their thinking with customers would lead them to commercial success. This meant putting themselves into the world customers live in and seeing it vividly, understanding occasions when a snack might be appropriate even if the occasions were not typically thought of as appropriate for snacking.

This customer-led attitude filtered into the entire core business beyond the brand extensions. For example, in the early 1990s, following PepsiCo's acquisition of Walkers, the organisation invested time and money to improve sales and distribution in the belief it would lead to increased sales in the future. At that time, packets of crisps were typically sold from boxes with holes punched in the top, or the packets were thrown onto shelves. Walkers persuaded retailers that moving from a cardboard box to a carefully designed fixture could increase sales by more than 20%. This involved extra labour cost for the stores but as belief in the Walkers team grew, the retailers were prepared to buy into Walkers' approach.

Similarly, Walkers' commitment to its long-running ad campaign with footballing personality Gary Lineker reflects customer-led thinking. As Glenn said:

> It doesn't take a genius to decide to stick with an obvious winner, but what surprises me is how few people do it. There are brand managers out there who get tired of advertising or pack design or strategy long before their consumers do.[18]

The Gary Lineker, 'No More Mr Nice Guy' campaign has run since 1995, when Lineker was famous for being a professional footballer; in fact, he was the golden boy of British sport. It parodies his squeaky-clean image as a player who was never cautioned by a referee (something that is almost unheard of in professional football) but behaves badly when faced with the temptation of Walkers. The fact that he was also a Leicester local hero turned national celebrity was even better. Staying loyal to Lineker has paid dividends for Walkers.

As we've shown with Tesco's story in Chapter 1, customer-led organisations grow in confidence with each Moment of Belief — seeing that increasing value for customers results in commercial success. This confidence is seen in other commercial decisions that add value for customers and do good things beyond merely selling them a product. For example,

Walkers' partnership with News International to create the Free Books for Schools programme was another example of a customer-led strategy that swallowed short-term costs in the pursuit of longer-term benefits. And it's not surprising to hear that Walkers was looking to emulate the success of another customer-led organisation's sales promotion – Tesco's Computers for Schools. Walkers' Free Books for Schools saw the company donate nearly seven million books worth more than £35 million to 36,000 schools.[19] Glenn believes this campaign turned Walkers into a loved British brand. 'And that is something that ad budgets just can't buy,' he said.[20]

Walkers sponsored hometown football club Leicester City FC, renaming the home ground Walkers Stadium. It teamed up with Umbro to introduce the Walkers Football Fund, which provides free soccer kits to clubs and schools.

This confidence led to the creative freedom around limited editions of Walkers crisps, from new flavours to even changing the name of the brand to get noticed. For example, it created a limited-edition pack to celebrate Leicester City's return to the Premiership in 1996, producing 7,000 packs of Leicester Cheese & Chive crisps featuring two of the players. The packs were only on sale in Leicester.[21]

The Walkers' story shows us that customer-led organisations are skilled and relentless at creating value for customers in new and better ways, continually improving the set of solutions on offer. Creating value for customers also creates value for the business. In the space of just 12 years from 1992, Walkers grew its revenues by £320 million. Let's explore how this happened in more detail.

Six activities fuelled by the outside-in leadership approach

During our examination of customer-led growth over many years, we have identified six activities that are disproportionately important in creating success, all of which are present in the Walkers story. This is what they look like in more detail.

1. **Making clear customer choices**. Which customers and which needs will you serve, and which will you ignore?

2. **Using guiding insight**. What do you understand about customers that is not obvious, but which explains their real motivations and behaviours in a way you can act on, and that gives you an edge?

3. **Developing innovative propositions**. How will you create a rounded offer that solves a customer's problem or gives them the outcome they want as fully as possible, ahead of alternatives?

4. **Empowering people**. How have you built teams so they are set up to be both consistent but also, crucially, flexible where it matters most to your customers?

5. **Rapidly learning**. How do you ensure you continually grow the value that customers receive and recognise? Not every interaction will go to plan and elements of the offer will need to be improved. How do you create and maintain systematic, distributed feedback about what's being delivered and how it rates with customers?

6. **Creating a business-wide customer plan**. How do you put the actions and performance management in place to help the organisation succeed in your customers' eyes, not just the business's?

These were arrived at empirically, but we feel it is useful to know what good looks like at this level. By examining each of the six outside-in activities and using other examples alongside Walkers, it becomes even clearer what customer-led organisations look like.

Making clear customer choices

We have seen how, by looking at the world through customers' eyes, Walkers was able to spot and choose to pursue fresh growth opportunities like evening snacking. Making clear customer choices is all about looking with new eyes and reframing markets. This can be tough to do when a company is dominated by inside-out metrics – building market share, growing shareholder value and the like.

Customer-led organisations make distinct decisions about the customers they choose to serve. They do not try to please everyone and satisfy all needs. For example, Ferrari understands its customers are genuine brand enthusiasts who desire a high-end image around performance, extrovert design and exclusivity. This appeal is maintained by making it hard work to become a customer and by choosing to limit supply. As Ferrari's former president, Luca di Montezemolo, said to *Businessweek* magazine:

> The quality of the sales is more important than the quantity ... Every company must grow, but growth isn't solely about getting bigger. If you increase volume too quickly, you can easily run into product or service quality issues and internal culture conflicts. By focusing instead on cultivating fierce customer loyalty, you can create not only a virtuous cycle of profit and reinvestment, but a growing sense of pride and satisfaction as well.[22]

In 1985, Unilever's male deodorant Axe (Lynx in the UK) single-mindedly targeted the male desire to get girls. 'Spray to get laid' became one of the most iconic global advertising ideas in the world and led to unprecedented brand growth for 20 years. However, by 2014, it became clear that 'The Axe Effect' was out of step with modern society. The notion that a fragrance was enough to compel women into voluntary sexual surrender was offensive as well as misplaced. The world had changed, and Axe needed to reinvent itself to appeal to a new generation without losing distinctiveness. A new campaign, 'Find Your Magic,' rewrote the rules of masculinity and told young men that being yourself was a more confident and contemporary way to appeal to young women. It worked, and positive sentiment on social media leapt from 14.74% to 41.35%, while purchase consideration among the target audience in the US increased by 25%.[23]

Using guiding insight

A critical element in Walkers' success was its team's reliance on insight. They looked at the category and the competition through the lens of calories. The opportunity was to encourage people to switch their evening calorie consumption from peanuts or chocolate or ice cream, and to do so by adding value to the social interaction.

Using guiding insight reveals something about customers that is not obvious, but which explains their real motivations and behaviours in a way on which the whole business can act. It can be tough for many businesses to achieve because it involves looking at an industry in a fresh way to discover motivations that can be understood and then acted upon. For example, Dove's insight that mature women find beauty a source of anxiety led to a celebration of real-life beauty that enabled Dove to become a confident and respected market leader. Similarly, O2's insight that existing customers felt taken advantage of, despite their demonstration of loyalty, led to a whole new customer-led business model that rewarded rather than penalised loyal customers.

Developing innovative propositions

It's much easier for organisations to make small tweaks to existing products. Walkers could have continued launching new flavours and creating news around its existing Walkers crisps, but this would never have created the same value as launching Doritos and Sensations.

Customer-led organisations create new markets and new business models. For example, Nespresso reframed the convenient coffee category by addressing a previously unserved segment. Nespresso's success can be attributed to insight, but its ability to address the opportunity required innovation at every step of the value chain and has become a much-admired case study in business model innovation. This wholesale re-invention outperformed cafetières, filter machines, percolators and the rest, in terms of enjoyment for customers and commercial value.

When Rolls-Royce Aero Engines, as number three in the market, needed to find a competitive edge, it developed an offering that answered the real needs of its customers. The usual practice was to sell jet engines to airline customers and then charge them again for servicing, maintenance and repairs. The more of this support the engine needs, the more it costs the customer. The new TotalCare offer meant that Rolls-Royce's customers now don't buy jet engines at all. Instead, they pay a rate for the jet engine thrust they use, which is the outcome they really want. This incentivises Rolls-Royce to make its engines as reliable as possible, so the revenue keeps flowing and the costs of servicing and aftercare are minimised. For customers, with fees known in advance, there is a more predictable cost of ownership and a minimisation of disruption.

TotalCare was first introduced in the mid-1990s, at which time Rolls-Royce entered into an agreement with Cathay Pacific. When Cathay Pacific's first A330s went into service, it meant combining initial sales with aftermarket support by TotalCare, which transformed the organisation from a product to a service business. Together, they created a revolutionary new business model that flipped the industry on its head and created a lot of happy customers. Over time, TotalCare has proven to be a game changer for the industry. As Mark King, the president of Rolls-Royce's civil aerospace business, explained:

> Providing real-time support and maintenance to its airline customers for decades after the original purchase is now the biggest part of the business, generating 55 per cent of revenues last year. Rolls-Royce is not alone in recognising that it pays dividends to listen to your customers. Its two main rivals, General Electric and Pratt & Whitney, have both introduced similar packages over the years. It is a decision that has revolutionised the industry over the past two decades. For every engine it sells, Rolls-Royce offers a long-term service arrangement, such as the TotalCare package for its airline customers. About 70 per cent of the company's airline customers have signed up to TotalCare. The system aligns the interests of the airline and the engine manufacturer.[24]

While the contract structure rectified an anomaly in the business model of the industry – rewarding manufacturers when their engines needed attention – aligning customer and manufacturer interests hasn't been the only benefit. Customers covered by TotalCare also profit from improved on-wing time, higher residual values for their engines, reduced risk and better oversight. That last benefit is the result of the reams of performance and reliability data that Rolls-Royce generates from its numerous service contracts, data that is then used to fine-tune engine health monitoring software to spot potential problems before they occur, something that is now very much in Rolls-Royce's interest.

Empowering people

We've seen how PepsiCo empowered the UK leadership teams behind Doritos and Sensations to meet its customers' needs in new, creative and valuable ways. And Walkers also empowered its sales teams to ensure retailers properly understood and engaged with the new brands. For example, Walkers invested heavily in sales promotions and extensive in-store merchandising with Sensations. Working with retailers, Walkers positioned its big sharing packs near soft drinks and alcohol because they are often consumed at the same time.

In contrast, many international organisations fall back into command-and-control mode without empowering local teams to set their own direction.

Customer-led organisations recognise that steering the way your offer makes it to customers has to be done by the people closest to them. For example, W.L. Gore asks individuals to earn the respect of their peers rather than bestowing it upon them by virtue of title and an organisational chart. The process of earning respect comes from finding new opportunities to solve customers' problems. There are no hierarchies, no titles and only high-level metrics. There are also transparent and frequent peer reviews and a strong focus on maintaining this culture.

Meanwhile, Transport for London (TfL) empowers its people to interpret its ethos that 'every journey matters.' This means people across TfL understand that in their different roles they each need to keep customers in a position to manage their time, and their emotions around time, well. Crucially they have freedom to do it their own way, leading to consistency of action but massive diversity in style and character across individual underground stations, bus drivers and digital service providers. It also leads to innovation, for example in lightening the mood with 'quotes of the day' shared on whiteboards at stations, something that grew spontaneously and organically throughout the organisation.

It began in Oval station in 2003, when customer services manager Anthony Gentles was inspired to perk up the 'blank faces' of commuters with a daily dose of wisdom from his favourite book *Tao Te Ching* – the key text in the ancient Chinese philosophical tradition of Taoism. 'Stations need not be sterile places,' Gentles told the BBC[25] (see Figure 2.1).

In a departure from the stereotype of the silent Tube user, passengers actually began chatting to staff. Some would stop to thank Gentles for writing the messages, while others started going out of their way to visit the station. Lunch clubs were even formed at workplaces to discuss the meaning behind the day's thought.

In 2007, he passed the baton on to his colleague Glen Sutherland. Since then the customer services assistant has written more than 3,000 thoughts – and says he's only repeated himself four times. Oval station now has over 20,000 followers on its Twitter account for thought for the day.

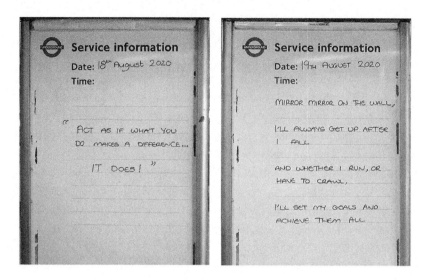

Figure 2.1 Transport for London, Oval Station, Thought for the Day. (Source: Transport for London – used with permission)

Moreover, Oval staff pipe out classical music and have installed plants and a book exchange to try to make the underground station a more pleasant environment for customers. Other Tube stations have followed, happily embracing ideas that have come from colleagues, not imposed from the top.

Rapidly learning

Customer-led organisations are on a quest for continual improvement. Not every business decision will be successful, and when this is the case, it provides an opportunity for learning. PepsiCo's initial failure to launch Doritos into the UK market is a case in point. Instead of giving up, PepsiCo used the opportunity to understand what worked and what didn't, then adapted for its second attempt. Learning from many sources and having a curious mindset were central to success. And critically Walker's second attempt to launch corn tortilla chips into the UK market came with the awareness that learning fast would be critical to making it work.

Developing an innate culture of curiosity within an organisation does not come naturally. It means results can take longer. It means encouraging risks and, therefore, increasing the likelihood of failure. It means taking a long-term view over the pressures of short-term financial reporting. It means putting mechanisms in place to encourage and nurture learning. It means hiring people who are curious.

Customer-led organisations recognise the importance of continually improving. They understand that not every interaction will go to plan and elements of the offer will need to be improved, so how can a systematic, distributed way to get feedback about what's being delivered and how it rates with customers be maintained? For example, Tata Group tackles one of the biggest barriers to learning by making its highest profile internal award all about failure, encouraging people to learn from their mistakes and take risks. This rapid learning or customer responsiveness is about being fast and right. The value of being right is obvious – customers get something that meets their needs. But the value also depends critically upon the speed with which the response is produced. The value of a course of action decays the longer it takes to be implemented. Sir Peter Davis, chief executive of retailer Sainsbury's at the beginning of the century, recalls speaking to an executive and his team about a test that was operating in a store. He asked when the outcome would be clear. The response surprised him:

> We'll probably know within two or three months; but we need to test it properly and we need to let it run for a bit longer to be sure.

Davis then asked:

> What would we do then?

The executive said:

> I expect we'll push it into another store.

Davis recalls:

> When I said it would take 434 years to make it into the entire network at that rate, they all looked terribly hurt.[26]

Creating a business-wide customer plan

PepsiCo, like Tesco in the previous chapter, set objectives and plans that focused on customers rather than financials as it was building its case to launch Doritos and Sensations. A customer plan helped them steer towards success as an extended team.

How do you put the plans and performance management in place to help the organisation succeed in your customers' eyes, not just the business's? This is a challenge for many organisations when faced with short-term financial and shareholder pressure.

While many companies will be familiar with the idea of a customer plan, an outside-in execution of one has some important characteristics. Customer-led organisations make space to focus on the customer in a planned and concerted way. Like Tesco, O2's customer plan turns specific customer needs and opportunities into a systematic way of working to meet them. The business defined a set of specific outcomes valued by customers such as 'the best network' and created O2 promises that set the company's ambition. This encouraged curiosity and the quest to work out what a headline idea really meant. For 'the best network,' an unexpected insight was that for customers, network quality was more about not dropping calls in cities than it was about reaching the remotest parts of the UK. Covering the map seems more obvious because it is easier to visualise, but it is product-led and ignores where people and their calls are. The call-dropping insight was picked up by the teams who could, together, make it happen, and in this case, a network strategy emerged that used a pizza analogy, to go 'deep pan not thin and crispy,' to grow capacity in cities rather than extending reach further into the countryside. This customer planning process proved to be a good way of uniting people and their work around customers and customer-led key performance indicators (KPIs) rather than business-led ones.

Customer-led leadership

We have noticed that that there are certain leadership traits that are disproportionately important in creating success for customer-led organisations.

Martin Glenn was a crucial character at Walkers, central to the team over many years. He started in 1992 as marketing manager and then from 1998 to 2006 he was CEO. He was joined by Neil Campbell who, as marketing VP, Glenn credits with taking the plunge to launch big bags of Doritos, adding a significant layer of growth that then encouraged them to build a dip business.

Glenn's transition from marketing specialist to CEO generalist is one clue to the way the marketing mindset became central to the company's ways of working. This meant the whole business naturally started with customers, and the marketing function was seen not as a pressure group but as the voice of the customer. We saw a similar phenomenon at Tesco when Terry Leahy was marketing director and made a point of stepping forward and becoming the voice of the customer for the business. According to Leahy:

> It's hard to argue with what the customer is saying and if you can bring that into the boardroom it's a very powerful tool ... All I had was the voice of the customer and made my argument to the decision makers on their behalf, which proved to be incredibly powerful in terms of persuading colleagues how the business needed to change.[27]

As we described in Chapter 1, Tesco's Clubcard programme enabled it to uncover the voice of Tesco's customers, giving it an unprecedented level of detailed insight into who its customers were and how they shopped. Having seen and believed in the feedback on what customers might really want, peers in other functions alongside marketing combined to create their response – one that provided value to customers and to the business. In the same way, under Glenn's leadership, the Walkers' leadership team was committed to customers and that ensured that the rest of the organisation was too.

Glenn was always very clear that Walkers needed to be bold. Customer-led leaders tend to be proactive. Rather than wait for the inevitable battle with own-label competition reducing PepsiCo's margins and eroding market share, Glenn and his leadership team took the decision to innovate. 'In crowded markets you don't grow unless you make bold steps,' insisted Glenn.[28]

The biggest call was the move to launch Doritos in 1994 into the UK, not least because it hadn't worked before. As Glenn recalled:

> We had a great desire to spread our business into broader segments. We'd been trying for years to find an angle and couldn't find one. The big difference between the US and the UK was the size of the tortilla category.[29]

And PepsiCo as a US company was confident enough to empower its UK team to do what it needed to do to make the brand extensions a success.

Walkers' leadership team was always looking outside the company for inspiration, reframing its market, redefining what success could look like. It's not surprising that Glenn recognises Tesco as a fellow customer-led brand. He cites its example as an established company that is never complacent:

> How do you keep a challenger mentality? For years, Tesco was chasing Sainsbury's and was good at creating new enemies. To always have an enemy is really helpful. Also, always create a new goal. Look for other opportunities in the day, look for benchmarks, define your market differently. We may have a good share of the salty snack market, but redefining what this looked like really helped the business too.[30]

We believe there are three leadership qualities that feature in customer-led organisations. We saw them in the Walkers case, and we have seen them work for customers at scale in a number of other businesses. They are:

1. **Committed**. Within the organisation, a strong sense of what matters that's set from top to bottom, exemplified by what people do, not just what they say, and the way they prioritise their time.
2. **Assertive**. Beyond the organisation into its markets, being prepared to lead, to proactively take action before competitors with the conviction that it's going to lead to the right kind of success.
3. **Externally focused**. Seeing the entire business from a customer's perspective, looking outside-in, not just occasionally but naturally. This means that the first two qualities are applied in service of this external focus. This matters – the internal commitment and external assertiveness can also, unhelpfully, manifest themselves in an inside-out way.

These three leadership styles are often misunderstood or uncommon. For example, while most leaders are committed, the difference lies in what they are committed about. An outside-in leader will clearly act as the voice of the customer and make it obvious that this is what matters around here. In terms of assertiveness, an outside-in leader looks to be market leading not market following. Being externally focused is an uncommon trait for leaders – for those who are, it means taking an external view of their company and the (small) place they have in their customers' lives, even when the leaders are buried deep within an organisation. It's no mean feat.

Taking each of these three leadership styles in turn, we have more examples that bring them to life.

Committed at Nespresso and Market Basket

Global brand Nespresso, launched by Nestlé in 1989, would never have come into existence were it not for the vision and commitment of Camillo Pagano, senior executive vice president. Pagano, an Italian whose family owned a huge espresso bar-cafe in Rome, knew his coffee and lamented Nestlé's lack of involvement in the lucrative roast and ground market. When he emerged as the champion of an ailing and long-running research and development (R&D) project aimed at addressing this gap, he initially found himself alone and recalled:

> There was a lot of scepticism about the possibility to commercialise Nespresso ... People thought I was a 'nut' to spend so much time on this small thing and to support the idea. I felt that developing this business would take time and patience. You need champions at the top for a new idea. You need to give an idea support against criticism. Any innovation immediately hits resistance in an organisation.[31]

Ironically, internal opposition grew as the concept began to gain traction, with other categories within Nestlé claiming they could achieve more if they were supported with equivalent investment.

> Why are you allocating resources to that project? It's proven that it's not going to work. If it was going to work, it would have worked before now.

Pagano attributed this resistance to how alien Nespresso's business systems were to the rest of Nestlé.

> Nespresso was developed as a totally innovative system ... (It) is so different from what the company does in its day-to-day business.

He was highly committed internally:

> It's going to require a different business model. It's premium. More or
> less everything else in the business is done as mass. We know mass
> marketing really well. But this is now about premium – a very different
> approach.[32]

And eventually, it worked – in a big way. Today its revenues are estimated
to be north of US$5 billion, and it is thought to be highly profitable.

Similarly, Arthur T. Demoulas, president and CEO of his family's grocery
chain, Market Basket, demonstrated remarkable commitment. In a little
over 10 years as leader, he grew revenues by 33% to reach $4 billion while
employees grew from 14,000 to 25,000. Demoulas' formula was a no-
frills strategy with an uncommon twist. Competitive prices were achieved
by smart sourcing together with eschewing common services such as a
website and loyalty cards, and the twist came with how employees were
treated. Market Basket's above-market employee package included higher
wages, profit sharing, healthcare and college support. This engendered
loyalty and enthusiasm. Arthur T's family benefited from handsome dividends. His commitment to the formula was tested when his board (of family members or their representatives) demanded higher dividends funded
by price increases and less generous employment packages. He rejected
their demands even though his job was at risk. Arthur T was fired by the
board in 2014. Over the next few months, employees and customers pro-
tested the firing of a man they saw as having the right approach. Some
of these employees temporarily lost their jobs during the dispute, which
was resolved only when Arthur T bought a controlling stake, returned as
CEO and reinstated his tried and trusted approach for his customers and
employees.

Assertive at M&S and Tesla

Stuart Rose, the CEO at M&S at the time of this development in 2006/7,
had an innate sense of what mattered to the brand. Through 'Plan A,' he
publicly committed to spending £200 million on a comprehensive sustainability plan. There was no return on investment calculation. This was a
brand-based, belief-led, outside-in leadership decision on what it would

take to go first and why it mattered. It was subsequently discovered that being sustainable also saved money. For example, a switch to LED lighting saved lighting bills (which was expected) as well as air conditioning bills (which wasn't) because LED lights gave off little heat. After five years, the original investment plus another £100 million in additional benefits had been returned. It was the assertive belief in what mattered to customers that created the space for this to happen.[33]

Similarly, Tesla's outside-in view of electric cars has made their offer desirable rather than functional. This required assertiveness – Tesla wasn't just competing with other premium car manufacturers but looking to grow and win in an entirely new category. This confidence led them to open patents and share technology with the rest of the market to help grow the competitiveness of electric cars. A project that Tesla entered into with Walmart in the US helps Walmart's retail outlets store electricity generated intermittently by solar and wind, creating a genuine alternative to the grid. As Apple started in computing and moved sideways into music, so Tesla is making a bet on leading in electric energy storage and assertively growing by seeing a virtuous circle outside the traditional market definition.

Externally focused at Tesco

Right from the very beginning there was an outside-in approach at Tesco. The senior directors all wore a lapel pin with the acronym – YCDBSOYA. Observers had been known to presume this might be a Yiddish expression, but it wasn't. It came from founder Jack Cohen's mantra, 'You can't do business sitting on your arse …'

Ian McLaurin also insisted that senior managers visit stores on Tuesdays, Thursdays and Fridays. The Monday board meeting had no agenda other than, 'What did we each learn last week in stores, and what can we do this week that would make everything work better?' With Terry Leahy and Tim Mason's encouragement, the business ran customer listening sessions across all stores with the store teams and senior management. This wasn't just market research. It was people from Tesco sitting down, talking to customers, listening and responding directly. Tim Mason remembered explaining to customers why the strawberries kept running out every Saturday, the embarrassment of having to go through the reasoning and not wanting to repeat it again next week. Compare this with sitting in a meeting room and seeing there is 91% availability of strawberries and next week 91.5% or 90.5% – the numbers just don't matter in the same way.

Similarly, at Walkers, Martin Glenn was a big advocate of getting out from behind the desk. As he explained:

> Don't confuse sending someone to the front to find out what's going on, to going there yourself. I've never regretted a field visit, a factory visit, a supplier visit. You always learn something.[34]

Some store visits are more effective than others. When we asked a large sample of British CEOs how they spent their time, those from the top 100 companies (in terms of their business performance) spent around 18% of their year in direct contact with customers. Execs from the bottom 100 companies spent 15% of their time directly with customers. Thinking this was a small difference, we followed up with some in-depth interviews and learned that the difference was accounted for by the quality of interaction (not the amount of time). The top performers' time was dedicated to observing the company's interaction with customers directly, seeing the customer experience unfiltered. The bottom performers spent their time socialising, for example at sports events, conferences and so on.[35]

Similarly, at US retailer Target:

> Store visits ostensibly intended as intelligence-gathering missions, were meticulously planned affairs, only slightly less formal than, say, a presidential visit. Every relevant national manager and local functionary would be notified in advance, each step choreographed, the 'regular shoppers' handpicked and vetted.[36]

Brian Cornell, who became Target's CEO in 2014, ditched this ceremonial visit process. Instead, he reached out to pals outside the company to put him in touch with a mix of Target shoppers with whom he visited a local store unannounced to management or staff. They gave him what he valued most – a grip on reality. There was no advance notice, no quota of visits, no specific schedule, no set visit plan – instead there were lots of basic questions. He would absorb reactions and answers, probe for better understanding, learning and also developing a more vivid, animated and powerfully informed perspective with which to engage his management colleagues. For Cornell, these visits were simply part of how he works.

We have some simple recommendations for being externally focused in a productive way. Scrap the official customer visits to instead make time to visit real customers spontaneously. Consider the concept *Genchi Genbutsu*, part of the Toyota Way. Roughly speaking, the phrase means 'go to the root (place) of the problem, see it for yourself and be moved to fix it.' At Toyota, you cannot 'sell' ideas internally unless you have the credibility of having lived the problem – in the shoes of the customer. It's also easy to learn directly from customers while seated at your desk. Rupert Soames, the CEO who led the turnaround of British temporary energy provider Aggreko, has described how 'whenever he had a moment' he called up 15 or 20 unhappy customers. Finally, it's worth evaluating your criteria and processes for promotion and hiring, ensuring that irrespective of function, your employees are genuinely interested in customers' lives.

Conclusion and recap

So, we now understand what good *looks* like for the customer-led business. The organisation and its set-up enable customer value to be delivered in new and better ways, at scale. We have discussed six elements that we have found matter – making clear choices about customers and customer needs, using guiding insight, developing innovative propositions, empowering people, ensuring rapid learning and having the discipline of customer planning – and they need to work in sync. The activities need to be tackled in a customer-led leadership style – outward-looking, committed internally and assertive in the market.

Although this formula or something like it is well established, leaders generally struggle to follow it as a complete set. We believe this is because it is more difficult than generally appreciated, and leadership teams are often insufficiently committed to and assertive about addressing the challenges involved and carrying it out thoroughly and consistently over time.

There is also a big difference between doing it all in an outside-in spirit and doing it in ways that are still effectively inside-out, whatever the lip service of protagonists. So now we move on to understand what good *feels* like – the customer-led shared beliefs that sit behind these ways of working when they operate well.

Notes

1   Henley, John. 1 September 2010. 'Crisps: A very British habit.' *The Guardian*. Retrieved from www.theguardian.com/lifeandstyle/2010/sep/01/crisps-british

2   Hyslop, Gill. 14 July 2017. 'Top 10 US salty snack brands in 2017 so far: Sales soar for Frito-Lay's Ruffles brand.' *Bakery and Snacks.com*. Retrieved from www.bakeryandsnacks.com/Article/2017/07/13/Top-10-US-snack-brands-Sales-soar-for-Frito-Lay-s-Ruffles-brand By 2017 Doritos achieved sales of US$2.1 billion and market share of 72.7% in the US alone.

3   Glenn, Martin. 2005. *The Best Job in the World: Shoulders of Giants*. Cobham: Compton House Publishing.

4   Glenn, Martin. 2005. *The Best Job in the World*, p. 26.

5   Glenn, Martin. 2005. *The Best Job in the World*, p. 26.

6   Glenn, Martin. 2005. *The Best Job in the World*, p. 28.

7   Glenn, Martin. 2005. *The Best Job in the World*, p. 14.

8   Glenn, Martin. 2005. *The Best Job in the World*, p. 10.

9   Glenn, Martin. 2005. *The Best Job in the World*, Companion DVD.

10 Glenn, Martin. 2005. *The Best Job in the World*, p. 11.

11 Glenn, Martin. 2005. *The Best Job in the World*, p. 26.

12 Glenn, Martin. 2005. *The Best Job in the World*, p. 22.

13 Interview with authors, 10 January 2017.

14 Glenn, Martin. 2005. *The Best Job in the World*, Companion DVD.

15 Glenn, Martin. 2005. *The Best Job in the World*, Companion DVD.

16 Glenn, Martin. 2005. *The Best Job in the World*, p. 28.

17 Glenn, Martin. 2005. *The Best Job in the World*, Companion DVD.

18 Glenn, Martin. 2005. *The Best Job in the World*, p. 14.

19 Superbrands. 2014. 'Superbrands case studies: Walkers.' *Superbrands*. Retrieved from www.campaignlive.co.uk/article/superbrands-case-studies-walkers/478730

20 Glenn, Martin. 2005. *The Best Job in the World*, Companion DVD.

21 Superbrands. 2014. 'Superbrands case studies: Walkers.'

22 McKee, Steve. 27 February 2014. 'Is your company a Volkswagen or a Ferrari?' *Bloomberg*. Retrieved from www.bloomberg.com/news/articles/2014-02-27/is-your-company-a-volkswagen-or-a-ferrari?sref=f1MkS6tP

23 Feeney, Danny. 2017. 'AXE: How an eternal teenager finally grew up.' *APG (UK)*. Retrieved from www.warc-com.ezproxy.imd.org/content/article/axe-how-an-eternal-teenager-finally-grew-up/112558/

24 Pfeifer, Sylvia. 5 June 2008. 'Rolls-Royce reaps the rewards of client care.' *Financial Times*. Retrieved from www.ft.com/content/2b1d2e0c-3032-11dd -86cc-000077b07658

25 Evans, Alice. 5 February 2018. 'Tube "thought of the day": The station where it started.' *BBC News*. www.bbc.co.uk/news/uk-england-london -42666628

26 Meehan, Seán & Charlie Dawson. 2002. 'Customer Responsiveness: Getting It Fast and Right Through Impatience and Intolerance.' *Business Strategy Review*, 13 (4): 26–37.

27 Baker, Rosie. 13 October 2010. 'Sir Terry Leahy says Marketers have great CEO potential.' *Marketing Week*. Retrieved from www.marketingweek.com /sir-terry-leahy-says-marketers-have-great-ceo-potential/

28 Glenn, Martin. 2005. *The Best Job in the World*, Companion DVD.

29 Glenn, Martin. 2005. *The Best Job in the World*, Companion DVD.

30 Glenn, Martin. 2005. *The Best Job in the World*, Companion DVD.

31 Kashani, Kamran & Joyce Millar. 15 December 2003. *Innovation and Renovation: The Nespresso Story* (IMD case no. IMD-5-0543). Lausanne: IMD Business School.

32 Kashani, Kamran & Joyce Millar. 15 December 2003. 'Innovation and Renovation.'

33 Gillies, Richard, Director, Plan A & Sustainable Business, Marks & Spencer from launch in 2008, interview with authors, 24 May 2020.

34 Glenn, Martin. 2005. *The Best Job in the World*, Companion DVD.

35 Barwise, Patrick & Seán Meehan. 2004. *Simply Better: Creating Customer Value by Delivering What Matters Most*. Boston, MA: Harvard Business School Press, p. 153.

36 Wahba, Phil. 1 March 2015. 'Target has a new CEO: Will he re-energize the retailer?' *Fortune*. Retrieved from https://fortune.com/longform/target -new-ceo/

3

WHAT BEING CUSTOMER-LED FEELS LIKE

There's a way to do it better – find it.

Thomas Edison

Sky: Believe in better

There was a popular joke during the early years of Sky TV:

What's the difference between Sky and the Loch Ness Monster?
Some people have seen the Loch Ness Monster.

Looking back, it's easy to imagine that the UK satellite broadcaster BSkyB, launched by Rupert Murdoch in 1988, was always destined to rule the world, yet, during its first few years, Sky had mounting losses of £14 million a week and anaemic subscriber numbers.

Murdoch always presumed that three pillars of content – sports, movies and news – would pull in crowds of subscribers with news being the big winner. But in the early years, it just wasn't happening. With so much free television on offer, BSkyB needed a 'killer application' for pay TV; it turned out that the only application the British would kill for was football.

'They've got four big sports in the US, but here it's football first, second and third. Everything else is so far down the track it's not funny,' said David Hill, head of sports at British Sky Broadcasting who had arrived from Nine Network in Australia to launch Sky Sports.[1]

And while ITV held the rights to top division football between 1988 and 1992, from '92 re-branded The Premier League, Sky Sports had to make do with cast-offs from lower levels of the game.

However, the tide turned in May 1992, thanks to an audacious £304 million deal that secured Sky live rights to five seasons of Premier League football while handing highlights to the BBC. It was a defining moment for Sky and a huge leap of faith for Murdoch and Sky's senior management.

Vic Wakeling joined Sky as head of football in 1991, and the following year, he was part of the management team, along with Rupert Murdoch and Sam Chisholm, that masterminded the deal that decisively turned the company's fortunes around and ensured its lasting success.

Andy Melvin, Sky Sports' deputy managing director joined the broadcaster as executive producer of football in 1991 and remembered the determination involved:

> When the Premier League came along, Murdoch took all the chips, put them on black, and said, 'Right, spin the wheel.' It was a huge gamble, and the sceptics said, 'This will be **** TV, real lowbrow stuff.' But we were a team of football people, making programmes for football people, and we were determined to make it work.[2]

The deal was struck on 18 May 1992, at the Royal Lancaster Hotel in Bayswater, London. Everyone expected ITV to win. Greg Dyke, head of ITV Sport at the time, was determined to keep Sky at bay saying, 'The Premier League would be the biggest dish-driver of the lot.'

But in a shock move, Sky stunned Dyke and the ITV companies by putting together a joint bid with the BBC. Dyke, furious, threatened legal action over the way the negotiations were conducted, calling the BBC 'Murdoch's poodle.' Alan Sugar, the chairman of Amstrad (which made Sky's dishes), was heard on the phone to Sky barking, 'Blow them out of the water,' after ITV offered £262 million for the rights.[3]

BSkyB did indeed blow its rivals out of the water, and the deal, for better or worse, reshaped the entire structure of the sport in Britain. It was also a moment that made every broadcaster sit up and take notice of the former upstart. Here was a company that was not to be underestimated. Here was a company that had a way of doing things that was different from its rivals.

The next day, one newspaper (a rival to Murdoch's own papers) summed it up with the headline, 'Future sold for pie in the sky.' With contracts signed, Sky splurged on a glossy advertising campaign to get armchair football fans signed up in time for the new season. With some of the best games no longer available on terrestrial TV, some expressed their wider concerns about exclusive deals, including Sebastian Coe, the newly elected Conservative MP, who said, 'I think it is wrong that only two million [satellite] dish owners get access to such major sporting events.'

In what became a long series of firsts for Sky, the first live English football Premier League goal seen by UK TV audiences was scored by Teddy Sheringham for Nottingham Forest against Liverpool on August 6, 1992. Showing 60 live games a year, Sky went on to revolutionise UK sports broadcasting with the money and resources it invested in its Premier League approach. For example, from the start of its Premier League coverage, Sky's outside broadcast units were running 16 cameras to the BBC's five. Today Sky deploys at least 24 cameras, most fitted with Ultra HD lenses, and many games have 'spidercams' offering a 360° perspective from any position on the field of play.

But it wasn't simply about financial clout being put behind an understanding of the customer in the form of a bid; Sky Sports' success has also been about customer-led innovation, about continually thinking about how to improve a sports fan's viewing experience.

Before Sky's deal, terrestrial sports broadcasting had been based around highlights drawn from many sources. To put it in perspective, on April 13, 1991, the last Saturday before the launch of Sky Sports, Bob Wilson had opened the BBC's Grandstand programme with a basketball championship in Birmingham.

Sky understood what a large number of people especially wanted to watch – that the real mileage and excitement lay in live events and especially football. Moreover, the broadcaster's technical innovation gave Sky customers the kind of viewing experience previously restricted to the players themselves.

For example, in 1992, the 'steadicam,' a stabilising bodysuit that allows camera operators to rush up and down the touchline without making viewers feel sick, was introduced. (This is now used in big budget movies like Harry Potter.)

More recently, Sky introduced the idea of adapting the ultra-slow-motion cameras used for crash-testing vehicles to enhance sports coverage.[4] All these broadcasting innovations have been subsequently adopted by other sports broadcasters and have become the norm, improving the experience for millions of distant sports fans all over the globe.

Financially, BSkyB was also turning the corner by 1992, moving into operating profit for the first time in March that year. By August, Sky dishes were in 3.3 million homes, and it had 1.6 million subscribers to its sport and movie channels.

Once BSkyB had bought the rights to Premier League football, it used them to build the strongest pay TV distribution system in the country. In September 1992, a handful of weeks after it started showing its exclusive live Premier League coverage, it started charging subscribers for the privilege.

As BSkyB's successful bid for the Premier League appeared to set it on the road to success, the naysayers sat up and started taking notice. Sky's customer base grew and grew. By 1996, Sky Sports had 3 million satellite subscribers and BSkyB controlled 90% of the revenues generated by pay TV in the UK.[5]

Sky's dogged belief that TV viewers would value better telly so much that they were prepared to pay for it paid off. This shared belief, part of a wider 'outside-in belief system,' helped the entire organisation have the confidence to make decision after decision that created customer value in new and better ways.

Nearly 30 years from launch, the broadcaster has grown from a bold upstart into an innovative, multi-platform technology and entertainment company with 22.9 million subscribers around the world.[6]

Sky's story, like Walkers and Tesco, is an example of a customer-led organisation challenging convention and taking big audacious steps in its quest to improve its customers' experiences. Vic Wakeling, by now the head of sport at BSkyB, confirmed its focus on customer choice in 1994:

> Sky Television is all about choice. It's about people who want to tune
> in and watch the news whenever they get in during the day or night.
> It's about people who want to watch a selection of movies ...[7]

In this chapter, we'll be looking at how Sky's outside-in beliefs lay behind the entertainment company's successive stages of success. Through the story of Sky, alongside others, we'll be examining why shared beliefs matter so much, and then in relation to our customer-led questions, how they vary between inside-out and outside-in belief systems. We'll see why the former is more common than the latter and what outside-in beliefs actually *feel* like within a company in order to better understand how to create and hold onto them.

Shared beliefs: The way we do things around here

Before we go further, we need to clarify what we mean when we talk about shared beliefs and why they matter.

When we first discuss shared beliefs, the response is often to view them as interchangeable with the idea of 'culture.' For us, the concept of culture as commonly discussed in business is somewhat imprecise. Our definition of shared beliefs comes from the anthropological concept of 'discourse,' which is often assumed to refer only to speech but is in fact a richer and more powerful concept. So, we decided to describe this idea as the shared beliefs of a group, or the group's belief system.

For us, the important aspects of shared beliefs are:

- That they describe the way a group thinks and the assumptions it makes – which may be different from the individual beliefs of team members. We are social animals and skilled at adapting to fit in with our tribe.
- That they define success for everyone in the organisation (especially important in our quest to understand customer-led practice and achievement). They explain *what people think they all need to do in order to win*, to earn congratulations, to get promoted and the like.

Shared beliefs dictate behaviour and can allow an organisation to take a leap of faith with confidence because there is a widely held conviction that 'this kind of thing works for us.' Academic literature analyses the way groups work together within an organisation to understand *the way we do things around here.*

MIT professor Ed Schein pioneered the field of organisational culture and defined culture as:

> The pattern of basic **assumptions** that a **group** has invented, discovered or developed, to **cope** with its problems of external **adaptation** or internal **integration**, that have worked well and are **taught** to new members as the way to perceive, think, feel and **behave**.[8]

He identifies three levels of culture:

1. **Artefacts** which are visible. These include anything tangible or evident from architecture and design of a workplace to dress code and office jokes with employees as an organisation's brand ambassadors. These tend to provide clues as to what the shared beliefs really are, but not the answer.
2. **Espoused beliefs and values** which may be visible in surveys. These are expressed in the mission, vision, philosophies and values of the organisation and serve as a guide for the company's decision making.
3. **Basic underlying assumptions** which are invisible. Unconscious beliefs and values that are in fact the most powerful of the three levels − far more so than espoused words on a wall that are often some distance removed from people's reality and experiences.[9]

John Kay, the economist, identified this same collective human quality and its importance in a speech he gave on the purpose of business in October 2014. He spoke to different groups of experts and described what could be learned from them as well as how useful it might be:

> So let's ... talk to the anthropologists because what the anthropologists understand in ways that none of the people I have talked to already do is that most of what happens in business as with everywhere else in our lives, happens in small groups of people. It is the relations between people in these small groups that determine the performance of the organisation and it is the interactions between these small groups that are what the structure of the business and the direction of the senior management should be intended to do. That's

a very different take on business from the one generated by the cult of the heroic individual.[10]

Toyota is an often-cited example of a strong culture or belief system. The beliefs and the ways of working that flow from them are codified in 'The Toyota Way.' This defines the company's expectations and guides its behaviours. There are two main pillars: continuous improvement (challenge, kaizen and genchi genbutsu) and respect for people (respect and teamwork). The company is: '...never satisfied with where we are and always improve our business by putting forth the best ideas and efforts.'[11]

Often a company's shared beliefs are revealed in the details, small actions that might seem insignificant or quirky from a distance, but which are of crucial symbolic importance in showing what matters to the group. An example comes from Amazon CEO Jeff Bezos's insistence that all company meetings begin in the same way with quiet reading. This is part of a whole system of unusual ways of doing things and reinforces the company's unusual belief system, a belief system that is ultimately all about being customer-led.

> Mr Bezos's recent letter to shareholders extolled the Amazon practice of starting all internal meetings by everyone present reading a memo of up to six pages, explaining what they are there to discuss. Instead of watching a PowerPoint presentation, or breaking into an immediate debate, Amazon's executives spend up to half an hour in complete silence, absorbing the briefing that one of them has prepared. 'This is the weirdest meeting culture you will ever encounter,' Mr Bezos admitted in one interview. The principle is that an executive must refine his or her proposal so fully to express it in narrative form that everyone will be able to understand it. Reading the memo means that all those in the room are informed for the conversation that follows, and are not merely bluffing.[12]

This concept of shared beliefs, or discourse, was proposed by anthropologists and influenced by Foucault[13] as an alternative to their traditional notions of culture.

While discourse doesn't only refer to language, the words we use and the expressions we articulate can very effectively reveal the system of beliefs of a group we might be part of. Some familiar examples include the difference between freedom fighters and terrorists, between immigrants and ex-pats, between a challenge and an opportunity, between 'we will' and 'we will try' and so on.

Gill Ereaut of Linguistic Landscapes describes discourse within a company as:

> An organisation's embedded habits of speech and writing, styles of expression, accepted slang and shorthand, and common terms for things, people and processes. It's the idiosyncratic language soup that characterizes an organisation and is invisible to those inside.[14]

Matthew Lieberman, professor and social cognitive neuroscience lab director at UCLA, found that belief systems are a way our brains have adapted to deal with too much information. In a conversation, the auditory system is receiving and passing on information at a phenomenal rate. One filter, among many that are applied, is the listener's beliefs or assumptions that guide a response, giving a better chance of an instinctive reaction that goes down well with the group. Beliefs provide stability. When new information arrives, it is assessed against the existing set of beliefs to determine whether it should be incorporated or ignored. You can see how 'groupthink' might arise as a team sticks together by removing uncomfortable truths that challenge the status quo.[15]

Kathleen Taylor, a neuroscientist at Oxford University, found it helpful to view beliefs and memories as similar. Just as beliefs get stronger by repetition and reinforcement across a group, so too do memories deepen as networks of neurons fire repeatedly when stimulated by an event.[16]

This all helps to explain why it is so incredibly difficult to change shared beliefs, especially in a large and extended group. Everyone involved is influenced by the prevailing beliefs, so everyone's behaviour is aligned. Seeing the behaviour all around you reinforces the perception of what matters to the group and how to fit in, how to stay safe. 'Fitting in' is a subconscious choice made over and over again that reinforces the belief at both the group and individual level each time.

Often a shared belief system only becomes visible when it clashes with another incompatible system, much to the confusion of all involved. For example, when a traveller used to paying for taxis by credit card in their own country takes a cab from the airport in a city where only cash is accepted, the two individuals will react with mutual incredulity when the time comes to settle the bill. Each is certain about the obvious 'rightness' of their own assumptions until someone from outside crashes in.

Specific belief systems: Inside-out and outside-in

Having explained why the shared beliefs of an organisation are the dominant determinant of its behaviour and that of its individuals, we return to the two very different systems of belief that relate to being customer-led – what we term inside-out and outside-in.

- Inside-out beliefs are conventional and not customer-led – they start with the business and what most obviously matters to it and to the people associated with it. They reflect the way people working in the business see the world – literally from the inside looking out, with colleagues close and customers distant, and with lots of assumptions about the way things are done that don't get challenged.
- Outside-in beliefs start outside the business. They begin with what matters to customers and with ways to do a better job for them, only then moving on to how the business can achieve these outcomes in ways that will be commercially successful as well.

We found that inside-out belief systems have two competitive advantages over outside-in belief systems, making these sets of beliefs the default setting in any organisation.

An inside-out way of defining success might be to sell more. And the way it might be assumed that this success will be achieved is to set higher sales targets, to promise people lots of money if they hit them, and to shout at them if they don't. The first advantage this way of seeing things has is that it sounds like common sense. This is what everyone does, right? The second advantage is that it works ... for a while. The focus, effort and alignment will produce results for a group, but eventually, as the sales targets rise, behaviour becomes 'pushier' in order to hit them – high pressure sales tactics, promotional marketing, obfuscation of a deal in the eyes of customers, and eventually mis-selling, cheating and regulatory if not legal trouble. The short-term success hides the long-term trouble, as we'll see later in the chapter when we analyse two inside-out examples – Wells Fargo and the Australian banking sector.

Another good example comes from a housing association. Under financial pressure, the organisation decided to stop mending fences on its housing estates. Fences don't need mending very often – there is a continual, slow flow of an issue here and then an issue there. This means the money-saving is immediate and ongoing and it is only years later that the customer cost starts to become clear in run-down neighbourhoods, diminishing pride, and as a consequence a spiral of other issues such as vandalism and graffiti. The business cost benefit was definite and immediate, the way it hurt what customers value was hard to spot and in the future. Putting it right costs a lot, but the people who made the original decision have long since moved on, no doubt believing they made a smart move.

In contrast, an outside-in way of defining success is to serve customers in some way, with the business seeing profit only as a means to that end, still crucial but not the ultimate goal. This already sounds like it might take more explaining than its inside-out alternative, and it gets harder when you look at outside-in initiatives as ways of achieving success. Often what matters to customers can't directly be linked back to what leads to sales. For example, Tesco's observation that customers didn't like to queue: an unarguable conclusion, and yet the business activity that would improve the situation is tricky to make a case for. The One-in-Front queuing promise cost £60 million, definitely and immediately. But, the customer response could only be determined by actually spending the money and seeing what happened. So, while costs are definite and immediate, benefits are probable at best and in the future. Outside-in initiatives usually have these characteristics, making them a hard sell in a business with inside-out beliefs.

Table 3.1 Outside-in versus inside-out beliefs

What does success look like?	
Inside-out	Higher sales, profit or shareholder returns
Outside-in	Greater value for customers – solving problems or achieving outcomes people care about in new and better ways
How is success achieved?	
Inside-out	Setting higher sales targets, rewarding employees for hitting them, penalising or berating them for failing
Outside-in	Innovating, leading the market with initiatives for customers that end up paying back for the business

Given the insight into this skewed playing field, let us get back to the Sky story to see how the broadcaster managed to make its belief system outside-in, against all odds.

From a wing and a prayer to Sky's the limit

At 6 pm on Sunday, 5 February 1989, Rupert Murdoch stood on a building site in an industrial estate in Isleworth, West London. In a frantic scramble to get on air before the official rival, British Satellite Broadcasting (BSB), he was about to switch on Sky Television for the first time.

'Is this going to work?' a journalist from *The Guardian* asked him. He smiled a crooked smile. 'It's a wing and a prayer,' he confessed.[17]

Sky's beginning as a scrappy upstart that set up shop in premises resembling a 'car-park on the way to Heathrow' offers a clue behind the shared beliefs that continue to shape the broadcaster's success today.

Sky challenged TV establishment norms from the very beginning. From different production technology, to different transmission technology and all things in-between, Sky zagged while the rest of the broadcasting world zigged. Let's not forget the fact it launched on a 'pirate' satellite called Astra, regulated not by Britain but by Luxembourg, and was able to reach virtually the whole of the British Isles.

This appetite for innovation remains part of the brand's DNA, with the broadcaster continually creating new ways to enhance its viewer's experience and push the boundaries of its industry.

Andrew Neil was pulled in from *The Sunday Times* to manage the broadcaster's launch and seemed to have the remit to throw money at the task. The service launched with four channels – Sky News, Sky Movies (initially unencrypted), Sky Channel (which became Sky One) and Eurosport (which showed tennis, skiing and cricket). As he said, 'Almost everybody said that we'd fail. It took Britain 60 years to get to four channels, within six months and we'd doubled that figure.'[18]

At launch, Sky News was fully formed with well-trained journalists who were longing to escape the terrestrial channels. They understood how CNN had already transformed news reporting as we knew it and were able to run live rolling news coverage of Nelson Mandela's release and the fall of the Berlin Wall in their first few years of existence.

But the forced entry into British television was not easy. For years, Murdoch and his team battled the established duopoly of ITV and the BBC, as well as the snobbery that initially greeted Sky's output, condescendingly dubbed, 'council house television.' Many people were up in arms about the unsightly satellite dishes on houses and the way this changed the appearance of Britain's towns and cities. In the early days, Murdoch and his leadership team batted away prejudices about ugly satellite dishes and presumptions that nobody would pay for television when they could watch BBC and ITV for free.

Murdoch used the MacTaggart Lecture in 1989 at the Edinburgh International TV Festival as an opportunity to launch an attack on the British TV establishment: 'Much of what is claimed to be quality television here is no more than the parading of the prejudices and interests of the like-minded people who currently control British television.'[19]

Yet, in these early years, British pay TV nearly sank Rupert Murdoch. Innovation came at a cost. In August 1990, New Corp's UK subsidiary, News International, Sky's parent, reported annual losses of £257 million, with Sky losing £95 million on top of start-up costs of £120 million.[20]

Dish sales were running at fewer than 10,000 a month. At great cost, Sky set up a direct salesforce to sell dishes, as well as a call centre in Scotland to sell subscriptions direct to customers. And rather than chasing advertising revenue, the broadcaster focused on securing paying customers.

In August 1990, Murdoch brought in Sam Chisholm from Australia's Nine Network who was later to describe his time as chief executive as 'an amazing experience, an absolute nightmare.'[21]

Meanwhile, behind the scenes, Murdoch was in secret negotiations to merge Sky with its arch-rival BSB. It soon became clear that this was less of a merger and more of a takeover. BSB's square dishes were ditched in favour of Sky's, most of BSB's staff were made redundant, and Murdoch loyalist Sam Chisholm was appointed CEO. Chisholm said:

> They had simply spent themselves into oblivion, all of them. The truth was that both businesses had been conceptual failures. It hadn't just been a failure, it had been an appalling failure.[22]

In 1991, the merged BSkyB was given a £200 million refinancing package to keep it afloat as the sheer cost of attracting customers to a whole new way of watching telly took its toll.

Sky's Moments of Belief

Sky's history is characterised by making big long-term bets – fundamental changes in direction that led the market and proactively created significant new value for customers.

These big moments of outside-in decision-making are key to understanding Sky's journey to customer-led growth and market leadership. They were Moments of Belief.

We have already outlined two Moments of Belief in Sky's history – its early launch as a satellite broadcaster and its audacious bid for the Premier League rights. There were many others that created and deepened its widely shared customer-led beliefs.

Let's explore some of these Moments of Belief in more detail.

Moment of Belief: A digital platform

BSkyB's launch of digital television in 1997/98 was a significant Moment of Belief for the broadcaster and spelled yet another new era in television. It required dismantling the existing tech platform and completely replacing it, based on the belief that customers would pay for a better offer and experience. Specific improvements included making the electronic programme guide easier to use and providing more than 200 new channels from Disney and Discovery to National Geographic. Beyond offering more choice, the new digital platform also offered viewers better picture and sound quality.

Britain was to become a testing ground for an experiment in consumer choice. BSkyB's launch of its digital services included pay-per-view films alongside bundles of channels devoted to different genres of programme. It was yet another demonstration that BSkyB was convinced by its guiding insight, originally from seeing the way TV worked in the US and then from its own UK learning, that customers would be prepared to pay for good quality content and a better TV experience. To encourage customers to join the digital revolution, BSkyB subsidised the retail price of the set-up boxes to the tune of £200 per unit.

Table 3.2 Sky's Moments of Belief

Satellite start-up

What?	Sky wins the race to launch a satellite broadcaster.
When?	1989–1992.
Who?	Customers grow from zero to 3.5 million.
How?	Sky challenges the establishment and subsidises customer acquisition to speed growth.
Why?	To shake up the status quo and offer better television in areas that matter to customers.

Winning Premier League TV rights

What?	Sky bets big on football.
When?	May 1992.
Who?	By 1996, Sky Sports on its own had 3 million satellite subscribers.
How?	Bidding £304 million to acquire Premier League rights.
Why?	Live football highly valued by large swathes of the British viewing public.

Digital platform

What?	Sky ditches entire analogue tech platform replacing it with a digital one.
When?	1998.
Who?	Customers grew from 3.5 million (analogue) in 1998 to 8 million (digital) by 2005.
How?	Brought specific experience improvements – the electronic programme guide (EPG), Sky+ and an explosion of choice.
Why?	Hungry for first-mover advantage and driven by a belief that digital brought lots that customers would love – vast choice, better quality transmission, easier navigation, the start of interaction with programmes and more. Biggest bet since launch.

Broadband and telephony

What?	Sky bundled broadband and telephony into deals offering extra value to customers.
When?	2005.
Who?	Customers grew from 8 million in 2005 to 11 million in 2012.
How?	Developed a strong value message for first time. Became more sophisticated at trading customers up.
Why?	Broadband helped customers have a whole solution for their home, putting TV and broadband together, a solution they can trust and which is easy to use.

Segmented brand offer and internet delivery

What?	Sky adds segmented brands to offering – Sky Go, NOW TV, Sky+ and SkyQ.
When?	NOW TV launched in 2012.
Who?	NOW TV customers grew from 239,000 households in Q1 2014 to 1.46 million households in Q1 2018.
How?	With NOW TV Sky offers a new value proposition to customers with pay-as-you-go to appeal to millennials alongside monthly packages.
Why?	To create value for a specific and different segment who would never value Sky's core offer – millennials – and who were starting to find value in disruptive competitors such as Netflix.

Yet again newspapers at the time were filled with forecasts of failure. Who wants a digital satellite dish? Why take 140 channels when 30 is enough for anyone? Rumours flew through media circles that Sky was losing more analogue subscribers than were being added through digital.

Digital would not be BSkyB's for the taking. The new digital terrestrial rival, ONdigital, was backed by two leading UK media companies, Granada and Carlton. They planned to spend millions of pounds launching a rival digital platform, using a mix of their own channels and premium programming bought in from BSkyB.

Its management at the time – Elizabeth Murdoch and Mark Booth – faced a daunting list of tasks: launch Sky Digital, compete against ONdigital, keep a wary eye on the cable industry (which planned its own digital launches in 1999) and do everything in their power to manage the decline of their analogue base while they effected the transition to digital.

No surprise that BSkyB's investors were unimpressed by the potential of digital. The broadcaster's share price fell from £6.91 in October 1996 to a low of £3.61 in February 1997, cutting the company's value by £5.5 billion. In June 1998, Neil Blackley, a media analyst at Merrill Lynch, the US investment bank, told the *Financial Times*, 'There is pain before the pleasure.'[23]

But Booth remained upbeat, arguing that digital technology gave BSkyB the opportunity to reinvent pay television. 'You don't go to a record store because you want to hear 10,000 records,' he said. 'You do it because you are confident they will have the one you want.'

He said capacity limits had previously prevented broadcasters from meeting the precise demands of consumers:

> You might like documentary programmes in general, but not the one you see when you switch on. If you have five documentary channels, there is bound to be something on that interests you.[24]

Moment of Belief: Broadband and telephony

In 2005 competition intensified in the broadband market among cable, satellite and telecommunications companies all looking to steal share. For Sky, this meant facing competition from big telecom players including France Telecom's Orange, retailer Carphone Warehouse, BT which had plans to launch a digital video on demand service in partnership with Microsoft, as well as the cable company ntl, which had partnered with Virgin Mobile.

Needless to say, Sky didn't see this as a problem but as an opportunity to increase value for its customers. Previously, customers had tended to buy broadband and telephony from one supplier and their TV from Sky. Now there was a chance to offer customers television, telephony and broadband services on one bill – a 'triple play' as it became known in the industry. As James Murdoch explained:

> [Consumers] want a whole solution for their home which they can trust, and which is easy to use. We hear a lot about telecoms companies 'we will offer video, it's all ones and zeroes.' We think it's trickier than that. It's about brand and customer focus. It's about making technology easier to use and making it resonate with the customer.[25]

In October 2005, BSkyB paid a hefty £211 million to buy Easynet, a broadband provider. The following month it signed a mobile deal with Vodafone, and within two months over 5 million streams of live television channels had been accessed through mobile phones.[26] Yet both these moves were described by Murdoch as a means to add value to a Sky subscription for existing Sky customers as much as a way of opening new markets such as online telephony or interactivity.

BSkyB surprised everyone with the scale of its broadband ambition. In July 2006, the broadcaster announced plans to invest £400 million over three years, double the estimates of outsiders. Sky's 'free' broadband offer, which encouraged existing customers to bundle their broadband and telephony into their TV deal, was offered to all the broadcaster's customers and not just to premium subscribers. For relatively small extra charges, Sky's subscribers could upgrade to faster upload and download broadband speeds.

The *Wall Street Journal* reported that while investors were concerned that BSkyB's leader, James Murdoch, was spending too heavily, his beliefs were something of a family trait:

> Just as his father News Corp chairman, Rupert, has done many times, James is taking steps that incur short-term losses in pursuit of a longer-term strategy.[27]

At the broadcaster's 2005 interim results, James Murdoch articulated Sky's outside-in belief system centred on customer-led innovation:

> It's about constant innovation, to continue to put innovative, new, easy to use products that bring things together for customers in a simple way ... it's about constantly moving forward and not staying still. And that really contributes to the brand position that the company has today, and it enables us to go through the cycle again around our customers. And all of these attributes lead to growth.[28]

Murdoch continually cited the customer in financial presentations to explain business decisions. Indeed, in a question and answer session with readers of FT.com, James Murdoch kicked off the discussion with the image of a family in their living room in Nottingham.

> Families want flexibility and control. They want to benefit from the wave of innovation that is sweeping across the communications industry. Our approach puts entertainment at the core and focuses on making things easy and intuitive for families.[29]

He also made the point that understanding customers was critical to Sky's strategy.

> We do 3.3 million unique house visits every year. That's a big number. Those are Sky+ upgrades, multi-room upgrades, service calls, sales and installation, moving home and so on and so forth. Those are quite big numbers. And every single visit is very unique. I can tell you myself and a number of [executives] we go out on these calls and we go on the road, and we go and visit customers and go and view these service calls. And every one is unique.[30]

Stretching Sky's business into broadband and telephony was about more than trying to lock in its existing 8 million customers. Its customers leapt at the chance to bundle their telephone, entertainment and broadband together. Between 2005 and 2012 the overall customer base grew to 11 million with broadband customers growing from zero to 5–6 million.

Moreover, it spelled a change in Sky's business model. Unlike betting the future on content, which is high cost and high risk, leading to either high profit or high loss, broadband offered a more dependable revenue, albeit with lower margins, and it was another reason for Sky customers to stick around.

Moving into the broadband market demonstrated outside-in thinking. As James Murdoch wrote in the 2007 Annual Report:

> Historically we had operated in an industry worth £7 billion. However, by moving into the adjacent sectors of broadband and fixed line telephony, we now operate in a combined sector whose value is over £20 billion today.

Critically, Sky's ground-breaking deals into broadband and telephony were also a step towards increased control of the customer's end-to-end experience. Today, the broadcaster has a carefully managed ecosystem. It makes its own boxes, develops its own technology, and manages all services and points of sale in order to control the customer experience. This means it gets hour-by-hour sales and churn data, immediate insight into customers' viewing consumption and more – all vital customer data to help it learn about what's valued and how to create more.

Moment of Belief: Segmented brand offer and internet delivery

Outside-in companies are always connected to customers and opportunities for value to be created in new and better ways. Their aim is to anticipate market changes, so they aren't taken by surprise. Since the launch of Netflix in 1998, and its subsequent pivot from loaning DVDs to internet streaming, which led to serious global success, Sky's competition now looks very different. Today, many customers are cutting the cord with their traditional entertainment provider and signing up to Netflix or Amazon Prime instead.

Sky was watching Netflix very closely from the beginning. It set up a small team away from the corporate centre to address a critical question – can we build a service that could sit over the top of subscriptions?

While the significance of Netflix is apparent today, when Sky entered the streaming market with NOW TV in July 2012, it was less so. 'The customer need wasn't that clear at that time,' recalls Nick Green, formerly director of internal communications at Sky.

> Netflix was interesting but there wasn't much on it unless you were 16. The Crown wasn't even a glimmer in the Netflix eye. It was hard to demonstrate the real customer demand beyond the logic that TV will go this way and we need to be in rather than out.[31]

Sky's subsequent fourth big Moment of Belief saw the broadcaster launch a different brand aimed at appealing to a different segment of customers and needs, recognising changing customer habits. With millennials uninterested in signing up to long-term subscription contracts, Sky's sub-brand NOW TV offered them flexibility to access content via a pay-as-you-go streaming service.

Critically, customers did not have to be a Sky subscriber to join. Thanks to Sky's existing movie rights, NOW TV could show the latest blockbusters months before its rivals.

This was a new value proposition that appealed to a very different audience. Before NOW TV was launched, there was a fierce internal debate about how it would fit in with Sky's business model – surely it competed. The verdict was that since competitors were creating customer value in new and better ways, Sky had to renew its own model proactively to respond. According to Green:

> The phrase Jeremy Darroch, chief executive, always used was, 'we must never think like the incumbent.' Because once you start thinking like that, you're writing your own death warrant.[32]

Like Sky's other Moments of Belief, the launch of NOW TV was both transformational and counterintuitive. This was an organisation that had been built around a subscriptions business model that employed a team of 800 engineers to install satellite dishes. As Green explained:

> Suddenly, with the NOW TV business model, you don't need an engineer, you don't need to call us; you get a box and you do it yourself and by the way, don't worry about anything dirty like a subscription. Running the internal comms function at the time, we had a real challenge to position this in a way so that people didn't think we'd gone completely mad and continued to do what they were employed to do.[33]

However, Sky's 'Believe in Better' mantra, literally summing up their belief system, meant that internal resistance was nothing more than a degree of head scratching. Sky's beliefs meant colleagues were open to challenging ideas because history and the broadcaster's track record suggested this outside-in approach worked. Green explained:

> There is a huge belief in the management of the organisation. In a 'Believe in Better' culture you're inspired to do stuff. You say, 'alright boss, sounds to me like you've gone slightly mad, but I'm up for the fight ... 'Big brassy Moments of Belief, initiatives that impact customers and maybe run counter to existing business models, really can work when everyone gets behind them.[34]

NOW TV created a new growth spurt from audiences such as students who had previously never considered a relationship with the Sky brand. They are hard to reach, perhaps in short-term rental homes where they can't install a dish and would never commit to a one-year contract. Their income might be low, but £10 for a football match split between friends can work – an example of re-framing the value conversation.

Other companies may have been concerned that NOW TV would cannibalise its far more lucrative existing subscription business. Not Sky, according to CEO Jeremy Darroch:

> You've got to step into consumer trends. The great thing about NOW TV is that we can suddenly get into parts of the market we couldn't have got to before. Perhaps some customers we would have acquired through Sky we now take through NOW TV, but any negatives of that are offset by serving more people.[35]

It's not surprising that Darroch had previously worked at Procter & Gamble and strongly believed that Sky needed to launch multiple brands in order to maximise value in the market, an important part of the P&G model.

Alongside NOW TV, Sky Q offers a premium service for Sky's most committed fans, while the Sky Go app (launched even before BBC's iPlayer) offers customers the opportunity to watch Sky across a number of different devices.

The lesson: Believe in better

Today, Sky's success at singlehandedly creating a whole new market is undisputed. The rise from a loss-making broadcaster into a multi-billion entertainment company is notable because of the many, many years of costly investments into big bets; not least because the pay-off was unclear and the time horizon was uncertain.

Sky has always been a pioneer and a rule breaker. Unlike its different groups of competitors, Sky's vision was never bound by industry norms but informed by a focus on the viewer and an understanding of macro trends. And as we've already explored, Sky's vision was shaped by an outside-in belief system that guided the leadership team to spot gaps beyond what was commonly defined as the market and gave it the confidence to take action to fill them.

Sky was successful because of one fundamental difference between it and other players across the British broadcasting landscape. While many in the industry only thought of TV with inside-out assumptions – few channels, free to air, something people sat down and watched together – Sky didn't have the same anchored view. It was quite literally thinking outside the box about how TV could be reconfigured to give customers what they wanted – what I love to watch, when and where I want to watch it, with high production values. This is outside-in thinking.

Indeed, BBC and ITV continually missed a trick, failing to spot Sky's potential and resisting change. For example, when Sky first launched, ITV took out disparaging full-page ads in the *Financial Times* showing rusty satellite dishes and the line, 'Money for old soap.'[36]

In 2007, Sky adopted the strapline 'Believe in Better,' publicly reflecting its positioning as a media company that makes life easier for customers. This was also an overt declaration of the fundamental beliefs held within the business. Customers will pay for better TV, so if we make TV better, broadly, we will succeed commercially as well. This is part of Sky's discourse. This is the articulation of Sky's outside-in belief system.

Nick Green elaborates on how this underpins Sky's internal culture:

> Three beautiful words – Believe in Better. It means you are constantly searching and always restless. Always looking for the next new thing. It is about the restless ambition to be able to do more for the customer and find better ways of doing stuff. The belief system is just there, it's palpable. It's in the water system. And the clues are there in the speed of transactions, in the style of leadership, in stuff on the walls. It is liberating because it enables constant challenge of the status quo, meaning there are very few sacred cows.[37]

This outside-in perspective is reflected in ambitions for growth. When Sky sees 60% of UK customers paying for TV, they also see 40% more to go for. Some will never want it, but there is clearly still much to play for, including selling more to existing customers by improving the offer, and looking to new international markets like Italy and Germany.

In November 2014, following the £6.88 billion buyout of its sister companies Sky Deutschland and Sky Italia in Germany and Italy, BSkyB reverted to its original name, Sky. Ditching the words 'British' and 'broadcasting' from its business after almost 25 years was an apt reflection of the company's evolution beyond TV into an international multimedia content company.

We've highlighted a number of these big bets throughout Sky's history, but it is useful to recognise the way the bets are taken, which is with a degree of balance. The business is an enthusiastic user of data, and its control of the end-to-end customer experience means it has a great deal to use. It tests and researches extensively, subjecting its insights to serious interrogation. Then the CEO decides. Indeed, because of the track record and the ultimate Murdoch owners, you are more likely to lose your job as the CEO if you are not bold enough, rather than if you are too bold. Feedback from patriarch Rupert is always 'go bigger, go faster, add more.'

Sky's culture is crucial. Akin to Jeff Bezos' continual reminders that Amazon must always stay as it was on day one – not resting on its laurels, keeping on driving forward with the energy and vision of a start-up – Sky is determined to keep alive the spirit of its beginnings as a scrappy upstart in a 'car park near Heathrow.'[38] Like many successful start-ups, Sky worries about complacency. It consciously nourishes its 'burningness,' the restless ambition that lies behind the way it thinks and behaves.

It works hard to woo investors in a way that is consistent with the belief system. Financial briefings always begin with customer metrics first around churn and average revenue per user (ARPU).

Its approach was aided by its ownership structure. Since Sky's flotation, it was owned 39% by Fox and 61% free float, which offered the sweet spot of public and private. Fox was large and supportive – and Sky was immune from takeover speculation other than from Fox. The free float meant there was also a focus on this specific business, a singular view on what was best for Sky and no danger of getting lost in the wider Murdoch group. The balance meant that investors' expectations were managed because it was clear the view was long term, including when that came at a cost in the short term.

So far, Sky has got it right. This was previously helped by having a supportive investor and owner in Fox and Murdoch. However, since September 2018, the company has been owned by US media firm Comcast, following Fox's sale of all of its shareholding. As we write, it's too early to say how this new ownership might impact strategy.

Moreover, despite success, Sky keeps having to make big bets, and some of them are getting bigger, not least the cost of UK Premier League TV rights, inflated by BT's ambition. Sky's success has been aided by the fact it operates in a growing market, so everyone wins to a degree. In contrast, Tesco, our story from Chapter 1, was in a mature sector where competition was defined by share, with winners and losers balancing out.

Sky's history is characterised by making big long-term bets – fundamental changes in direction, proactively creating significant new customer value and leading the market. Usually there are no precedents, something that comes with genuine leadership. The original launch was a gigantic bet that involved outsmarting regulators. Going digital was huge. It tore up the established analogue business at significant cost at a time when the whole enterprise was not yet especially big or valuable. As scale has grown, the bets have still been large, but smaller compared to the scale of the business. Their track record helps the belief that each bet will succeed. Indeed, the £30 billion Comcast paid for Sky in 2018 made it the most valuable UK company to be sold in the past 30 years.

The contrast of an inside-out belief system

Sky's story demonstrates how outside-in beliefs propel a company to long-term success, even when short-term initiatives that focus on customers may appear difficult, expensive and risky at the time. In this world, success is genuinely creating more value for customers, pioneering on their behalf, and success is achieved by leading a market in this direction in a way that is also commercially sustainable.

At this point it's helpful to contrast what an inside-out belief system looks like and how it might lead to a different business outcome. As a reminder, an inside-out belief system tends to feel more natural for a company. Success is defined primarily in financial terms, as sales or profit, and success is achieved by setting increasingly stretching sales targets, rewarding through bonuses and punishing for failure. These sales targets mean that customer value is not a primary concern.

As we covered earlier in the chapter, inside-out beliefs are natural, although they may eventually be unhelpful. In contrast, outside-in beliefs are difficult to establish. They require faith that the costs will eventually be justified by a future return.

Let's return to the metaphor we introduced in Chapter 1 that we find helpful in characterising the relationship between inside-out and outside-in beliefs. It describes the organisation as a planet and the pull of 'gravity' making it hard to escape from inside-out forces. It describes the way these forces get stronger as the size of the planet grows, what it takes to lift off, establishing outside-in beliefs to begin with, then how falling back is remarkably easy unless something deliberate is done to prevent it.

A start-up company is tiny. Like a small planet, it has hardly any gravitational pull and it is easy for all involved to escape the natural perspective to see their world the way customers see it; outside-in with a clear view of their competitors and alternatives.

But an established business is huge, and the bigger it gets, just like a larger planet, the stronger the pull of gravity holding everyone in place. To escape takes serious effort, and like the challenge of getting a satellite into orbit from Earth, you need a powerful rocket with a number of stages to propel you fast enough and far enough to break free. Burningness provides the fuel and then our rocket stages are Moments of Belief, each one propelling the beliefs of the business and its people's perspective to be progressively more external. Eventually, after enough Moments of Belief are seen for real and appreciated by all, the business and its beliefs are flying high, circling the planet, taking a view that is outside looking in.

Having made it this far, the battle is far from over – gravity is a relentless force. A satellite over time and without intervention slowly loses speed, starts to descend and eventually crashes back to Earth. So it is with outside-in beliefs. Only taking a particular kind of action can maintain them, a stream of Moments of Belief and paying attention to where the beliefs really are.

The ease with which organisations can fall back to inside-out thinking and actions can be seen with a closer look at the global banking industry.

Inside-out for real: A natural disaster waiting to happen

The Australian banking sector has been exposed as an industry that abused customers and took them for granted. A relentless pursuit of profit diverted Australia's five biggest banks from considering how they could simultaneously create value for customers. A Banking Royal Commission established in December 2017 by the Australian government looked at National Australia Bank (NAB), Commonwealth Bank (CBA), Australia and New Zealand Banking Group (ANZ), Westpac (WBC) and AMP. These five banks control more than three-quarters of the domestic market. The five biggest financial institutions have had to refund customers to the tune of AUS$222.3 million for failing to offer advice while charging ongoing advice fees.[39]

AMP, a 170-year-old institution, was under investigation following evidence that the bank misled regulators on at least 20 occasions and systematically charged customers fees without providing the service they were paying for. Its chief executive Craig Meller was forced to quit.

Meanwhile, NAB admitted in May 2018 that its staff routinely falsely witnessed client forms, describing the practice as a 'social norm' in the bank (a neat description of shared, inside-out beliefs). CBA, the country's biggest bank by assets, confessed to charging customers fees for services it never provided as well as charging clients who were deceased – in one case for up to a decade. CBA is under investigation for more than 50,000 alleged breaches of money laundering and counter-terrorism laws, to which the bank has partially admitted, resulting in the departure of its chief executive Ian Narev and a revamp of its board. According to Mark Johnson, a former deputy chairman of Macquarie, an Australian bank:

> What has shocked people the most is the extent to which banks have become indifferent to their customers, all the way through to engaging in dishonest behaviour.[40]

The problem lies with the culture. Justin O'Brien, a professor at Monash University said that the banks' historic strong reported performance promoted, 'light-touch regulation and the emergence of a banking culture which prioritises profits and shareholders over customers.'[41]

This is not an Australian problem. The reputation of the global banking industry is in shreds with repeated, extensive bad behaviour towards customers. Wells Fargo was fined $1 billion in the wake of a US investigation which found that thousands of colleagues signed up customers for bank accounts without their knowledge in order to meet impossible sales targets – the stated inside-out aim was eight products or accounts per customer.

Wells Fargo rose from a San Francisco headquartered regional bank to one of the top four US banks via a number of mergers. It had traditionally been a locally oriented bank very engaged in and supportive of local communities. Its business model was simple – buy low, sell high. It eschewed investment banking, preferring to generate funds from its customers while at the same time earning a reputation for fair pricing, never chasing business by low-balling terms.

Cross-selling was at the heart of its strategy championed first by CEO Dick Kovacevich and continued by his successor John Stumpf. The data was impressive. Wells Fargo outperformed all its major competitors in terms of total shareholder returns. It was able to demonstrate to analysts that 52% of its customers had more than eight products and that profits per customer rose dramatically in line with the numbers of products held. Customers with eight products were five times more profitable that those with three products.[42]

In August 2018, in a section of a 173-page securities filing, 'Additional Efforts to Rebuild Trust,' the San Francisco bank admitted that due to a computer glitch, more than 600 customers who might have qualified for easier terms on their mortgages did not get them. Of those, around 400 went on to lose their homes. This technical glitch went undiscovered for five years.

And the issue with Wells Fargo, as with many other inside-out organisations, is that an inside-out belief system is tough to change. Erik Gordon, a professor at the University of Michigan's Ross School of Business told the *Financial Times* that many of Wells Fargo's 260,000 or so employees thrived in the old culture, or at least got used to it. 'You're mostly working with people who built their careers based on doing things the old way,' he said.[43]

A former personal banker at Wells Fargo, Mike T, who worked in a branch outside Philadelphia, told the *Financial Times* that he left the bank because he was dismayed by how many colleagues who bent the rules to meet aggressive sales targets were promoted ahead of him. A district manager ordered him to target (mostly Mexican) construction workers who were refurbishing a shopping mall across the street. Whenever a worker tried to cash his pay cheque at the branch, he was made to sit down with a banker to discuss opening a new set of accounts before being given the money.

To hit the sales targets, it was easier, indeed it was only possible, if people acted in a pushy, hard-sell way, fundamentally inside-out. Putting customers first would never hit the numbers in a given month – only something much bigger, that created a significantly more attractive offer, would have a chance of doing that.

In most organisations, outside-in thinking feels unnatural and requires a constant stream of Moments of Belief to change people's beliefs. The success of Zalando, the European online fashion retailer, shows this well.

The unnatural outside-in success of Zalando

From the outset, German-based retailer Zalando's founders defined success in terms of long-term growth and customer value creation. They believed in prioritising these over short-term sales, profits and share-price. Unified by an ambition to create something meaningful from the opportunities in the market, the founders' burningness gave them the energy and momentum to create a new kind of European online retailer. In its first decade, Zalando surpassed the likes of Amazon and ASOS to become Europe's largest online fashion retailer, with 2018 revenues of €5.39 billion, profits of €119 million and a market capitalisation of €11.5 billion.

Launched in 2008 and inspired by, among others, Zappos, the successful US online shoe store that offered free shipping and free returns to customers, Zalando's founders saw a future for a European online retailer that invested in service and was led by free delivery and returns. The concept of free shipping and free returns is commonplace today, but as Filip Dames, Zalando's former chief business development officer and co-founder of its highly popular shopping club Zalando-Lounge points out, it was revolutionary in 2008. Especially the idea that customers could return goods after 100 days – an eternity in the fashion industry.

> The 100-day return policy doesn't economically make sense, if you look at the fashion industry in terms of seasonality, stock and turnover. You buy something and then three months later you can return it. It created a lot of trust for the customer.[44]

This was a breakthrough Moment of Belief for Zalando. Such a bold move illustrated to all employees, as well as to customers, that Zalando was putting the customer first. Customers could try on their purchases and if they weren't happy, they could send them all back, for free, no questions asked.

Despite the risk, Zalando wasn't caught out, said Dames:

> Most returns came back within the first two weeks. Only a single digit percentage of sales were being returned after month one, two or three. Internally and externally the 100-day return was a very strong signal about what kind of business we were and how we planned to succeed.[45]

Dames called out an early bold marketing strategy as a second Moment of Belief that imbued Zalando with confidence in its home market Germany. The founders wanted to capitalise on the daily growth of customer visits and orders by raising awareness. They benefited from a scaling back of media spend by their competitors in the wake of the onset of the global financial crisis in 2008. With a subdued media market, they could buy TV ad spots at significant discounts and by running a basic ad they had scripted themselves they kept the production costs to around €5,000. The reaction was very strong – driving visits, opening new accounts and boosting sales. TV advertising worked for them. The next time Zalando ran a TV ad, it had an even bigger impact, breaking rules and expectations around its industry. As Dames recalled:

> We took a bold decision, hired a top creative and created a spoof spot like the film The Blair Witch Project. It was dark and polarizing, featuring a man who locks himself inside a closet full of his partner's shoes. Because it wasn't about the product, styles or even fashion, it stood out in a sea of jaded fashion ads. It gave us a clear direction and tone of voice which enabled us to build 90% brand awareness across Germany.[46]

Seeing the ad's response and immediate impact strengthened team members' belief in Zalando's overall approach – put the customer first. As Dames explained:

> You see these types of decisions working and they give you confi-
> dence. This confidence was important for Zalando's growth … Next,
> we decided to launch into seven to eight new countries in one year,
> which is crazy if you think about all the different payment methods
> and regulations and return policies.[47]

Hence, Zalando took on the challenge of Europe with its maze of different languages, regulations and fashion tastes with characteristic
gusto. Zalando takes a customised approach to each country, including
website, payment and delivery methods, products and communication.
While Dutch customers use electronic payments, some French customers prefer cheques, and in parts of Italy and Poland, shoppers can pay
the postman in cash.[48] By 2014, at great expense, Zalando had created
15 country-specific websites and established three fulfilment centres,
including Europe's largest e-commerce distribution warehouse. It was
another reinforcing Moment of Belief, sustaining employees' understanding that success needs to be measured in terms of customer-value
creation.

Another Moment of Belief cited by Dames was Zalando's decision to
extend its brand into new categories including sport, beauty and its own
range of clothing. Today, Zalando is one of the biggest sports retailers in
Europe and one of the largest customers of Nike in Europe. According to
Dames:

> There was a unifying ambition and an underlying strategy. We saw
> what was possible in this market to create something meaningful … if
> you feel this, it drives you and allows you to make different decisions
> and think in terms of the long term rather than optimising the next
> quarter.[49]

All these customer-led strategies are born from outside-in beliefs – long-
term customer satisfaction will in the end prove more valuable than short-
term margin protection. Thinking from a customer perspective has become
the default, leading to many small but significant outside-in decisions that
make Zalando an unusual company.

For example, by 2019, Zalando had taken its very first Moment of Belief
– 100-day returns – and stretched it to neatly solve another customer problem while addressing the thorny industry issue of sustainability. Customers

are now able to return old used clothes that they no longer want. They're reimbursed in Zalando vouchers (not the original price but a fair amount), and the second-hand clothes are recycled on Zalando's used clothes marketplace. Dames explains, 'This is an important and timely evolution of our original promise, "we've got you covered."'

As Zalando grew from start-up to publicly listed market leader, it had to pay close attention to its culture – staying customer-led, fast and innovative. According to Dames:

> We hired very young people, which was a bold move ... It was often their first job, so they were inexperienced but with a high ambition. We made sure that the people who joined back then had the same enthusiasm about what we were building. That gets harder as you get bigger.[50]

Zalando has successfully protected its outside-in approach as it has grown. From the outset the founders have been clear about what they regard as success. When the company's share price dropped after its successful IPO, Rubin Ritter sent out an email to all employees who were concerned by the falling stock price:

> Please, don't look at the share price day-to-day – the company did not change. Look in the long term. Yes, we need to think of profitability, but we will not become corporate.[51]

And when the company was marking its first 10 years and hit a bad quarter at the end of 2018, the founders noted:

> Our 10th Anniversary reminded us to think in longer time periods than quarters or seasons. When we hit challenging times, we worked hard to fix problems that needed fixing, but at the same time we made sure our team focussed on what really matters: the needs of our customers and how we intend to serve them in the future. That way, having a bad quarter never kept us from having a great decade.[52]

This customer-led approach has paid off. Zalando is now active in 15 European markets, offers its customers more than 20 local payment options, collaborates with different regional logistics service providers and speaks 12 languages, not only in its online shop but also in customer service.

Selling the wares of close to 2,000 international brands to 26.4 million active customers, sales grew a further 20% in 2018.[53] When a series of Dutch shoe stores went bankrupt in 2017, many pointed to 'the Zalando effect,' echoing the impact that Amazon has had on bookshops.

Tell-tale signs of outside-in versus inside-out belief systems

If big Moments of Belief are the rocket stages that create, nurture and grow outside-in beliefs, there are also smaller details of behaviour that become more local stories within companies, perpetuating their beliefs – mini Moments of Belief if you will. This is the way we do things around here. For example, at Orange under the leadership of Hans Snook in the 1990s, you had to talk about the customer. If you failed to mention customers in the first five minutes of a board presentation, you would be asked to stop and leave the boardroom. It didn't need to happen many times to become a rule the business ran by.

Gordon Campbell-Gray, founder of luxury London hotel OneAldwych, only recruited waiting staff who he felt really cared about customers. Did they really want a guest to enjoy their experience? One tell-tale for him was when people served a cappuccino. What did they say? The words didn't matter, but he wanted the feeling that they genuinely wanted this to be a moment of enjoyment, and for this to be shared with conviction. He absolutely didn't want his team to use the same words as each other. That would be inauthentic. He wanted people who meant it and expressed it their own way, and a German would have a very different style to an Italian.

IKEA's founder Ingvar Kamprad famously embodied the furniture retailer's frugal spirit, sleeping in his battered, old Volvo rather than staying overnight in a hotel, flying economy and wearing clothes from flea markets. His thriftiness was reflected in the Swedish company's philosophy to offer 'democratic design' to people with 'thin wallets' and make good home design affordable to all.

Tell-tale leaks that reveal an inside-out system tend to betray a disregard of customers

Many companies are organised around and celebrate products. The main functions are product-led, the pictures on the walls are of products (often pristine without a human to mess up the view) and the main events each year are product launches. Store visits are to check on the store and the staff rather than to listen to and meet customers, finding out what they really think about what's going on. And customer contact means watching focus groups from behind a one-way mirror eating sandwiches, drinking wine and laughing when they say something silly.

Behavioural leaks that reveal the belief system can be seen in the way a company uses language. As we touched upon right at the beginning of this chapter, the study of language or 'discourse analysis' can be highly revealing about an organisation's underlying beliefs, something that linguistic specialists like Gill Ereaut of Linguistic Landscapes has been analysing for years.

An outside-in language leak is seen in the way Disney calls its theme park customers 'guests.' An example of inside-out comes from the automotive industry. In mapping a customer's relationship with the business, a marketing team described the sales steps with energy and then labelled the next stage 'the fallow period'... This is when the customer owns and uses the car, the whole purpose of the customer's investment. For the customer it is the point – the value of their investment. For the salesperson, it's the dull bit where you can't sell anything. The term 'fallow period' tells you the organisation is inside-out.

Ereaut describes how language characterises a business and is invisible to those on the inside. She writes:

> Habits of language in an organisation matter, because they sustain certain ways of thinking, especially basic ideas such as who we are, what we do, who 'those people out there' (customers and stakeholders) are and – crucially – what the relationship is between 'us' and 'them.' Are 'we' knowledgeable experts and 'they' a somewhat ignorant nuisance? Are 'we' so polite that we cannot possibly challenge 'them,' even when we should? Are 'we' the guardians of a moral high ground?[54]

When analysing the discourse of the prostate cancer charity Prostate Cancer UK in late 2011 to help spark radical change, Ereaut discovered some subtle but persistent patterns in the charity's language. There was habitual indirectness and distancing, and a marked use of euphemism and hyperpoliteness. While there were occasional bursts of outrage (at the plight of men with the disease) and fighting talk, especially by individuals in conversation, this was submerged. 'We characterised it as a 'muffled' discourse – soft, quiet, civilised and caring – but muffled,' she said.[55]

This analysis gave the charity the confidence and clarity to move to a powerful new way of speaking and acting – bolder, more energetic and more strongly advocating on behalf of the men it was fighting for. The new culture was one we would call an outside-in belief system.

Conclusion and recap

Shared beliefs are crucial in determining the ways a group of people behave.

Inside-out beliefs are natural but unhelpful; outside-in beliefs are the other way around. There is a kind of organisational gravity that pulls people towards being inside-out.

Through the story of Sky and others, we have seen how Moments of Belief can overcome this gravitational pull, showing people that outside-in choices and actions work. In so doing, they gradually build a shared outside-in belief system.

Moments of Belief challenge easy assumptions. They address a customer issue – for Sky, offering a paid-for viewing experience that was better, with more choice, Zalando offering a country-specific online fashion retail experience with exemplary, easy service centred on free delivery and returns.

By innovating, by leading the market, by taking leaps of faith to commit significant resources to solving customer problems in new and better ways without knowing whether they would work, these two companies created a stream of Moments of Belief, securing a company-wide outside-in set of shared beliefs. They have shaken up whole industries as a result.

Some common outside-in shared beliefs include:

- The belief that addressing things that frustrate customers in a market proactively, in smart commercial ways but without a concrete business case or research evidence, will pay back and will lead to business success, not just to happy customers.
- That customer retention and concentrating on genuine value improvements for existing, good customers is hugely more worthwhile than

focusing most strongly on customer attraction and using sales tactics reactively when people try to leave.

- That there is always a better way, it just has to be found or invented, leading to breakthroughs like the iPhone, Tesla, Amazon, and Ford. This is about how success is achieved.

- That business exists first to serve customers – to make people's lives better in some way, large or small – and that profits are a means to that end. This is fundamentally what success is understood to be.

So now we understand what good *feels* like for customer-led businesses.

The importance and power of outside-in shared beliefs is critical – they guide everyday behaviour and decision-making. These beliefs help employees understand that this is the way we do things around here. This is what success is, and this is how success is achieved.

These outside-in shared beliefs are developed and maintained by Moments of Belief – big bets that prove putting customers first will pay off in the end. These Moments of Belief are critical to the success of outside-in thinking because it can feel unnatural and costly from the inside.

Shared beliefs often reveal themselves through the language and behaviour of an organisation and the varying importance placed on customers versus products, or on customer value versus short-term sales.

Having defined the playing field and the central importance of shared beliefs, in Chapter 4 we explore how organisations change these beliefs. In particular, we look at how they shift from the conventional inside-out to the remarkable outside-in.

Notes

1   Lander, Richard. 11 March 1992. 'Why Sky is over the Moon.' *The Independent*, p. 21.

2   Briggs, Simon. 18 April 2011. 'How Sky Sports became one of the most influential sports broadcasters over the last 20 years.' *The Telegraph*. Retrieved from www.telegraph.co.uk/sport/8459452/How-Sky-Sports-became-one-of-the-most-influential-sports-broadcasters-over-the-last-20-years.html

3   Byrne, Ciar. 25 February 2003. 'Corrie climax sparks power surge.' *The Guardian*. Retrieved from www.theguardian.com/media/2003/feb/25/broadcasting

4   Johnson, Sarah. 20 April 2011. 'Sky Sports celebrates 20 years of broad-casting.' *Campaign.* Retrieved from www.campaignlive.co.uk/article/sky-sports-celebrates-20-years-broadcasting/1066652

5   Johnson, Sarah. 20 April 2011. 'Sky Sports celebrates 20 years of broadcasting.'

6   Hill, Louise. 25 January 2018. 'Customers flock to Sky as sport chan-nels shake-up helps broadcaster to a 24% leap in profits.' *This is Money.* Retrieved from www.thisismoney.co.uk/money/markets/article-5310997/Sky-boasts-soaring-customer-numbers-sports-shake-up.htm

7   King, A. 1998. 'Thatcherism and the emergence of Sky Television.' *Communication Abstracts*, 21 (5): 277–293.

8   Schein, Edgar H. 1985. *Organizational Culture and Leadership.* San Francisco, CA: Jossey-Bass, p. 12.

9   Schein, Edgar H. 1985. *Organizational Culture and Leadership*, p. 12.

10 Kay, John. 21 November 2014. 'A blueprint on better business.' A Blueprint for Better Business 2014 Conference: Putting Purpose into Practice. Retrieved from www.blueprintforbusiness.org/tag/john-kay/

11 Toyota. 2001. 'Toyota Way 2001: Sharing the Toyota Way Values.' Retrieved from www.toyota-global.com/company/history_of_toyota/75years/data/conditions/philosophy/toyotaway2001.html

12 Gapper, John. 9 May 2018. 'Memo from Amazon: Tell a good story.' *Financial Times*, p. 12.

13 Michel Foucault's inaugural lecture, 'The Order of Discourse,' at the Collège de France, given on 2 December 1970, and published in French as *L'Ordre du Discours* (Paris: Gallimard, 1970). It deals with the way dis-course is controlled, limited and defined by exercises of power.

14 Ereaut, Gill. 2013. 'How language reveals barriers to success.' *WARC, Market Leader*, Quarter 1, pp. 34–36.

15 Jha, Alok. 30 June 2005. 'Where belief is born.' *The Guardian.* Retrieved from www.theguardian.com/science/2005/jun/30/psychology.neuroscience/
     Lieberman's research was originally published as: Lieberman M. D., A Hariri, J. M. Jarcho, N. I. Eisenberger, & S. Y. Bookheimer. 2005. 'An fMRI investigation of race-related amygdala activity in African-American and Caucasian-American individuals.' *Nature Neuroscience*, 8 (6): 720–722.

16 Jha, Alok. 30 June 2005. 'Where belief is born.'

17   Brown, Maggiek. 5 February 2009. 'Sky's TV launch: A wing and a prayer.' *The Guardian*. Retrieved from www.theguardian.com/media/organgrinder /2009/feb/04/sky-tv-early-years/

18   Darby, Ian. 6 February 2009. 'Sky – Twenty years of revolution.' *Campaign*. Retrieved from www.campaignlive.co.uk/article/sky-twenty-years-revolut ion/879684

19   Murdoch, Rupert. 25 August 1989. McTaggart Lecture, Edinburgh International Television Festival. Retrieved from www.thetvfestival.com/ website/wp-content/uploads/2015/03/GEITF_MacTaggart_1989_Rupert _Murdoch.pdf

20   Darby, Ian. 6 February 2009. 'Sky – Twenty years of revolution.'

21   Beale, Claire. 27 June 1997. 'Sam Chisholm and BSkyB: The Sky chief who held the future of TV in his hand – Sam Chisholm took BSkyB from loss maker to major innovator.' *Campaign*. Retrieved from www.campaignliv e.co.uk/article/live-issue-sam-chisholm-bskyb-sky-chief-held-future-tv -hand-sam-chisholm-took-bskyb-loss-maker-major-innovator/28844

22   Horsman, Mathew. 1 February 1999. 'Sky: The first decade … the biggest television revolution since colour.' *The Guardian*. Retrieved from www.t heguardian.com/media/1999/feb/01/bskyb

23   Gapper, John, 18 June 1998. 'Digital TV's brave new world.' *Financial Times*, p. 21.

24   Gapper, John, 18 June 1998. 'Digital TV's brave new world,' p. 21.

25   25 October 2005. 'Dynamic fresh thrust from BSkyB: Easynet, plus 300GB PVR.' *Broadband TV News*. Retrieved from Factiva database.

26   Edgecliffe-Johnson, Andrew. 19 January 2006. 'Murdoch aims for clear blue sky.' *Financial Times*. Retrieved from www.ft.com/content/2d66537a -8916-11da-94a6-0000779e2340/

27   Lupinacci, Paul. 18 August 2006. 'Shareholders strike back over private-equity deals.' *Wall Street Journal*. Retrieved from www.wsj.com/articles/ SB115587016646939159/

28   1 February 2006. 'Interim 2005 British Sky Broadcasting Group plc Earnings Presentation.' London. Fair Disclosure Wire, Voxant Inc. p. 4. Retrieved from Factiva database.

29   Edgecliffe-Johnson, Andrew. 19 January 2006. 'Murdoch aims for clear blue sky.'

30   Factiva. 1 February 2006. 'Interim 2005 British Sky Broadcasting Group plc Earnings Presentation.'

31   Nick Green (Director of Internal Communications from July 2009 to September 2012, later head of Property Services until August 2016), interview with authors, 15 August 2018.

32   Nick Green, interview with authors, 15 August 2018.

33   Nick Green, interview with authors, 15 August 2018.

34   Nick Green, interview with authors, 15 August 2018.

35   Gale, Adam. 25 January 2018. 'How Sky CEO Jeremy Darroch plans to resist Netflix – with or without a Fox/Disney takeover.' *Management Today*. Retrieved from www.managementtoday.co.uk/sky-ceo-jeremy-darroch-plans-resist-netflix-without-fox-disney-takeover/leadership-lessons/article/1455498

36   Burrell, Ian. 8 June 2014. 'The BBC was impervious to the launch of Sky News. Now they have to take notice.' *Independent*. Retrieved from www.independent.co.uk/news/media/press/the-bbc-was-impervious-to-the-launch-of-sky-news-now-they-have-to-take-notice-9509609.html

37   Nick Green, interviews with authors, 15 August 2018 and 18 January 2019.

38   Darby, Ian. 6 February 2009. 'Sky – Twenty years of revolution.'

39   Hutchens, Gareth. 7 August 2018. 'Australia's big four banks and AMP have had to pay or offer $222m to customers.' *The Guardian*. Retrieved from www.theguardian.com/australia-news/2018/aug/07/australias-big-four-banks-and-amp-have-had-to-pay-or-offer-222m-to-customers

40   Smyth, Jamie. 1 May 2018. 'Probe exposes Australian banks' abuse of customers.' *Financial Times*, p. 16.

41   Smyth, Jamie. 1 May 2018. 'Probe exposes Australian banks' abuse of customers,' p.16.

42   Tayan, Brian. 6 February 2019. 'The Wells Fargo cross-selling scandal.' *Harvard Law School Forum on Corporate Governance and Financial Regulation*. Retrieved from https://corpgov.law.harvard.edu/2019/02/06/the-wells-fargo-cross-selling-scandal-2/

43   McLannahan, Ben. 15 August 2018. 'Wells Fargo's apologies leave customers unmoved.' *Financial Times*. Retrieved from www.ft.com/content/dbc1d692-9fa6-11e8-85da-eeb7a9ce36e4?accessToken=zwAAAWWzXktQkdPbwdaSn6YR6NOF2u63qc425A.MEYCIQDUSSLxnXGF9uPTup_wMqc5EZFTmYXMxut8yVGRuJl2OQIhAOwsvy5j6-ok4TvCIDuA1q6RRHIjaSQfZZG1aHMNPg47&sharetype=gift

44   Interview with authors, 19 February 2019.

45   Interview with authors, 19 February 2019.

46   Interview with authors, 19 February, 2019.

47   Interview with authors, 19 February 2019.

48   'Zalando: Fashion forward.' 1 September 2016. *The Economist.* Retrieved from www.economist.com/business/2016/09/01/fashion-forward

49   Interview with authors, 19 February 2019.

50   Interview with authors, 19 February, 2019.

51   Boris Radke, CCO. 15 September 2017. 'Inside Zalando: From startup to IPO in 6 years' (Video file). Retrieved from www.youtube.com/watch?v =UvUng5YAlpM

52   Zalando. 25 February 2019. 'Letter to Shareholders.' *Zalando Annual Report.* Retrieved from https://corporate.zalando.com/en/investor-rel ations/letter-shareholders

53   Zalando. 2018. 'Key Figures.' *Zalando Annual Report 2018.* Retrieved from https://corporate.zalando.com/en/investor-relations/key-figures-2018

54   Ereaut, Gill. 2013. 'How language reveals barriers to success,' pp. 34–36.

55   Ereaut, Gill. 2013. 'How language reveals barriers to success,' pp. 34–36.

4

CREATING CUSTOMER-LED BELIEFS

We are what we repeatedly do – excellence then is not an act, but a habit.

Aristotle

easyJet: The airline that moved from inside-out to outside-in

Short-haul travel was revolutionised in the noughties. In the age of the national flag carriers, flying was an occasional luxury, but a new wave of pioneers, building on Southwest Airlines' breakthrough in the US, saw the opening up of the regulated market in Europe as an opportunity for disruption. And disrupt they did, with Ryanair and easyJet becoming two of the world's most profitable airlines. It was a new model – point-to-point routing between high-demand destinations, eight flights per day per aircraft, short turnaround times, no free food and drink, stripped back fares with add-ons, dynamic pricing based on timing and demand and a pared-down boarding process with no allocated seats or boarding cards, making it faster and cheaper.

But this new model brought a cloud with its silver lining. The experience of flying was increasingly unpleasant. Passengers complained that the advertised price could never be achieved in reality. They felt stung with pricing that was perceived as tricky, having high and hidden charges for 'extras' like luggage or having your boarding pass printed at the airport rather than at home.

The stress of boarding was one of the most painful parts of the experience. Because seats weren't allocated, there was a race to get onto the flight to get a good seat, and for parties to sit together. This was a battle that favoured the fit, the strong and the organised. For most, especially older people and families, this part of the trip had become a nightmare.

easyJet had done well in the first wave of discount airline growth, but by 2010 it was struggling. While the initial spirit of discount air travel was customer-led, that purpose had been lost and the experience had instead become dominated by cheapness, a consequence of an internal inside-out cost-cutting mentality. Cutting back on crew had led to flights being cancelled creating irate customers and demoralised staff.

It took easyJet's new CEO, Carolyn McCall, nine months to get the operation back on track, reinvesting, listening and doing what she promised. But while this moved the airline out of crisis, people's beliefs were still that the business was transactional, all about pricing and cost.

So, when an idea was proposed to do something proactive to make customers' awful experiences better, the audience was suspicious rather than receptive. McCall was changing her team, making it more customer focused, and the fresh eyes identified the introduction of allocated seating as an opportunity to make a statement, to make a giant leap to improve the flying experience and in so doing show that easyJet could take a lead in the sector, working with customers not against them.

The idea did not go down well with everyone. In operations, steeped in the practicalities of making the planes run on time, they were convinced it couldn't be done. The low-cost business model relies on completing eight flights each day. This involves getting passengers and baggage off, cleaning, replenishing, then boarding passengers and loading luggage in 25 minutes. It was self-evident to many that boarding would take longer when passengers had to queue for and find a specific seat rather than taking the first one available, and that, plus the extra administration of boarding cards, made it look like a bad idea. As Peter Duffy, easyJet's marketing director at the time, explained:

> The economics of the business is all about turning planes around and we didn't want to blow a hole in profitability. Operations had a well-founded concern that these establishing principles were being torn up for an unproven outcome.[1]

But McCall was insistent – she wanted to set a customer-led tone and was convinced that easyJet could challenge assumptions and innovate within the low-cost model. She couldn't do this without her operations team and so she asked them to participate in a trial codenamed BOSS (bums on selected seats). The first attempt saw a 40-minute turnaround and the sinking feeling that maybe the objectors were right. Looking for inspiration from organisations that know all about fast turnarounds, easyJet turned to Formula 1 team McLaren. If an outfit capable of routinely changing the four wheels of a racing car in less than three seconds couldn't provide a breakthrough, then no one could. As McCall said:

> We went to Formula 1 to learn how they shave tenths of seconds off pit stops. Our team started learning from that [and finding where] we could save time on the turnaround to do allocated seating.[2]

The ah-ha moment was the recognition that while it DID take passengers longer to find their allocated seats, easyJet DIDN'T need to follow the conventions of larger airports where only one of the aircraft's two doors were used to get people in and out, with the air bridge sheltering them from the elements. Instead, ignoring the air bridge, easyJet hit on the simple idea of boarding passengers through both front and rear doors simultaneously, according to their seat numbers. They took longer to get seated but filling up the two halves in parallel effectively cut the plane's size in half.

That put the 25-minute turnaround in reach, and in November 2012, the airline replaced the survival-of-the-fittest boarding scrum with free allocated seating on all its flights (customers could pay extra to choose their seat but every person now had a specific seat reserved for them at no extra cost). Of the 800,000 passengers surveyed, 70% said they preferred allocated seating.[3]

Duffy was at Gatwick airport the day the initiative was launched.

> I was excited. I thought it was revolutionary. I walked up to a customer and said, 'What do you think?' 'You're just doing what every other airline does, aren't you?' she replied. This was levelling but it was important. Yes, it was what every other flag carrier airline did, but it wasn't what any budget airline did. It was a repositioning and it marked us apart.

Allocating seating was a symbolic move that completely turned perceptions of the business around by 180 degrees. It showed colleagues that customers don't have to just accept the conventions of the low-cost model, and the business benefited as the less stressful boarding experience brought in increasing numbers of older customers and families. According to McCall, '… allocated seating was the single most successful thing easyJet had done for its passengers.'[4] For easyJet, it was a critical first Moment of Belief that kickstarted a succession of customer-led innovations that we will return to shortly.

Moving from inside-out to outside-in in four stages

We have shown why belief systems are central to the way a business behaves and have distinguished between their inside-out and outside-in variants – the former being deceptively 'natural' but ultimately leading companies astray, the latter being uncommon and 'un-natural,' yet a prerequisite for customer-led success.

All customer-led successes have to somehow establish these difficult outside-in shared beliefs. This chapter is about how, against the odds, it is done, how an organisation moves through four stages to go from an inside-out belief system to one that is outside-in:

1. The first stage is recognising burningness – pain, fear or ambition that is so strongly felt that the current position is untenable, the current model obsolete. Business as usual is not an option.

2. The second stage is when a company achieves its first Moment of Belief – using the burningness to justify a business initiative that is bold, expensive, good for customers and risky, as the costs are definite and now, the benefits probable at best and in the future if at all. Then, when this single significant outside-in initiative is seen to work, it creates the belief that outside-in ways of doing things can, sometimes at least, be valuable for the business too.

3. A flow of Moments of Belief – encouraged by the success of the first, the execution of a second, a third and so on becomes a succession of outside-in initiatives with belief growing that each time the organisation is brave enough to act on what customers want, and smart enough to find an innovative solution that could potentially be commercially sustainable, the outcome is positive. The pattern is established – the more the business creates value for customers, the better the business does commercially and competitively.

4. Making outside-in activities systematic – establishing organisation-wide mechanisms for showing colleagues what matters to customers, where there are gaps or opportunities, how to go after them, then making it easy to respond in a distributed, widespread way.

This process of changing conventional to unconventional shared beliefs is seen not just in business and the world of work. It occurs in some of our biggest historical shifts in society's norms and beliefs, and in particular where a specific Moment of Belief has stood out as pivotal in a wider sea-change in opinion and behaviour.

Examples include the moment Rosa Parks refused to give up her seat on a segregated bus in Montgomery, Alabama, thereby sparking a chain of events culminating in a historic advancement of civil rights for African Americans; the moment Henri Dunant witnessed the horrors of war and provoked an immediate organisation of medical relief leading to the creation of the Red Cross; the moment King Henry VIII refused to recognise papal authority and declared himself Supreme Head of the Church of England, now a significant and respected branch of Christianity; and the moment the Bolsheviks overthrew Russia's Provisional, post-Tsar government and established what would be the USSR, one of the most significant world powers of an era. These examples seemed particularly relevant as they are not only famous and varied, but they also brought about significant change through what can be interpreted as single acts – Moments of Belief.[5]

Looking more carefully at the example of Rosa Parks, we can see the four stages of this journey across the shift from narrow, self-interested inside-out beliefs to broader, more generous outside-in ones. When Rosa Parks boarded James F. Blake's bus in Montgomery, Alabama, on 1 December 1955, she set in motion a series of events that would determine the fate of the civil rights movement and alter the trajectory of American society. Parks' protest – ignoring Blake's order to give up her seat in the coloured section of the bus for a white passenger – was quiet and non-violent, and she did not resist arrest when the police intervened. Her act sparked the now famous 380-day Montgomery bus boycott. It provided a platform for the emergence of the influential human rights leader, Martin Luther King, then president of the newly formed SCLC (Southern Christian Leadership Conference), an African-American civil rights organisation.

Contrary to popular belief, Rosa Parks was not an accidental heroine but a politically active citizen and secretary of the local chapter of the NAACP (National Association for the Advancement of Coloured People). Here we get a sense of 'burningness' – the pain, fear or ambition that something had to change and that none of the accepted actions would be enough to make a difference. For as Parks insisted:

> People always say that I didn't give up my seat because I was tired but that isn't true. I was not tired physically, or no more tired than I usually was at the end of a working day ... No, the only tired I was, was tired of giving in.[6]

Parks' action demonstrated that it was possible to resist without violence, and that apparently a negative immediate outcome – her arrest – could be a pivot, something that could be built on, eventually developing a momentum that was unstoppable. It was a Moment of Belief. It was a practical and visible action. It was bold and risky. The bus driver Blake disregarded advice from his boss to make Parks leave the bus and called the police instead. After a stand-off Parks was arrested and charged. But encouraged by Parks' bold protest, the Civil Rights Movement organised a 380-day Montgomery bus boycott ending only when desegregation on public buses became enshrined in law (Browder v. Gayle 1956). The legal victory was a second, bigger Moment of Belief, and it was the start of our third stage, a self-reinforcing cascade of Moments of Belief, each building on the last and making success more likely.

Finally, exemplifying the fourth and final stage of the journey when more systematic ways of building shared beliefs emerge, we saw how this train of events provided a platform for the emergence of Martin Luther King and all that followed under his leadership.

Rosa Parks changed the face of history, her decision to stay in her seat led to an important change in the beliefs of large groups of people, both the disempowered black community who could see that they could make a difference, and the suppressing white majority who saw that they could not continue in the ways that they had been used to. This is what Moments of Belief can do. And, this is why they're important within business today. One bold customer-led action can lead to another and another, transforming the way a company thinks and behaves.

The remarkable turnaround of easyJet

When Carolyn McCall joined easyJet as chief executive in 2010, the European budget airline was in crisis. Following a breakneck expansion, it was suffering from low morale, a reputation for frequent delays – more than one third of its flights were late – and poor customer service.

There had been a very public spat between Sir Stelios Haji-Ioannou, its larger-than-life founder and largest shareholder, and the board leading to the resignation of McCall's predecessor, Andrew Harrison, alongside the airline's chairman, chief financial officer and a number of other managers.

While easyJet was initially established as an outside-in challenge to flag-carrying airlines by opening up the world of air travel to passengers previously priced out, the discount market had gradually become more competitive. Harrison had been appointed to bring more order, rigour and focus on finances. His efforts, recalled Andy Caddy, an executive who in nine years with easyJet worked for three different CEOs, led to easyJet losing sight of its customers.[7] It was no longer a plucky start-up pioneering cheap air travel. It was now an airline making good profits from unpleasant customer experiences.

As McCall spent her first few weeks visiting the airline's main hubs in Milan, Paris, Madrid and Gatwick she found easyJet staff hiding their lanyards for fear of being targeted by irate customers frustrated by delays and cancellations. Staff morale was at rock bottom.

In McCall's first year, air traffic controller strikes, volcanic ash clouds and snowstorms added close to £100 million in unanticipated operating costs.[8] A *Sunday Times* article showed easyJet had worse on-time performance than Air Zimbabwe. Rival Ryanair made the most of the opportunity, running an ad in the UK national press with an image of Zimbabwean president Robert Mugabe under the headline 'Here's easyJet's New Head of Punctuality.' As McCall recalled:

> My first six months were about as bad in terms of adverse events as any CEO could have ... We had a terrible crew shortage, which led to cancellations during the vital summer months. That was followed by the worst winter weather in 30 years. The next year, we had the worst in 40 years. The summer brought us awful air traffic control strikes in Europe. Then, just after Christmas, oil prices went through the roof and the hedge that we'd done was working against us. So that first year was really, really tough.[9]

McCall clearly had burningness – extreme pain felt across the business. None of the conventional or accepted inside-out business moves like further cost cutting, promotional offers or new routes would be enough to make a difference. Something more fundamental had to change – McCall was determined to make easyJet see things once again from a passenger perspective. In the air travel industry, customer satisfaction is directly related to punctuality, and it was essential to get on-time performance right before going any further. Indeed, research showed that if the plane was late, passengers would say that the sandwiches didn't taste as good and the crew were ruder. Punctuality was essential.

For something so serious and so apparently hard-edged and operational, McCall took an unconventional approach. She began by engineering a shift in thinking that started with language. From the beginning, McCall chaired a daily operations meeting in order to understand the causes of poor performance. She asked questions every single day of the operations team, not just about flights but about how many customers were impacted by flight delays and cancellations.

By stopping referring to delayed aircraft or flights and starting to talk about '180 delayed customers' she was changing the discourse. She was helping her management to get into the habit of talking about people, not planes, thinking about families, not logistics.

Early on, McCall also made a habit of speaking to pilots and assisting the cabin crew whenever she flew, generally several times a week. It was not uncommon for passengers to see her making her way through the centre aisle with a plastic bag to gather the rubbish. 'Because they are so busy on the flight, it's the easiest way to talk with the crew,' she said.[10]

One of McCall's first acts on arriving from Guardian Media Group in 2010 was to write to pilots to reassure them that although she was looking to change direction, she did not plan to create an 'Orange Ryanair'[11] – a reference to the harsher employment terms of easyJet's low-cost rival – which previous management had wanted to introduce. She listened to their comments about the crew's food, rosters and scheduling.

easyJet's pilots were furious about many things, not least the fact that overzealous managers before McCall's time had withdrawn free in-flight meals and drinks to save money. Symbolically, as a final straw, instead of being given full-size Mars bars to fuel them in the cockpit, they were given one that was fun-size and they were not happy. So, she reversed it:

> When I started, I had so many negative emails from pilots and cabin crew, all saying 'this is wrong, that is wrong, no one listens to us.' It was a constant barrage.

She received so many emails in the first six months that she took to addressing her inbox at night. But she also started taking action. She reintroduced free food and drink, insisted on better rostering to provide a more predictable schedule for workers and added more standby staff.

Finally, there came some encouragement. As McCall recounted:

> It was Easter 2011, and I was on the first day of a holiday. I saw an email from a pilot and groaned, but, of course, opened it – you can never really be on holiday in this job.

Instead of the kind of email to which she was now accustomed, McCall was relieved to read a message from a pilot thanking her for his stable roster, which meant he could spend Easter with his family for the first time in five years.

'This was the turning point for me,' said McCall – confiding, however, that the pilot still concluded his email with, 'PS crew food is still shit.'[12]

Andy Caddy, the easyJet veteran, remembers McCall in stark contrast to Harrison's financially focused approach:

> From the start she was clearly different. She said easyJet was in the business of delighting customers, making it possible for them to do things that hadn't been offered before. Customers had become used to the pain of discount airline travel and easyJet has lost its purpose. She said, 'we're going to get back to what we're good at, doing what's right for the customer.'[13]

Given the multiple levels of costs associated with cancellations, the changes she made worked economically too, countering the apparent attractiveness of the initial cost cutting, which reflected an inside-out mentality and that had in practice led to the unintended consequences of costs rising. It worked. easyJet's average punctuality rate was 51.3% in mid-2010, 79.0% in 2011 and 94.2% in March 2012.[14]

In parallel, McCall was establishing a new leadership team. easyJet's operations director lasted only three months of her new regime. She believed he 'had lost the confidence of the pilots.'[15] He was the one executive from whom she took advice before agreeing to join. 'He told me then the company had lost sight of its own people, and its passengers, and wasn't working as a team.'[16]

To grow the company's focus on customers and champion the leadership philosophy that easyJet was more interested in people than planes, McCall recruited two directors who understood this perspective. She appointed Peter Duffy, previously at Audi, as director of customer, digital and marketing, and Paul Moore who had previously worked at Virgin, as director of communications. This meant McCall went from being the lone outside-in voice on the board to having two others on the team who 'talked customer.' James Millett, a senior marketing executive who spent seven years at easyJet, reflected that this acted as a catalyst for other executives to take a customer perspective with accountability being shared across the wider executive leadership team. McCall got the community (the top 40 leaders) together on a monthly basis and facilitated an informal straight-talking sharing of progress. Subsequent critical initiatives like replacing 'drip pric-ing' (the practice of adding an admin charge at the end of a booking) with a headline price you could rely on, allocated seating and a loyalty pro-gram, were all cross-functional and cross-team in a spirit that was firmly customer-led.[17]

She worked with them to 'reset the agenda for easyJet.' That started with clarifying easyJet's purpose, the reason why people who work for the busi-ness – 'get out of bed in the morning.' As McCall explained:

> What we found was we wanted to make travel easy and affordable for all people. That was founded in the core of what easyJet was at the very beginning. For us it had quite a lot of stretch in it, we had always been about affordable flying, but did we really make it easy for our passengers?[18]

It's not a coincidence that McCall sat as a non-exec on Tesco's board on Sir Terry Leahy's watch until the retailer sued *The Guardian*, where Carolyn was CEO, for libel, and she had to resign. She learned some valuable lessons about customers from her time there.

As at Tesco, in the run-up to Christmas, she made her top team go back to the floor, manning check-in desks and tagging luggage. 'Terry would go back to the tills every year – same sort of business, about value and customers.'[19]

It was important for the easyJet team to recognise both parts of the purpose – this wasn't about going from being affordable to being easy, it was adding ease to affordability. 'We are low cost in everything we do. It's in our DNA — look at this hangar we work in. But it doesn't mean you have to be cheap to passengers.'[20] In fact, the team took low cost to great lengths, proudly staying in a Premier Inn and celebrating with cans of beer from the neighbouring off-license when they started winning awards.

The purpose mattered for another reason. The team took this challenge of pioneering on behalf of customers to change the world of discount air-lines seriously. They really had a chance to make a mark on the industry. To begin with, easyJet's burningness came from pain – they simply HAD to change, reinvesting in their operation. Now, with a renewed sense of purpose, they added ambition. There was no way on Earth that they could make discount airline travel easy as well as affordable doing only what was conventional. If they were going to succeed, they would have to be bold, and to begin with, most of the people in the organisation would not believe this was going to work.

As described at the start of this chapter, easyJet's first big Moment of Belief, their first demonstration that they could change the rules of their sector to make it work better for customers and then also for the business, came with the introduction of allocated seating. It didn't come easily. But it was far from alone as a candidate for reinvention.

For an airline that at the time was just 15 years old, 'quite a lot of things had become sacred cows. There were quite a lot of things that had not been reviewed or reassessed,' said McCall.[21]

The idea that budget airline passengers could have an assigned seat was considered radical. It was a symbolically crucial step forward for the whole easyJet team and for the business in the eyes of customers too.

Like many Moments of Belief we've described in this book, it was a business initiative that was bold, expensive, unarguably good for customers and yet risky for the business, with costs definite and now, benefits probable at best and in the future if at all.

In fact, while allocated seating was taking shape, the team was working on what became another Moment of Belief. For this, easyJet tackled 'Gotcha Pricing.'

'Gotcha Pricing' was a description of the way discount airlines had come to make money. They advertised a very low rate for a flight but made it almost impossible for customers to actually buy a ticket for that price. Instead customers ran into add-ons of various kinds. Some were reasonably transparent like paying extra for luggage. But many were not. Passengers would effectively be fined if they forgot to print out a boarding card. People would be automatically opted into add-ons like travel insurance that they had to opt out of again manually, and they would be charged extra for paying by any means at all other than the airline's own brand credit card. Perhaps the worst example was being allowed to add a second bag but without the weight limit changing, something that was counterintuitive and that would lead to people's luggage being overweight and charged for at the airport at eye-watering rates.

The easyJet team wanted to do something about it, but acting on their own would have been commercial suicide. So they decided to go about it with a bit more cunning, looking to change the way the whole sector operated. They began to build a relationship with the Office of Fair Trading (OFT), but when they first lobbied for a regulation change, they weren't trusted – even the OFT assumed there must be a catch. It took 18 months, but when it came, it was applied to the market as a whole – to competitors, not just to easyJet.

This meant lost revenue for all, but what easyJet then set out to do was to find opportunities for customers to pay more but this time by buying services they valued and for them to be offered as genuine choices. Allocated seats meant a choice could be offered to upgrade to the best ones. Luggage rules were made generous and fair, but luggage going in the hold was still paid for. On board, the food and beverage offer was upgraded to become genuinely appealing featuring premium brands – Segafredo coffee, Clipper teas, Hendricks gin, Fever Tree mixers.

All this meant easyJet had price transparency – the price customers paid at the end was the price they expected, and it would match the advertised price more easily and more often. They were providing additional customer value alongside additional revenue, happily.

After burningness, the first element of the inside-out to outside-in journey, these two formative Moments of Belief (the second stage) were followed by an accelerating flow of improvements and innovations (a flow of Moments of Belief, the third stage) all adding value for easyJet customers. They included a smart app that featured a real-time view of where a plane was in the sky so customers could understand any delays transparently. The app featured mobile boarding cards, easy to achieve for global airlines, tough in reality for easyJet with its multiple small European airports. 'The app was leading the low-cost industry, it felt like a quality product for consumers and saw us competing on a different tangent to competitors,' said Duffy.[22]

Each customer innovation took easyJet further from its inside-out rivals who seemed to go to war with their passengers as soon as they entered their website and continued the battle until they disembarked at their destination. Now belief was growing that every time easyJet was brave enough to act on what customers wanted and smart enough to find an innovative solution that could be commercially sustainable, the business got better. According to Duffy:

What Carolyn did brilliantly was relate the success of the airline to the success of the customer strategy. It came through again and again in all internal and external communication. Then the Operational team created a Customer Charter. It was self-generated because customers are owned by everyone – it had become democratised.[23]

In time, this took easyJet to the fourth stage of the outside-in journey, becoming more systematic in the ways the business was being customer-led, using data and processes to understand even better what mattered to customers and how this differed between them, then acting on the insight to fill gaps or take opportunities to create value in new and better ways.

This meant easyJet started to see that there were more segmented customer needs. For example, offering additional options for luggage instead of just having above and below 20 kg. It recognised the weekend traveller as having distinct needs from a longer holidaymaker. This led to the creation of a 32 kg super-premium offer, increasing the 20 kg limit to 23 kg, offering a lower 15 kg level, and offering a paid-for service to drop hand luggage off at check-in to be reunited with the passenger on boarding the plane. Duffy likens this systematic innovation to the way the soap powder brands in the 1970s grew to have a more segmented offer, supplementing powders to launch liquid products, tablets, combinations of soap powder and fabric softener and so on. 'Combining our data with being systematic meant we could see new areas of value for our customers that we could also turn into value for the airline in smart ways.'[24]

This even led to insights that surprised Duffy himself. On a trip with his wife, they were over the weight limit with their luggage and at the end of the holiday he complained that she hadn't worn half of what she'd brought. 'But I like choices,' she said, and the light bulb went on – choice was worth paying for beyond the functional need of packing enough clothing.[25]

The central element of this fourth systematic outside-in step was about gathering and using data from easyJet's digital services and then also from a loyalty scheme, the easyJet Flight Club. Loyalty offers are tricky with the discount model. The airlines don't have the currency of empty seats to use as the main reward because every seat is part of the dynamic pricing approach. But easyJet realised there were other options – that flexibility was also valued and that this was something it could offer its best customers, allowing late changes without penalty or access to priority boarding without booking or paying for it in advance. Duffy explained:

> Research told us that while customers knew we offered value for money, they were looking for recognition. If it was the 20th time you'd jumped on that plane you wanted it to mean something. Our regular travellers were second homeowners or worked away from home. We offered them flexibility so they could change dates and that was very popular. It was about recognising our most valuable customers in a way that was appropriate.[26]

These changes opened up new segments to easyJet, which now started to appeal to Europe's legions of business travellers, people who already knew the airline from their leisure trips. With business hats on, they are a more lucrative segment. McCall estimated that easyJet's average business traveller pays 10 to 15% more than someone flying for pleasure. 'That's definitely worth having,' she said.[27]

With these significant changes to easyJet's belief system and business model came some striking results. In March 2013, following nearly three years of McCall's leadership, the no-frills airline flew into the FTSE100 valued at more than £4 billion. Passenger numbers had jumped by 43% to 65 million a year, of which more than 12 million were business travellers, up from 8 million in 2010.[28]

McCall presided over a remarkable turnaround, the share price moving from £4 to £19 between 2010 and 2015, revenue from £3 billion to £5 billion and net profit from £121 million to £548 million. And this was all achieved in the spirit of a growing belief that being customer-led meant the business worked better, not worse. In her words: 'We have taken customer service to a new level and – I say this with no hubris – we have redefined what customer service is for the low-fares market.'[29]

Indeed, easyJet's customer-led approach revolutionised the entire no-frills airline industry, with even Ryanair CEO Michael O'Leary deciding it was time for his airline to start 'being nice to people' in 2016.[30]

While insisting easyJet was 'probably five years ahead' of its competitor, McCall applauded the changes made by the Irish airline. 'We've changed the way they behave with customers,' she said. 'It's actually better for the sector, there are benefits to them emulating what we've done for customers.'[31]

And like many of the other outside-in companies we've profiled, this wasn't an easy journey for easyJet. As Duffy admitted:

> It's hard changing the way things are done ... It's hard, hard work and takes a lot of energy. And the hardest thing is just staying with it. You have to be pragmatic about knowing this is the right way to behave.[32]

easyJet's turnaround was characterised by the four stages this chapter has at its heart as it transformed from an inside-out to an outside-in organisation. The burningness and pain when the airline was compared unfavourably with Air Zimbabwe, which became ambition as a sense of purpose grew, successfully introducing allocated seating as a first Moment of Belief followed by a sequence of customer-led successes that gathered momentum, growing shared belief around what the airline was and how it operated, leading eventually to a systematic and more data-led way of creating value for customers.

Next, we'll explore these four stages in more detail as an organisation moves from an inside-out belief system to an outside-in one. Through an analysis of DBS Bank, we'll show the critical role of burningness and how it can be used productively to give a leadership team the conviction to take a risky decision. This leads to a first Moment of Belief – a business initiative that is bold, expensive, definitely good for customers yet risky for the business and, crucially, that is seen to work for customers and in time for the business too.

The story of AO.com, the online white goods retailer, reveals the second and third stages – how a first Moment of Belief followed by a subsequent flow of Moments of Belief can create a growing shared conviction that outside-in ways of working lead to the growth of an exceptional customer-led business.

Finally, Deliveroo, the restaurant food delivery service, shows the fourth stage as outside-in activities become systematic, making it easier for people across the business to make all sorts of aspects work for customers in new and better ways.

Exploring burningness at DBS

We look at burningness through the lens of DBS Bank – a leading financial services group headquartered in Singapore that operates across 18 markets – and the decisive steps taken by its CEO, Piyush Gupta. When he joined DBS in 2009, the bank was seriously underperforming and losing traction. Its ATMs frequently ran out of cash, wait times at the branches and call centres were long, customer complaints were growing and market share at home was under pressure.

Burningness is a critical first step in a company's journey towards outside-in thinking. It is a visceral state, a time when a company feels like something is on fire, a raging force that simply has to be responded to decisively. It might be pain, fear or ambition, but something has to change. And this need for change is so overwhelmingly crucial, so urgent and so important that conventional approaches, and continuing with the current model, have to be ruled out because they will never be enough.

Burningness creates the conditions that mean outside-in initiatives, with their definite costs and uncertain benefits, become the only way forward.

Not all types of burningness are equal – there is a hierarchy across pain, fear or ambition. The most effective is pain. It is unarguably present, and it means something different has to be done. This is what easyJet experienced at the start of its journey. Fear is a step less effective – it is a shared view that there is a need to change, but it might not be now. If the first step is risky for the core business – think digital photography and Kodak – then a team might choose to wait. Ambition is the least pressing. Things are fine and may carry on being so. But the team has a burning desire to be somewhere else, somewhere better. There's an enemy to defeat, a cause to pursue and they will do almost whatever it takes to get there.

In 2013, DBS was experiencing the most acute burningness – pain. The underperforming Singapore-based bank was four years into an ambitious transformation programme to become a world-class, multinational bank. Under the new leadership of CEO Piyush Gupta, a lot had been achieved but much remained to be done.

Operations and technology were 'in a disastrous state, with no real metrics, no clear targets of where you wanted to be, and zero aspirations around customer service,' said Dave Gledhill, head of group technology and operations since 2008.[33]

Everything was going wrong. An expensive project to fix operations had failed with four years still to go and costs running to S$300 million, 50% over budget. DBS's market share was falling. The bank's overseas growth strategy wasn't working. And Gupta was acutely aware of the growing threat from nimble technology companies like China's Alibaba, which had been offering micro loans to its customers since 2008.

The situation was exacerbated on August 1, 2013, when the Indonesian government blocked DBS's much-needed breakthrough deal to acquire the country's Bank Danamon. This was a major setback to DBS's expansion plans. The acquisition would have helped grow DBS's presence in Asia's growth markets, but it was not to be.

Despite Gupta's earlier hopes, DBS had not been able to increase its presence in growth markets where the Singapore bank already had a footprint – China, India and Indonesia. High costs, regulatory uncertainty and scarcity of suitable targets were making mergers and acquisitions (M&As) in existing markets look impossible. In China and India foreign banks were limited to an ownership stake of 20% and 10% respectively. Acquisitions were no longer going to be a viable path for DBS's growth.

Alongside all of the pain from the bank's overseas growth strategy not working, Gupta also felt fear that financial technology companies (fintechs), could deliver many of the same services as DBS without expensive branch networks or legacy technology issues. As Gupta explained:

> Alibaba scared the living daylights out of us. They were raising money, making payments and making loans with zero branches and completely electronically. They were reaching millions of people. We knew that the change in our industry was upon us, that the discontinuity had arrived.[34]

This sense of burningness was acute during a 2013 meeting with DBS's executive board. Gupta was convinced that something fundamental had to change to safeguard the bank's future. In the meeting, Gupta asked for the board's support to change his original transformational ambition of creating a world-class multinational bank into something significantly different. He wanted DBS to become a 22,000-person start-up, a bank fit for the future that could complete with fintechs like Alibaba and Atom Bank on their own terms.

The board supported Gupta completely. They agreed DBS would need to act boldly to transform three elements of its business: its technology, its customer journey and its culture. Burningness had propelled DBS's leadership to radically change the bank's growth strategy, a decision that would require a huge investment of time and resources and one that had no guarantee of working. The bank was setting out to move from inside-out to outside-in.

This dramatic shift in mindset saw the birth of a number of big initiatives, including fixing the technology and rethinking the customer journey, which would later include the idea of making banking joyful. They redesigned branches with seating for customers and launched a queuing system so customers could be sent an SMS message when it was their turn. They also made changes to encourage new beliefs, for example allowing employees to work with start-ups on hackathons to solve business problems from a customer perspective and make the company tech-literate.

DBS conducted over 1,000 experiments in 2015, in which teams tried new ways to find solutions for customer and business problems. More than 100 prototypes were developed across the bank as a result. The bank also established start-up accelerators, which allowed colleagues to interact with people who had very different mindsets. These programmes touched about 2,000 people across the bank in 2015 and 5,000 in 2016.

In 2014, the bank set a target to improve a hundred customer journeys and conducted over a thousand 'looking' activities, including customer interviews, surveys and immersions, to understand consumers better. It set up a Human-Centered Design Lab and trained 700 staff in human-centred design. It partnered with A*STAR[35] to support its use of big data.

In 2015, the bank trained all 250 managing directors in customer journey techniques and asked each of them to lead a customer journey project. As a result, DBS had more than 300 customer journey projects running in every part of the bank. Thousands of bank staff across functions, levels and geographies were involved in these projects, which pushed them to think and act differently.

DBS's burningness propelled the bank to launch India's first mobile-only bank in April 2016 – DBS digibank India – targeting 125 million English language speakers with smartphones. The pain of overseas expansion could be overcome with a digital-only strategy. And taking its cues from fintechs rather than the traditional banking industry, the new bank was completely branchless and did not offer cheques, which were popular in India.

With Sachin Tendulkar, a popular Indian cricket star, as its brand ambassador, the platform had three key features. First, account opening was completely paperless and electronic, with customer authentication using biometrics and the Aadhaar card, a unique identifier for every Indian resident. DBS partnered with a popular national café chain, allowing potential customers to visit over 500 designated outlets to complete the authentication process. Second, customer service was delivered through an artificial intelligence driven virtual assistant developed in partnership with Kasisto, a US-based software company serving the banking industry. Third, it used a dynamic soft token security system embedded in the customer's smartphone which was more secure than inputting one-time passwords received via SMS.

In its 2017 Annual Report, the bank revealed it had signed up over 1.8 million customers since its launch. The burningness experienced by DBS four years earlier had led it ultimately to expansion into India with an entirely new business model fit for the future – a true customer-led success. Moreover, digibank subsequently launched into Indonesia, the market that had prompted Gupta's bold change of strategy in 2013.

DBS's burningness propelled the bank in a new direction. But in our description of the journey to outside-in beliefs this is just the start. The next step is about specific, bold action through Moments of Belief.

Exploring Moments of Belief at AO

The second stage of an inside-out company's journey towards becoming outside-in comes with a Moment of Belief.

AO.com, a start-up online retailer selling white goods, grew to a valuation of more than £1 billion in 15 years, propelled by a number of bold Moments of Belief that transformed the company into a big customer-led, outside-in success.

Founded in 2000 by entrepreneur and salesman John Roberts, AO.com started with quite a basic customer-led premise – better prices. Roberts saw an opportunity in the growing world of online retailing, and he believed, controversially at the time, that big ticket items such as fridges and washing machines could be sold over the internet as easily as CDs and books. In the early days, when most felt this couldn't be done, AO allowed its intrepid customers to save 35–40%. But as the idea of e-commerce took off, Roberts realised he didn't have an advantage that would last.

As a hugely ambitious character, he brought his own version of burningness to the challenge. Knowing how competitive the white goods sector was, with powerful and ruthless physical retailers, and how online retailing in general was low margin and tough, he had palpable fear. He responded by deciding that his business had to be more than just a little bit better than the alternatives. Unless he built something exceptional, he would be crushed, so from the start, there was no lack of boldness even if there was a lack of sophistication.

Although AO had early traction, its brand was unknown. Working with big names, providing a white labelled service for its customers, looked like a route to accelerating growth, and Roberts worked hard to attract partners. In the end, both Boots and Sainsbury's proved keen to enter the category without the risk of setting up their own operations.

There were still challenges. Before allowing sales to start, Sainsbury's insisted service be delivered their way, formalising the approach with clear procedures and rules. Because AO had only one service team, this new approach was applied to everything including AO's own brand customers.

The structure brought some benefits – not only were customers happy but, to Roberts' surprise at the time, it was a route to reducing costs as well. By having better ways of handling customers' problems, he discovered much more quickly what his customers' problems actually were – and they were costing him money. So, he fixed them. And as he worked through these problems, complaints diminished and demand rose. Better service might look like it costs more, but in fact, it costs less eventually. Not only that, but also because customers are happier, they leave positive comments, recommend to others and growth accelerates.

All was going well – and then Sainsbury's gave Roberts six months' notice. They wanted to move their business to Comet, which was prepared to offer what Roberts viewed as an unsustainable level of commission. ('They got worse service when Comet went bust,' he noted wryly.)[36]

In a race against time, Roberts and the team transferred all of the lessons from selling for Sainsbury's into their own AO-branded approach. By the end of the period, AO's sales were higher and their service better than had been the case through Sainsbury's.

Although Roberts had learned a first lesson about customer-led success, he still knew that being good wasn't enough. AO had to be exceptional to survive. The original burningness was just as strong but now he had some ambition as well. His belief, and that of the people around him, had shifted, altered by the first Moment of Belief on their journey, provided by Sainsbury's, that better service was better for the business too.

Now he searched for more ways to be exceptional, placing customers front and centre.

His next big Moment of Belief was around a customer insight that with hindsight sounds obvious (many customer-led examples do). A fridge or a washing machine breaking down in most households constitutes a minor emergency. Suddenly a high-cost decision needs to be made fast and the value of getting a working replacement up and running is huge.

Roberts knew that the industry had an inside-out mentality — they got by with low-cost distribution, relying on suppliers to provide stock and third parties to deliver. But with suppliers supporting multiple retailers, AO could never be certain what was available for immediate dispatch. Similarly, having haggled the price down, the delivery service was pared back, making it unreliable and not especially friendly either.

Roberts made a big bet. His belief was that being able to offer next-day delivery on the whole AO white goods range would be a breakthrough, a proposition that would be hard to match. He invested in AO's own warehousing, AO's own stock not shared with any other retailers, and the acquisition of a warehousing and delivery operation called Expert Logistics. This meant AO could offer bulletproof rapid delivery for the first time to customers, promising that every product listed could be in the customer's home the following day, wherever in the UK they lived.

David Wilkinson, at the time trading and purchasing director (and formerly Roberts' boss in pre-AO days), explained:

> Up to now our logistics providers had been mis-aligned. While our priority was wowing customers, theirs was the P&L. At last the model could be integrated. We identified a logistics company that sounded like they had pride in customer service. Once we bought them, we had total customer ownership from order to receipt. Manufacturers were so impressed that they started using Expert Logistics (now AO Logistics) for home deliveries to consumers on behalf of other

> retailers. Now there was competitive advantage behind being bet-
> ter – we used it in relentless weekly meetings to improve our deliver-
> ies. Our customers were very happy.[37]

The delivery teams enjoyed their sense of purpose too, being on a mission to get their customers' orders to them when and where they wanted,
come what may. Today, there are many AO tales of mythical proportions,
from delivering a washing machine to a customer on an island using a
rowing boat to persuading a mechanic driving a recovery vehicle to tow
a broken-down AO van with its customer's cargo to its final delivery.

The next big Moment of Belief saw AO offering its customers free
returns for any reason at all for 100 days after purchase. Roberts' long-
suffering CFO, subsequently CEO, Steve Caunce, was sure that this time
Roberts had gone too far. The business could be bankrupted by customers
borrowing washing machines at no cost – the cost and risk seemed out
of all proportion to the benefit. And yet ... it turned out that customers
could be trusted and once again hidden value emerged after taking the
leap.

It turned out there were only two big reasons why customers returned
products – they were damaged, or they'd bought the wrong one. Customers
appreciated the no quibble spirit with which they were replaced or refunded
and relieved to be able to sort it out without a lot of arguing.

The value for AO came from this discovery. It meant they could systematically iron out all of the reasons why products were damaged in transit,
and they could also learn how to make it easier for customers to choose
what was right for them first time. The customer and the business very
often have aligned interests if the set-up is outside-in – win-win – where
success is defined as being good for the customer, not win-lose where success is the money made from an individual transaction and what it costs
the customer.

The fourth Moment of Belief on AO's journey was perhaps the most cul-
turally significant – giving AO's customer service teams complete freedom
to do what they felt was right in sorting out customers' issues and to look
for ways to be memorable and thoughtful too.

Roberts certainly felt this was the most crucial – others could eventually copy next-day delivery or a 100-day guarantee, but if he could instil
a genuinely customer-led set of beliefs in the way the business operated,

then he knew that would be all but impregnable. He simply couldn't imagine his inside-out competitors ever being able to copy this way of thinking.

Roberts summed up his intentions in a way that would be instantly understood by the front-line teams. 'Treat the customer as if she was your gran but then after the call you need to explain what you did to your mum.' That was his human way of asking people to put customers first but not at any cost.

Because he trusted them – the front-line teams no longer had to ask supervisors for permission – they took responsibility. Roberts had effectively stripped out layers of management from his customer call centres. In his language you'd have to give away a lot for free before costs were higher than the layers of management he wasn't paying for. Moreover, this new approach meant that 95% of customer issues were dealt with immediately and usually with a warmth and character that customers loved.

The power of this approach becomes clear hearing stories from the front line. In one exchange, AOer Abi helped customer Gerald, a disabled pensioner who relied on his broken microwave for meals. Gerald only had a cheque book and AO doesn't accept cheques. So, Abi asked her colleagues for a contribution and together they treated Gerald to his new microwave for free. This act of kindness, the epitome of 'treating your customer like your gran,' was only spotted during a routine check of customer calls.

Here was another big investment for the company that was un-natural but that worked. It clearly demonstrated outside-in beliefs to customers and, even more importantly, to colleagues as well. The string of Moments of Belief showed that being customer-led also meant winning big. In 2014, AO listed on the London Stock Exchange, valued at more than £1 billion with John Roberts' share valued at more than £400 million.

Exploring systematic ways of working outside-in at Deliveroo

Finally, in the last stage of becoming an outside-in company, as Moments of Belief gather momentum, an organisation finds more systematic ways of working outside-in, something that Deliveroo shows well.

Deliveroo is a start-up that has disrupted the food takeaway business in multiple countries. They bring high-quality meals from restaurants that often don't deliver straight to customers. This has been achieved at the same time as establishing an outside-in belief system.

While Deliveroo's journey as a start-up is not quite the same as a company moving from inside-out to outside-in, it can be just as tough to move from nothing to operating at scale at breath-taking speed through multiple fundraising rounds while avoiding an inside-out, target-led set of beliefs.

Deliveroo shows how introducing more systematic ways of being customer-led can reinforce outside-in beliefs leading the company to spot gaps and opportunities in what customers receive and in what the business can offer. In 2018, five years since it was launched, Deliveroo was valued at $2 billion.[38]

The business was founded by Will Shu, an investment banker who worked long hours and was sick of eating unsatisfying supermarket ready meals every night for dinner. Coming from New York, he knew takeout food didn't have to be this way. 'I was literally working the same hours as in New York, but I had to go to Tesco's every night ... it just became really depressing,'[39] he told one interviewer. Like so many breakthrough innovations coming from the personal experience of a gap or a bad service level, Shu's burningness was a mixture of complete dissatisfaction (pain) at his choice of after-work dining options and ambition that it could be better. The city was full of great restaurants, but he was amazed that so few of them delivered food.

Shu had a belief that people would pay well for good food delivered as distinct from lower quality offerings from takeaway outlets. By establishing Deliveroo's own fleet of delivery riders, he was able to create rapid access to genuinely good hot food. This was a big bet. The main competition just provided an ordering platform and relied on the restaurants and takeaways to provide the delivery service. That meant the loss of quality control for both the food and the service with customers unable to see where their order was on its journey towards them.

Deliveroo is one of only a handful of companies that have overhauled an entire ecosystem, participating in the gig economy, changing the look of the roads with its fleet of delivery riders. It has been a catalyst for change in many cities, altering the way we eat.

From the beginning, Deliveroo challenged assumptions, taking an outside-in approach. In February 2013, ignoring sceptics who told him

'English people don't want good food delivered!', Shu launched Deliveroo in Chelsea, his home neighbourhood. As Shu recalled:

> I was the first delivery guy and for eight months I delivered food every single day for five hours, not because I really needed to for money's sake but because I really wanted to understand what the customer went through.[40]

In the early days, Shu's banker friends kept ordering from Deliveroo because they found it hilarious that he was their delivery guy. A hedge fund trader who Shu hadn't seen for five years was shocked when he delivered a pizza to his big house in Knightsbridge thinking he must have fallen on hard times, saying, 'Will, what are you doing? Are you okay?'

Six years in, Deliveroo was earning revenues of more than £350 million through 60,000 riders in 500 cities and 13 countries from over 80,000 restaurants with no more than 30 minutes from order to receipt.[41]

Deliveroo's first big Moment of Belief was investing in its own delivery and logistics operation to ensure that they were in control of food arriving hot and within thirty minutes for its customers. Deliveroo makes money by charging restaurants a commission and customers a simple low fee on its app. It offers restaurants who don't normally deliver an extra source of revenue by outsourcing the job to Deliveroo. Indeed, the company says that restaurants who partner with the delivery firm see their revenue increase by up to 30%. For example, Sunday, Deliveroo's busiest day, tends to be the day when many restaurants are empty.

Deliveroo's focus on logistics has fuelled its rapid growth. Being a nearly full-time delivery driver in the first 10 months of the business, Shu learned about efficiency. 'I did it seven days a week. You do that and you get pattern-recognition in minutes. You can shave off elements of the journey,' he said.[42]

Today Deliveroo has systems that give it control and also feedback on how the system is performing. It uses a routing algorithm that picks the right driver to collect an order from a restaurant then deliver it to its destination. A team of data scientists looks for efficiencies by breaking down the delivery process; this includes the interaction with the customer, the process of cycling or driving to the restaurant, picking up the food at the back door, or punching in a code at the restaurant to get in and then getting the food swiftly and safely to the customer who ordered it, through often complex entry systems, doors and stairs.

The data-led learning can be highly actionable. Shu explained:

> If you tell the restaurant precisely when the [delivery] guy is going to be there, that's better than saying he'll be there in 10 minutes ... You give them precision. A Neapolitan pizza takes 90 seconds to cook. A steak takes 10 minutes. How do you pair that so the food is piping hot when the guy gets there? We have a million tests going on all over the place.[43]

Deliveroo uses real-time data, constantly calculating and recalculating the best combination of riders to orders through a dispatch engine affectionately known as 'Frank.' It can change decisions in response to live new information like a sudden accident and subsequent traffic jams.

Taking seriously its customer-led purpose to provide the best restaurant-quality food to its customers, Deliveroo has designed its own food containers to protect the food on its travels while keeping it piping hot. It has individual compartments for different parts of the dish and this packaging has become another revenue stream, being sold to Deliveroo's restaurant partners.

Deliveroo then found there were unexpected insights available from its data pool that showed new opportunities to better meet customer needs. The business now has a new perspective, seeing where demand lies, where suppliers are and how these pieces of the puzzle fit together across a city. It revealed cuisine blackspots in big urban areas. For example, despite the demand in similar neighbourhoods, there were very few good-quality burger restaurants in Camberwell, an area of South London.

So Deliveroo created an outside-in response. Deliveroo Editions became an entirely new part of their business model. Seeing a cuisine blackspot, Deliveroo now establishes kitchens with restaurant partners in shipping containers in unused local spaces. These low-cost, low-risk outlets are purely focused on Deliveroo deliveries and do not operate as restaurants in their own right. In high-demand areas, Deliveroo funds the cost of the new kitchen set-ups. Its plans showed 134 of these kitchens in the UK by the end of 2018 and openings in Madrid, Paris, Sydney and Amsterdam, alongside existing kitchens in Singapore, Dubai and Melbourne.[44]

As a poster child for the gig economy, Deliveroo has inevitably faced criticism for its fleet of self-employed delivery riders. While Deliveroo pays above the minimum wage in the UK (£10 an hour), riders have no contracted hours and don't get sick pay or paid holidays. In outside-in fashion, Deliveroo is working with governments to change employment legislation so that it can offer its riders both flexibility and security. Until then, Deliveroo provides warm, waterproof visible uniforms, gets involved in local community groups, organises casual meetups for riders in Nando's and hosts dinners for riders during Ramadan.

Deliveroo's outside-in growth was based on its understanding that good food delivered fast and hot was what mattered to customers, then finding systematic ways of using data at scale to do this more effectively. In so doing it has created whole new business opportunities and business models.

Conclusion and recap

When Rosa Parks took her seat on the bus in Montgomery on that December day, she set in motion a train of events that would determine the fate of the civil rights movement and the future of America. There was a burningness that made her act this way, and her decision to take her seat, then the subsequent positive action and coverage was a Moment of Belief that created momentum that snowballed towards significant change.

In the same way, we've seen the outside-in momentum that came from intense moments of burningness in the business world: easyJet's pain as delayed planes and disgruntled passengers threatened its future, and then the ambition that was ignited when the team realised they could be a force for good more widely; DBS's pain as a strategic acquisition fell through at the last minute, and then the fear that it might be disrupted by digital competition; AO's fear that it just couldn't last given the competition, then the additional pain from Sainsbury's service standards that it couldn't meet became ambition as confidence grew; and Deliveroo's William Shu, with his personal pain and company-wide ambition that there had to be something a whole lot better than supermarket ready meals when working late.

With each of these companies, these intense beginnings led them to innovate on behalf of customers, taking big, bold bets.

Some of these bets crystallised into Moments of Belief – light bulbs popping on that suddenly illuminated how serving customers better, from their point of view, was the right thing for the business too. easyJet learned from Formula One how to provide allocated seats to passengers without slowing down aircraft turnaround, DBS transformed itself into a 22,000-person start-up, an invisible bank with a key role in customers lives, fit for the future and ready to compete with fintechs. AO provided next-day delivery for its customers and created a culture of caring at scale, and Deliveroo built a logistics operation and a digital platform that allows it to bring restaurant food into customers' homes, even in areas that lack the restaurants its inhabitants want to buy from.

We have shown how organisations that become customer-led successes establish an outside-in belief system. Yes, it is against the odds, but as the stories of these companies demonstrate, it's entirely possible with the right conditions and a motivated, capable team.

As we have seen, there are four stages that flow together to form a real customer-led transformation. Burningness creates the impetus for a first Moment of Belief, then confidence from seeing it working motivates another, then another, deepening conviction and changing behaviour across the organisation until, eventually, outside-in beliefs and behaviour become systematic, learning what matters to customers and acting on it to solve their problems in new and better ways in a seamless flow.

What could possibly go wrong?

In our next chapter we will answer that question by showing how falling back to earth from outside-in to inside-out is a great deal easier than becoming outside-in in the first place.

Notes

1   Peter Duffy, interview with authors, 21 November 2018.

2   Ghosh, Shona. 27 November 2014. '"We weren't making travel easy for our customers," says easyJet chief.' *Campaign*. Retrieved from www.c ampaignlive.co.uk/article/we-werent-making-travel-easy-customers-says-easyjet-chief/1324047

3   Calder, Simon. 6 September 2012. 'Now boarding... calmly. easyJet ends the scrum.' *Independent*. Retrieved from www.independent.co.uk/travel/news-a nd-advice/now-boarding-calmly-easyjet-ends-the-scrum-8107102.html

4   McCall, Carolyn. 26 November 2014. The Marketing Society Annual Conference, Inspirational Resetters panel.

    Elen Lewis (formerly Digital Editor, The Marketing Society), interview with authors, 19 October 2019.

5   Meehan, Alice. August 2016. 'Moments of Belief.'   IMD Research Report. https://www.imd.org/contentassets/e60e4c757a6e49ddb-f86daa6302f9348/imd_article_momentsofbelief_round4-1.pdf

6   Theoharis, Jeanne. 2013. *The Rebellious Life of Mrs Rosa Parks*. Boston, MA: Beacon Press, p. 62.

7   Interview with authors, 1 May 2020.

8   Clark, Nicola. 15 June 2015. 'easyJet Chief leads airline through turnaround.' *The New York Times*. Retrieved from www.nytimes.com/2015/06/16/bus iness/international/chief-of-easyjet-leads-airline-through-a-turnaround .html

9   Gwyther, Matthew. 25 April 2013. 'Queen of the skies: easyJet CEO Carolyn McCall on piloting into the FTSE100.' *Management Today*. Retrieved from www.managementtoday.co.uk/queen-skies-easyjet-ceo-carolyn-mccall-piloting-ftse100/article/1179006

10 Clark, Nicola. 15 June 2015. 'easyJet Chief leads airline through turnaround.'

11 Hollinger, Peggy. 21 November 2014. 'Carolyn McCall: Flying high at easyJet.' *Financial Times*. Retrieved from www.ft.com/content/8e57d15e -70ac-11e4-8113-00144feabdco

12 Eleftheriou-Smith, Loulla-Mae. 25 April 2012. 'easyJet's Carolyn McCall on putting clear blue sky between the airline and its budget rivals.' *Marketing Magazine*. Retrieved from www.campaignlive.co.uk/article/easyjets-carol yn-mccall-putting-clear-blue-sky-airline-its-budget-rivals/1128281www. campaignlive.co.uk/article/easyjets-carolyn-mccall-putting-clear-blue-sky -airline-its-budget-rivals/1128281

13 Interview with authors, 6 April 2020.

14 Eleftheriou-Smith, Loulla-Mae. 25 April 2012. 'Easyjet's Carolyn McCall on putting clear blue sky between the airline and its budget rivals.'

15 Davidson, Andrew. 20 November 2011. 'Rookie pilot with an Armani smile.' *The Times*. Retrieved from www.thetimes.co.uk/article/rookie-pilot-with-an-armani-smile-7fq62hk7vrs

16 Davidson, Andrew. 20 November 2011. 'Rookie pilot with an Armani smile.'

17 Interview with authors, 6 April 2020.

18   Vizard, Sarah. 26 November 2014. 'easyJet CEO: "Marketers should be at the centre of all consumer businesses."' *MarketingWeek*. Retrieved from www.marketingweek.com/2014/11/26/easyjet-ceo-marketers-should-be-at -the-centre-of-all-consumer-businesses/

19   Davidson, Andrew. 20 November 2011. 'Rookie pilot with an Armani smile.'

20   Davidson, Andrew. 20 November 2011. 'Rookie pilot with an Armani smile.'

21   Clark, Nicola. 15 June 2015. 'easyJet Chief leads airline through turnaround.'

22   Peter Duffy, interview with authors, 21 November 2018.

23   Peter Duffy, interview with authors, 21 November 2018.

24   Peter Duffy, interview with authors, 21 November 2018.

25   Peter Duffy, interview with authors, 21 November 2018.

26   Peter Duffy, interview with authors, 21 November 2018.

27   Clark, Nicola. 15 June 2015. 'easyJet Chief leads airline through turnaround.'

28   Clark, Nicola. 15 June 2015. 'easyJet Chief leads airline through turnaround.'

29   Medland, Dina. 26 April 2017. 'easyJet CEO Dame Carolyn McCall on Transformative Leadership.' *Chartered Management Institute*. Retrieved from www.managers.org.uk/insights/news/2017/april/easyjet-ceo-dame -carolyn-mccall-on-transformative-leadership

30   Wall, Robert. 23 March 2016. 'Ryanair's new strategy: Being nice.' *Wall Street Journal*. Retrieved from www.wsj.com/articles/ryanairs-new-strate gy-being-nice-1457862512

31   Gwynn, Simon. 26 April 2017. 'easyJet's Carolyn McCall: When you've done something wrong, apologise.' *Campaign*. Retrieved from www.campai gnlive.co.uk/article/easyjets-carolyn-mccall-when-youve-done-something -wrong-apologise/1431750

32   Peter Duffy, interview with authors, 21 November 2018.

33   Meehan Seán & Pallivathukkal Cherian Abraham. 7 July 2017. *DBS Transformation (A): Becoming a World-Class Multinational Bank* (IMD case no. IMD-7-1836). Lausanne: IMD Business School.

34   Meehan Seán & Pallivathukkal Cherian Abraham. 7 July 2017. 'DBS Transformation (A).'

35   A*STAR is the Singapore government's agency that promotes science, technology and research.

36   Interviews with authors, 20 February 2018 and 25 May 2020.

37   David Wilkinson and John Roberts, interviews with authors, 5 and 20 February 2018.

38   Garrahan, Matthew & Aliya Ram. 28 November 2018. 'Uber and Deliveroo talks "miles apart" on valuation.' *Financial Times*. Retrieved from www.ft .com/content/53fe1324-f271-11e8-ae55-df4bf40f9d0d

39   Dunsby, Megan. 17 June 2018. 'Will Shu: How I went from investment banker to founder of $857m-backed tech start-up Deliveroo.' *Startups*. Retrieved from https://startups.co.uk/will-shu-how-i-went-from-investm ent-banker-to-founder-of-200m-backed-tech-start-up-deliveroo/

40   Dunsby, Megan. 17 June 2018. 'Will Shu'.

41   Deliveroo. 5 February 2019. 'Deliveroo growth soars, with 80,000 restaurants across the world' (press release). Retrieved from https://uk.deliveroo .news/news/delvieroo-rx-growth-2019.html

42   Olson, Parmy. 17 February 2016. 'Here's how Deliveroo built an army of 5,000 drivers in just 3 years.' *Forbes*. Retrieved from www.forbes.com/sites /parmyolson/2016/02/17/deliveroo-army-5000-drivers-3-years/#38fb2 1ed2obd

43   Olson, Parmy. 17 February 2016. 'Here's how Deliveroo built an army of 5,000 drivers.'

44   Ram, Aliya. 18 May 2018. 'Deliveroo launches £5m fund to invest in UK restaurants.' *Financial Times*. Retrieved from www.ft.com/content/335391 d0-5a8c-11e8-bdb7-f6677d2e1ce8

5

LOSING CUSTOMER-LED BELIEFS

As a jumper I try to defy gravity for as long as I can. But no matter how far I jump, I'll always hit the earth eventually.

Greg Rutherford (British Olympic gold medallist
– long jump, 2012)

O2: From outside-in to inside-out

As with our first example, Tesco, the spectacular rise and subsequent decline of O2, the UK-based mobile telecom network, demonstrates that a customer-led approach that leads to great things at one point in a company's lifecycle is no guarantee that it can sustain it in another. At the height of its success, O2 was responsible for a succession of customer firsts as it rewrote the rules of the mobile industry that had traditionally thrown all its efforts at recruiting new customers and almost none at keeping existing ones happy. In September 2002, less than a year after BT demerged mmO2, as it was called then, analysts called it 'a perpetual value destroyer' and valued it at £3.65 billion.[1] It was sold to Telefonica three years later for £17.7 billion.

O2's decision to reverse the standard industry practice by focusing on loyal existing customers rather than buying new ones with costly acquisition programmes constitutes a massive Moment of Belief. A stream of Moments of Belief followed in its wake, including an innovative sponsorship deal that transformed the maligned Millennium Dome in London into the world's most popular entertainment venue offering priority tickets to O2 customers.

However, the combination of O2's takeover by Telefonica in 2005 plus the pressures of the financial crash of 2008/9 on the Group and an ambitious diversification programme made it increasingly hard for the mobile company to maintain its laser-like focus on creating customer value above all else. Its distinctive outside-in beliefs were eventually undermined by Telefonica's need for profit and the lure of ambitious expansion beyond the core. Like an invading virus attacking a healthy body, the outside-in beliefs were weakened, diluted and eventually killed off. O2 is a vivid illustration of reversion to the norm; even when a firm achieves outstanding success by establishing widely held customer-led shared beliefs, without superhuman effort, it can expect to lose its advantage as those beliefs weaken over time.

The inevitability of falling from outside-in to inside-out

This chapter is about the inevitability of being pulled back down to Earth from the soaring heights of customer-led success. It is about being extraordinary and then becoming ordinary – not through incompetence or hubris, but as a natural process. O2, the airline Virgin Atlantic, US retailer Market Basket, and Nokia, the Finnish mobile handset and technology company, all achieved great things in ways that were entirely customer-led, based on deeply-held shared beliefs. Yet their exceptional customer-led success was temporary, and all of them eventually came crashing back to earth.

The rise and fall of these companies shows that even when they appear unchallengeable, outside-in beliefs are never secure. Being customer-led took all four companies to market leadership and enviable levels of performance. Yet, despite this great success, the shared beliefs behind what led to that success proved fragile. Some recovered to have another period of customer-led success but only after rescue and turnaround.

Why is this arc inevitable? We have uncovered three types of challenge to a company's belief system, issues that over time, if unaddressed, will undermine even the most strongly held outside-in beliefs. As Gerald R. Salancik once said, 'Success ruins everything.'[2] The more the company's approach seems to work, the more the 'burningness' fades. As success becomes taken for granted, the pull of the comfort zone increases, and the appetite for remaining in the customer's orbit shrinks. There is strategic and operational drift as managers switch their attention from the customer's quest for better quality and higher value to the less stressful option of exploiting their current happiness to please investors. In time their outperformance, as judged by customers, erodes with inevitable but delayed consequences for market share, earnings and valuation.

A company's shared beliefs are constantly under attack from three different quarters:

1. The inside, as common sense and the natural way of seeing the world from behind an office desk every day attempt to reassert themselves.
2. The outside, as newcomers join the pioneering group of leaders and blur their customer focus by bringing conventional doubt and risk aversion into the mix.
3. The competition, as it keeps on improving and eventually throws up something better than the model used by what is now an incumbent. The first two factors will have taken the edge off the company's customer-led zeal, prompting a defensive, protectionist response in place of previously confident customer innovation.

These challenges emerge seemingly naturally in different ways, sometimes to dramatic effect, as the examples in this chapter show.

Virgin Atlantic was an exceptional, entrepreneurial challenger to the traditional flag carrying airlines on long-haul routes. It was created in the mid-1980s and broadly had two eras – the first where it punched well above its weight and created a pioneering series of innovations that customers welcomed in the long-haul air travel sector. And the second as the business grew to another level of scale, ownership changed, objectives became more commercial and the whole enterprise matured. As newer competitors produced their own market-leading innovations, Virgin Atlantic retained its identity but applied it in more professional ways. Compared to its heyday, it lost its maverick spirit and it was no longer an outright market leader, but it remains a good business – more conventional but with more substance too.

Market Basket was an outstanding grocery retailer with a way of working that both customers and colleagues revered. It had strong leadership and a family ownership structure, but many of these owners were distant from the reality of the way the business operated. These shareholders couldn't see or didn't appreciate the way the outside-in beliefs led to the performance they enjoyed, and many of the ways of doing things at the retailer looked expensive. So they pushed for higher margins, greater efficiency, becoming preoccupied with faster and better financial returns. They could only see the golden eggs, not the goose that was laying them. And as a result, they almost killed it.

Nokia was an apparently impregnable global market leader. But even though it had insight into what customers cared about in a traditional mobile handset back in the 1990s and early 2000s, it became attached to the particular solution to what it saw as its customers' problem. When it asked about phones, its customers talked about phones – buttons that were easy to press, batteries that lasted forever, sending texts and making calls. It was drifting from being customer-led to becoming product-led, unaware of the ways new types of competitors saw the opportunity for mobile technology and many different kinds of data. It only became obvious when Apple launched the iPhone. Now what mattered was the operating system, the way data could be shared across devices, plus an interface that was visual … the rules had changed, and for Nokia, it was too late to respond.

O2 faced all of these challenges. Its success meant it was highly valued, and it was acquired by Telefonica, a traditional ex-public sector telecom player that wanted to learn from O2's magic touch. For a while, Telefonica gave the O2 team space, but when the financial crash of 2008/9 arrived, there was a need for urgent financial contributions from every quarter, and all involved were forced to prioritise cashflow and question investment. Now the O2 business faced significant inside-out financial targets that needed short-term, financially led action to hit them.

In parallel, the success and power of its reputation led its people to subtly shift from focusing on customers and the essentials of what they cared about to focusing on the O2 brand, trying to expand it into multiple markets from its mobile network base.

While this was going on, the competition moved on, and the forces of Apple's and Google's operating systems, global handset brands and punishing commoditised competition for supplying bandwidth meant O2's performance at the core lost its edge.

Telefonica's involvement unavoidably led to bureaucracy increasing, causing management to look inwards. The well-intentioned innovation efforts were less effective than in O2's heyday. Resources were diverted from the core. Despite all of this, O2 is still a strong player in its market, but it is closer to being a utility than the pioneer it envisaged in its youth.

From remarkable customer leadership to conventional utility at O2

O2's Customer Plan is one of the most vivid examples of a Moment of Belief we've discovered in our research. The idea that a mobile company would invest hundreds of millions of pounds to give existing customers the best deal was revolutionary.

Unusually for a company that became an outstanding customer-led success, O2 started life as part of a nationalised industry – the UK's British Telecom. In 1984 it was privatised and as the potential for mobile telephony emerged, Cellnet was created – a 60:40 joint venture between BT and Securicor, a business with a background in security services.

The mobile market was initially limited in appeal, with high costs and large handsets that needed big batteries or a connection to a car. Cellnet and Vodafone, both quite technical and business orientated, led the UK market. In the early 1990s, consumer branding overhauled the sector, first with One-to-One (later taken over and rebranded T-Mobile) and then Orange. Independent distributors like Carphone Warehouse and Phones4U became winners through smart trading, an understanding of brand, of tactical marketing and a wave of consolidation.

Growth was rapid but not for the incumbents who were seen as old-fashioned and uncool. Cellnet's customer base was business orientated, and its consumer customers tended to be older and low value. In 1999,

BT bought out Securicor's share, and in 2002, Cellnet was spun off from BT completely. At this stage the view in the mobile telephony sector was that Cellnet was close to being worthless, known for 'glovebox' customers – people who kept a switched off handset in their car's glovebox just in case their car broke down.

This was the first stage of O2's customer-led journey and their burningness was pain – they were out of business unless they acted very boldly indeed. The team had been together for a while, and they felt they had something to prove personally too.

The management had a very clear, basic customer challenge. They needed to find a way of attracting high-value consumers and this meant young people for whom the mobile phone was becoming an essential part of life – they used texting as much as calling to stay connected to their social group. Recognising the need for complete reinvention, Cellnet rebranded as O2 – the oxygen you need for modern life, where heavy users would rather be without their wallet or keys than their phone.

O2's early years were successful as it employed some of the best marketing talent to build a dynamic, youthful and appealing brand. It made bold decisions, such as sponsoring the edgy TV programme Big Brother, which was controversial but loved by the customers it needed.

Initially, it had a following wind. The Orange brand had vacated its position as an early customer-led pioneer following acquisitions that took it from entrepreneurial Hutchison to ex-state-owned France Telecom. The market was also fast-growing with room for competitors to have some success by taking different paths.

The customer base changed and grew but the market was maturing. As competition intensified, the industry was not in a good place. The whole sector was set up in an inside-out way – the convention was that the critical growth metrics were customer numbers and average revenue per customer, leading to a continual fight to acquire new customers in 'tricksy' ways. This approach relied on the hope that tempting offers would attract new people and grow share, and then when their introductory discounts expired, their inertia would stop most of them cancelling their contracts, a point at which revenue from each of them would increase and they would become profitable.

By 2004, it became clear that the market and O2 had issues. Profitability was falling as this intense competition spiralled. Existing customers woke up to the way the market favoured switching, and there was increasing resentment that unless they left, or threatened to leave, which prompted their existing network to give them a much better deal, they were taken advantage of. O2's leadership needed to react.

In 2004, Matthew Key was promoted from CFO to CEO. He was an accomplished strategic thinker who had been an integral part of the O2 success story. The shift in role allowed him to take a broader perspective and a longer-term view across the years he was going to be in charge. Among others he could rely on was Cath Keers, O2's CMO with a background in customer service, marketing and sales. She naturally cared about customers and spent considerable time at the front line to stay connected to what was really going on. Mark Stansfeld was O2's commercial director responsible for sales. He was open to customer-led thinking, not focused on price as would have been common with most of his peer group at the time.

This was a difficult period. Key and his senior team needed to develop their strategy and it was clear that more of the same was going to lead to diminishing returns at best. Previously profitable customers on long-term contracts were leaving at the rate of 25–30% a year and more and more had to be spent to attract people to replace them. Margins were falling while independent retailers who sold multiple networks were getting showered with money in a zero-sum game to buy customers' choices, making their owners very wealthy in the process. O2's own call centres were multiplying as existing customers called not just with problems but also when they renewed, playing a game to get the offers they knew were at the discretion of the people they spoke to.

Costs to attract, retain and run the business were spiralling with the customer bucket full of leaks. Burningness had returned in the form of increasing pain and a growing fear that this just wasn't sustainable. As a contemporary described it:

> Cath Keers personally championed the customer-centric agenda. She had a belief that doing the right thing for customers would win out. She had ambition for the business and wanted the brand to do something meaningful. She was also not fearful of having a go.[3]

She initiated work on what became called the Customer Plan, a central plank of the leadership team's turnaround strategy. Instead of focusing on new customers, it proposed that O2 would put existing customers at the front and centre of their priorities. This would end the practice of giving new customers better deals than those already with O2. However, in order to keep customers in the face of the competition, it would mean giving the entire customer base a better deal. The only way this might work would be if retention rates stepped up and customers became happy to have a more positive, trusting relationship with O2, buying more from the brand instead of counting down the days until they were free to leave.

This was a true Moment of Belief. The cost of taking this step would be huge and immediate, estimated at around £150 million. (In practice, it turned out to be more like £250 million!) The benefits would only be visible in time, and no one knew for sure whether they would materialise.

To pay for this plan, another big decision was made – to stop work on technology where O2's aim was to compete with hardware and software businesses. Instead, they invested in a range of things that existing customers valued – prices that were fair and reasonable, new stores, better call centres and a better digital customer experience.

The period when the plan was developed and debated was considerable and the timing in some ways fortunate, as CEO Matthew Key was in a position to apply his judgement as well as knowing the numbers inside out. The market model was broken, and it was worth betting on changing it; in the medium term it should help O2 outperform. This move was also in line with the values of the kind of business he said he wanted to run – putting customers first. After a month of debating the plans, they were eventually signed off by the plc board but with the clear expectation that either this worked, or the senior team would be looking for new jobs.

The boldness came from three kinds of burningness:

- Fear of the future and the competition, making it clear that change (or failure) would be inevitable at some point, as shown by the numbers.
- Ambition of one kind, closer to Tesco's determination to beat Sainsbury's, in this case fuelled by the success of the indirect distributors in the market, Carphone Warehouse and Phones4U, whose owners were doing very well; O2 wanted to grow its own direct business alongside them.

- Ambition of another kind, for customers, seeing the potential in investing in what customers really valued, rather than trying to push them towards a mobile network's bottom line.

Once the decision was taken, there was a lot to do. Beyond identifying the headline areas that mattered, the O2 team executed brilliantly. The customer experience mattered, with carefully designed customer journeys and attention paid to the touch-points that mattered most; call centres and stores hired differently – people were selected because they displayed the values and attitudes that fitted with O2's beliefs. This meant they could be given more freedom and broadly asked to do the right thing for the customers they served. The underlying holistic approach was that 'it only works when it all works.'

Having embraced the direction and made the investment, there was an anxious wait to see whether it would pay off. In practice, it worked far more quickly and decisively than anyone imagined. Four months in, surveys showed O2 leaping from the bottom of the customer satisfaction charts to the top, and they had started to grow swiftly. Existing customers loved the initiative, even just hearing about it and in advance of experiencing the joy of an easy renewal. The team were surprised to find the degree to which customers of other networks loved it too – unsurprisingly, with hindsight, they were just as frustrated as O2's customers.

Deb Corless described the effect at the sharp end in contact centres working on renewals:

> Before the Customer Plan, we were in a deal-making environment. Call handlers would try to offer the best deals only to the best customers, giving less to others, and they would be steered by the latest offers and subsidies, looking to cross-sell to get profits up whether the deal was right for the customer or not. The customer's mindset was to battle hard to get a good result. After the Customer Plan, customers called and actually liked their O2 experience. There was trust, and they were open to seeing what the offer would be. Colleagues loved it too. They wanted to feel proud of their work and now they saw their job as doing the right thing for the customer. They could be generous, offering little bundles of goodness like free texts at any point in the conversation. All this, and it worked commercially as well – I was sceptical at first, but the evidence built people's belief.[4]

For O2 this meant a leap in retention and also a leap in new people being attracted. Far from taking five years to have an impact, it had happened in months.

As ambition grew, some more big Moments of Belief followed. In London, the great structure built to house a year of Millennium celebrations – the Dome – had been through a period of sporadic use as a venue for fairs and one-off shows. Then it was bought by AEG, the entertainment business, with a vision to turn it into Europe's leading purpose-built venue for music concerts. They wanted a headline sponsor, but the lasting image of the Dome was as an unloved mistake.

Corless remembered O2's decision to become that sponsor being announced at the annual marketing conference 12 months in advance. 'There was a lot of rah-rah and clapping, but we were all thinking they'd lost the plot.'[5] As the launch got closer, the team saw more details emerge that were encouraging, but doubts persisted. Eventually, in the run-up to the public launch of the new O2 venue, 18,000 O2 colleagues, families and friends were invited to a preview evening.

> There was comedy, there were bands and it was amazing. It set new standards for any venue in the UK, and it was an O2 branded experience. It was the proof of the pudding and another pivotal moment for O2.[6]

Clearly, this was another true Moment of Belief – a market-leading action based on customers that ended up working commercially for O2 as well. They took the big bet because the team felt customers would value the bold endorsement, and they would also value their priority access, something that the business built into a valuable and unique property.

There were more big and impressive Moments of Belief along the way:

- An innovative deal with Tesco to create Tesco Mobile as a 50/50 joint venture, a way of reaching a different set of customers with a more relevant proposition that became the biggest and most successful MVNO (Mobile Virtual Network Operator) in the world with 5 million customers and plenty of awards for customer service.
- Reinventing the whole pay-as-you-go offering into an option seen as classless and easy – for people who wanted to control their spending – rather than cheap and second-best.

- Winning the Apple iPhone launch in the UK and insisting they changed their plans from working with two networks to only working with O2. Apple and iPhone had huge cut through especially among early tech adopters. O2's UK exclusivity gave people happy with their existing network a reason to join O2, it added to O2's image as the most forward-thinking operator, and it generated pride with colleagues. Peter Erskine, Group CEO at the time, and Matthew Key had recognised the potential in this deal and then landed it too.
- Buying an independent retailer (The Link) to grow more direct relationships with customers.
- Launching giffgaff, the world's first mobile network where service was largely provided by customers through a customer community, again hugely innovative and boldly executed leading to a lasting success, 10 years in and counting.

The list goes on and on. But the reason O2's story is in this chapter is because the outside-in beliefs couldn't and didn't last.

The most obvious challenge to the company's beliefs came with its purchase by Telefonica, announced late in 2005. The issues weren't immediate though and not for the direct reasons you might assume from a distance.

Telefonica admired the customer centricity of O2. In Spain, Telefonica was originally the state-owned telecommunications monopoly. A large organisation not used to intense competition, the Telefonica culture was financially driven and dominated by engineers in top roles.

To begin with they recognised that the value of O2 would be diminished if they got in the way of its bold, customer-led ways of working. So O2's base was broadened internationally both as O2, for example re-branding a recent Czech acquisition, and in many Latin countries as a guiding spirit behind the Movistar brand.

The period from 2006 to 2009 was good, a honeymoon perhaps. O2 was doing well and the Telefonica share price was strong. But slipping from outside-in beliefs back to those that are inside-out can come from the inside, from the team itself, as much as from outsiders imposing their views.

One force comes from the natural process of running a business. Around the board table the conversation is about the here and now, the plans and the quarter-by-quarter progress. Talking about customers can feel like a distraction. And then, when the company is succeeding and the numbers keep rising, it can feel easy. There are calls to speak at conferences, awards and a constant flow of compliments.

O2 started to diversify. It had won in mobile telecoms and it started looking for growth beyond the core, partly in obviously linked markets such as broadband and fixed line telephony, and partly more boldly, looking to take mobile into other areas of customers' lives such as health and financial services.

Both parts of the diversification proved challenging:

- On broadband, there was a lot of debate over the entry point the business should take and by the time a plan had been agreed, the window of opportunity had largely closed; others, like Sky, moved faster and invested more. Broadband also turned out to be a more operationally complicated undertaking than expected, and so the distractions continued as market entry proceeded.

- On wider diversification, good work was done to understand where the O2 brand could play a valued role in customers' lives. But the risk with brand extension is that it is easy to become brand focused rather than looking outside-in, from where customers stand. A big mural appeared in O2's new UK headquarters depicting 'O2-ville,' a village of O2 services. It seemed to be centred on O2 rather than the customer. As someone in the business remembers feeling at the time, the intention was good, trying to invest ahead of a maturing mobile industry. O2 was looking to fix problems customers had in other areas of their lives. But perhaps because of the huge success of the brand, the team found themselves assuming too much strength and having not enough humility. An example might be looking to fix issues with the way money works for customers by applying customer insight when it's a truly complicated market to change, especially for a single country-based mobile operator.

Now, fighting on a broader front, but in a core market that was relentlessly competitive, O2 was losing momentum.

When the takeover had happened, a few of the core team left or stepped back having had a financial windfall. Then in 2008/9 the financial crash hit

Spain especially hard. Telefonica was naturally in trouble given its exposure to the whole of the Spanish market. Growth rates across Western Europe slipped back to low single figures, and to Telefonica, South America was more attractive. O2 became a cash cow, providing much-needed income and, under pressure to produce more cash, investment slowed.

This made a material difference:

- In 2010/11, there was an auction for the new 4G spectrum, but Telefonica set conservative ceilings for O2's bids. As a result, O2 came out with not much additional bandwidth meaning they could offer customers less capacity and carry less traffic. The network subsequently cost more to run and gave customers an inferior experience.
- By 2012, what was 'core' was changing. Newer businesses like challenger Three saw the future of mobile in data and using the internet. That was the focus, not making calls and sending texts. As a result, they were on a journey to deliver the best mobile internet experience, while O2 judged itself on call performance stats.
- In 2013, O2 outsourced its contact centre operations to Capita, worth a rumoured £80 million annually to the O2 bottom line. After a protected period, the service was moved to South Africa despite what one employee described as a 'car crash trial' and customer satisfaction never recovered to the O2-owned levels.

Corless had left O2 at its peak, joining mobile challenger brand Three for four years, then returning to O2 as part of a new customer experience team and expecting great things. Instead, she described what she found:

> ... a group that felt downtrodden. Part of the role was to update the exec on metrics and actions, but it felt like going through the motions, looking to tell good news stories, not highlighting areas to do better. If issues mattered to customers but addressing them would have little commercial benefit, they felt unimportant. There had been lots of patting on the back about O2 being an amazing customer-centric business, but to be good at this you have to be paranoid and we'd lost our paranoia.[7]

O2 had moved from being a proactive, maybe paranoid challenger to being more of an incumbent. The more you have, the more you have to protect, especially when it is difficult to justify riskier investments. And riskier investments are exactly what outside-in initiatives look like – definite costs, uncertain returns, costs now, returns in the future. The new challenger gathering strength was Hutchison-owned Three who, as we have just seen, had recruited plenty from O2 and was recruiting more as O2 people felt held back from pursuing their best ideas.

Meanwhile the day-to-day experience for leaders within O2 had evolved – as it would in what was now an international company. A business looks to lower costs in areas that are shared, and functions like running the company's IT platforms and networks were brought together. It meant more frequent negotiation with the centre for the O2 UK team, taking time and shifting attention inside the business. The centre has to manage by numbers and so the conversations and meetings are more about metrics and less about customers, what matters to them and whether new and better alternatives are emerging.

By 2013/14, Telefonica was seriously thinking about selling O2, and this proved destabilising. Two other big competitors, T-Mobile and Orange, were also looking for new owners and so immediate profitability really mattered. It was even harder to get a yes to investment requests. An agreement was reached with Three, but having had a year trying to maximise profitability to ensure the best price, an objective that is a hugely inside-out force for a business, the European competition regulator blocked the deal in 2016, a decision overturned rather academically by the European courts in May 2020.

As we write this, O2 soldiers on in the UK, a good strong business in what is now, on the network side, a mature sector with another merger rumour swirling around it and Virgin Media. O2 is good, but it is no longer an outside-in leader. This has been arrived at not by making big mistakes, not through hubris or complacency, but simply in the natural way of things.

Next, we'll look at the inevitable arc of companies falling from outside-in to inside-out through the stories of three exceptional companies. Virgin Atlantic, whose outside-in beliefs were challenged by internal forces; Market Basket, whose outside-in beliefs were challenged by external forces; and Nokia, a market leader who drifted away from being customer-led and was taken by surprise by a competitor changing the rules of the game.

The challenge of internal forces at Virgin Atlantic

When Virgin Atlantic started flying between the UK and the US on June 22, 1984, it ruffled plenty of feathers. It came offering not only better, friendlier service and lower costs for passengers, but also a commitment to put the customer first.

Reflecting the values of its founder, Richard Branson, Virgin Atlantic was a pioneer, bringing a stream of innovations that competitors sought to follow. These included individual seat-back televisions for all Economy passengers, a team of on-board beauty therapists for Upper Class and a new cabin called Premium Economy for cost-conscious business travellers. Branson himself was sometime seen massaging the backs of Upper Class passengers or pouring them drinks.

In 1999, Branson sold a 49% stake in the company to Singapore Airlines, valuing Virgin Atlantic at £1.225 billion.[8]

On Virgin Atlantic's 30th anniversary in 2014, Branson told *The Telegraph* he had always wanted to do things differently in the airline industry.

> I made sure that 95 per cent of our cabin crew hadn't flown with other airlines and would have a fresh approach. We took our skills from the entertainment industry and translated them to work in airlines.[9]

Virgin Atlantic swiftly built a reputation as a different kind of airline with an insatiable appetite for fun, glamour, innovation and customer service. Without the network or golden handcuff loyalty programmes of established airlines, Virgin Atlantic had to make its mark through product differentiation.

When Joe Ferry joined the airline in 1996 as a designer (becoming head of design in 2002), he recalled a vibrant start-up culture. Richard Branson and many of the original directors were still on the board. It was a place that cultivated a healthy disrespect for the status quo, a 'screw it, let's do it' mentality. 'I'd come up with ideas and Steve Ridgway, the CEO, would say, 'yes, let's do it.' It was like the parting of the waves for many innovations we had.'[10]

Ferry's final year project as a student at the Royal College of Art was to design an airline seat that could transform into a flat bed. It was an industry first. Every seat company said it was impossible, but Branson took Ferry's ideas to a friend who built Formula 1 cars and they made it happen within the constraints of an aircraft cabin.

However, during the four-year development phase, British Airways wheeled out something similar, the prototype for a business class bed. Virgin Atlantic's design team was devastated. 'Brand Virgin was all about being innovative, we'd invested millions and spent so much time and effort and then the person we were trying to beat had beaten us,' said Ferry.

But instead of resting on its laurels and making good with the existing investment, Virgin Atlantic's design team went back to the drawing board to develop an even better seat. It was a Moment of Belief. 'The bravery of Steve and Richard was remarkable – they said, 'No, it's not good enough,' and wouldn't take no for an answer,' said Ferry.

And this time around, Ferry's team invented a revolutionary concept. The configuration of the seat had a different surface to sit and sleep on. It was the first fully flat bed in business class that gave all passengers aisle access and didn't face backwards. This was unheard of. The Holy Grail. Virgin Atlantic filed the patent in August 2001.

The following month, 9/11 happened and the airline industry, indeed the world, changed overnight. People stopped flying and many airlines collapsed. At the time, 70–80% of Virgin Atlantic's flights were transatlantic.[11] The American airlines – United, US Airways, Northwest and Delta – all filed for Chapter 11 bankruptcy protection, and Swissair, Belgium's Sabena and Australia's Ansett all failed.[12] Airlines suffered combined net losses of more than $35 billion (£18.4 billion) from 2001 to 2004, according to the International Air Transport Association (IATA).[13]

Amidst this industry turbulence, Virgin Atlantic steadfastly invested in customer innovation. A series of Moments of Belief made it clear to stakeholders that Virgin Atlantic remained customer-led. This bravery was extreme. Virgin Atlantic had gone from flying full planes to having no customers for weeks on end. Nobody was entirely sure that anyone would ever fly again. Ferry recalled:

> We made loads of redundancies, and I was asking for $2 million for the new seat. Steve said, 'We've got to invest in innovation. Either the world will end, or we'll have a better product and seize market share.' At the time, I was expecting to lose my job. Even Singapore Airlines had stopped its design efforts, and no one was doing development.

> We were under a lot of pressure, but there was bravery and devotion
> to the brand. It was that dynamic that made Virgin shine ...[14]

Thankfully, passengers did begin flying again, and Virgin Atlantic took a more systematic approach to development, taking care to retain its entrepreneurial spirit. It was still David to British Airways' Goliath, railing against the newly built Terminal Five in Heathrow with a revolutionary clubhouse, limousine pick-up and drive-through check-in that could take passengers through security from car to lounge in three minutes. Ferry explained:

> We created a service design team, looking at our guest journey
> through their eyes and all the touch points we could affect like the
> security check and queues. How could we pick up a guest after a bad
> experience and turn it into a good experience again?[15]

Indeed, in 2003, Virgin Atlantic's Upper Class suite changed the face of business travel with a reclining leather seat for take-off, a place to eat a proper meal opposite your partner, a fully flat bed, on-board bar and private massage room.

While these innovations delighted customers, they also impacted the return on investment (ROI). If Virgin had been the kind of company to look only at the short term, the on-board bar and flat bed would never have been signed off. 'Our first fully flat bed meant we were losing two or three seats,' said Ferry. 'And we could have fitted three seats in there instead of an on-board bar, that's hundreds of thousands of pounds per seat per aircraft across the fleet. That's what a bar costs in terms of lost revenue ...'[16]

By May 2003, Virgin Atlantic was flying more than a million passengers annually from its bases at London's Gatwick and Heathrow airports to 22 destinations including LA, Barbados, Cape Town and Tokyo, and it was profitable too.[17]

During this period of Virgin Atlantic's growth, its management team – CEO, Steve Ridgway, COO, Lyell Strambi and CFO, Julie Southern – created the perfect climate for customer focus, says Ferry:

> We had a Coca-Cola budget with champagne aspirations. And some-
> times we were quite maverick. Leadership was fired with belief and
> optimism that we were doing the right thing.[18]

Outside the aircraft, Ferry and his team created a 2,000 square metre lounge for passengers. The Clubhouse opened in Heathrow in March 2006 and featured a spa, cocktail bar, Jacuzzis, hair salon, games room and a brasserie – all associated with modern luxury brands like private members club Soho House.

Meanwhile, quirky design innovations delighted Virgin Atlantic's guests in economy class, including a rubber duck in their bath kits alongside the toothbrush. The amenity kits cost hundreds of thousands of pounds a year, and were created to answer the design question, 'How could the on-board loos feel more like bathrooms?' Even today, passengers reminisce about the duck. Similarly, the salt and pepper pots had labels on the bottom saying, 'pinched from Virgin Atlantic,' and the Upper Class butter knives were engraved with the words 'stainless steal' because of passengers' propensity to take them home as envelope openers. There were 1930s champagne glasses, which were horrendously impractical to load and store on a flight. But these design choices were all about delighting customers, harking back to old-school glamour, fuelling big picture brand appeal, freed of the common constraints of proving narrow or short-term ROI.

Change was one day inevitable. 'Organisations have to grow up as they scale up,' says Ferry. 'How do you hold onto that spirit that got you there in the first place? It's a challenge.'[19]

Pressures from external markets started to change the focus of the team. The price of oil spiralled from around $30 a barrel in 1996 to $140 in 2010. The brand benefits of adding new products to the airline cabin were tougher to justify with higher oil prices. Fuel and weight in the airline industry are proportional. Anything on board that increases weight, like an on-board bar, also increases the fuel bill.

In this tougher business climate, Ferry's design team had to change its mindset. It was no longer about layering product into the airline cabin; instead, it was about what could be taken away without guests noticing. Innovation became about investigating materials that could strip 30% of the weight from an economy seat and therefore reduce fuel bills. And these design challenges that linked innovation so tightly to an economic spreadsheet were not necessarily the kinds of challenges that motivated the original team.

In December 2012, Delta Airlines bought Singapore Airlines' 49% stake in Virgin Atlantic for £224 million and in 2013 an executive from American Airlines, Craig Kreeger, became CEO. Jeremy Brown had joined Virgin Atlantic's design team in 2004 and stayed until 2018. He describes the nature of the shift:

> When Singapore had 49%, they were quiet, but Delta was much louder, and outside factors were having more and more effect on the airline's room for manoeuvre. As margins shrunk, we had to become more streamlined in the ways we worked.[20]

Alan Penlington was at the airline from 2005 to 2017, in roles including leading on customer experience, innovation and change. He described the benefits of the new approach – there was more structure, with clearer objectives to make a profit, a set strategy and shared plans. It was clear that product-driven innovation would no longer be a sustainable way for Virgin to compete and a shift was made to the softer qualities of the customer experience: people and service.

The experience was mapped out end-to-end and attention paid to having a Virgin way of doing things. This included investing in development for the on-board crew to help them tune in to customers' different emotional states, having more to say about the provenance of the food and drink provided and using digital technology in smart ways to help give colleagues data to tailor their approach, underpinned by a new Microsoft partnership.[21]

Luke Miles, who took over as head of design from Joe Ferry, played a leading role in this different kind of innovation, developing 'tools for conviviality, creating uniforms designed by Vivienne Westwood that celebrated Virgin's people and changing the design feel to become more muted and elegant, creating a canvas for the crew to shine.'[22]

Attention was also paid to aspects of what customers value, but in areas where Virgin Atlantic needed to catch up rather than continuing to add to strengths. The Delta deal led to a true joint venture, opening up their domestic flows of passengers from across the States. Before the JV, 90% of Virgin's transatlantic flyers were just shuttling between London and their US destinations. After the JV some flights had half their passengers coming from locations across the US. Virgin customers went from having a limited choice of purely Virgin Atlantic flights to having flexibility across hundreds of options. New York to London flights available to Virgin Atlantic customers went from three a day to fifteen, a huge difference if your meeting over-ran and you wanted to get back as swiftly as possible.[23]

The focus had moved from the burningness of beating big brother BA to a more conventional balanced scorecard considering customer satisfaction alongside on-time performance, colleague engagement and profitability. This was a more subtle shift than it first appeared.

As Alan recalled:

> Perhaps for the first time there was a genuine belief that Virgin could not only make customers happy but also be commercially successful. To make profit for future investment and to secure the long-term future of Virgin was inspirational to all, and Craig Kreeger had set out a plan to do this.[24]

Customer innovation was becoming less 'screw it, let's do it' and more data driven. But not everyone was happy with the evolving approach, as Alan described:

> HQ bought into it, but cabin crew never felt the same way. They tended to have a lot more long-serving people, many with 25–30 years of service. They wanted the airline to succeed but perhaps in the old way more than the new way.[25]

It's important not to characterise this as a loss of all the shared beliefs that had made Virgin Atlantic great. But the spirit was definitely changing, and it mattered that what was done for customers made sense financially as well. In a debate about reducing cabin crew numbers from 12, a view that considered the customer experience was that Virgin needed 10, not the industry norm of 9. Although BCG, brought in to review the business, pushed hard for the lower number, the executive team agreed to a trial to see what effect the changes would really have, and with some more traditional smart innovation in parallel – in Premium Economy an extra glass of bubbly with the meal, which was served on china plates for example – passenger ratings went up not down.[26]

Nonetheless, there was definitely less of a burning sense of leading the market. Alan talked of going from 'glitz and glamour for glamour's sake to grown-up, acting like a 30 year old.'[27]

Clearly, it's not black and white. The airline is still a distinctive business and it still innovates in a Virgin kind of a way. But is it exceptional like it was? Perhaps it never could be as a grown-up business in a difficult industry. Although other examples in this book show scale alone is not necessarily an impediment to customer-led success. As Ferry sees it:

> The challenge is that good isn't really good enough for a brand like Virgin; it has to be exceptional. When you're not constantly innovating, the competition catches up and satisfaction from guests reverts to the norm. If you don't do crazy, exciting things, you become a conventional airline.[28]

In March 2019, Virgin Atlantic reported its 2018 results, a Group loss before tax and exceptional items of £26.1 million, with a £49.0 million loss in 2017. It is clearly tough for a challenger brand like Virgin Atlantic to continue pioneering as it matures and deals with industry pressures outside its control.

Looking in from a distance, our judgement is that Virgin Atlantic went from an exceptional, customer-led success to something more mature, a little less pioneering, a little more holistic in its view of what matters to customers and how to provide it.

As the airline grew, it needed different people to run the business well, just as easyJet had beyond its early founder-led growth phase. These people brought different beliefs about what success looked like and how it could be achieved. The oil price made the environment MUCH harder to innovate in, and as the business evolved the leadership team's character changed too.

Virgin Atlantic's success was an amazing achievement, not just in the early days, but repeatedly as a stream of incredible Moments of Belief happened again and again. As Ferry sums up:

> Our accolade was that we invested in innovation in the darkest of dark times. That was down to the bravery of the senior leadership. We were genuinely living the brand. Lots of companies say they are. But are you

when the going gets tough? We did, and I'm very proud of my time with the airline.[29]

The challenge of external forces at Market Basket

The saga of Market Basket, a supermarket chain with 72 stores in North-Eastern USA, involves a bitter billionaire family feud between two cousins both named Arthur Demoulas – Arthur T. Demoulas and Arthur S. Demoulas (Arthur T and Arthur S from here on in). The battle over the spoils of the successful retailer has swept up employees, shareholders and politicians and demonstrated the colossal consequences of board members and executive management not sharing the same beliefs. It's a story that shows how tough it is for a successful business to hang onto its outside-in beliefs even when everyone within believes in them.

Today, Market Basket is led by Arthur T. He's a highly respected and popular leader with outside-in beliefs, who knows that investing in two elements of the business – his employees and his customers – will create long-term success for the retailer. In little over 10 years as leader, he grew revenues by 33% to reach $4 billion while employees grew from 14,000 to 25,000.[30]

Market Basket has a long reputation as a low-cost food grocery retailer that provides great service and cares about its people. The wages are good, generous benefits are provided including healthcare, and all employees participate in a profit-sharing plan. On average cashiers at Market Basket make $40,000 – well above the national average of $21,370.[31]

Motivated, happy employees create a community feel in the stores that is appreciated by Market Basket's loyal customers.[32] They love the combination of great value, excellent product selection and top-notch customer service. There are no self-checkouts, but extra staff employed to pack the shopping and unload your groceries into the car if you're struggling. Many customers rely on the low prices of speciality items like gluten-free breaded chicken pieces to feed their families. In 2018, consumer reports rated Market Basket in the top five US grocery stores and supermarkets on customer satisfaction. It's a virtuous circle – high employee morale creates a positive customer experience, boosting customer satisfaction and loyalty, subsequently boosting profitability, which is reinvested and which helps to boost morale.

The *Boston Globe* estimated that Market Basket's employee benefits include an average of four bonuses a year, totalling six to eight weeks pay, a $1,000 scholarship for all workers enrolled in college and an extra 15% of annual pay invested in a retirement account. Store managers and truck drivers could retire with a nest egg of $1 million or more.[33] Arthur T has a reputation as a father figure. He remembers names, birthdays and milestones, attending many of his team's weddings and funerals.

Market Basket is unconventional, with no place for loyalty cards, online shopping, or self-checkout aisles. They prefer to stick to a formula learned from Arthur T's late father, Mike, known as *Telemachus*, whose name he invokes repeatedly while explaining his outside-in beliefs.

> We keep it as simple as possible for people. We keep costs low and quality high. We keep the stores clean and offer service with a smile. And if at the end of the day you have some success, then you share that with the associates.[34]

Market Basket has been hugely successful generating some $4.8 billion in sales. But hidden problems, rooted in the complex ownership of the business, can be traced back through its history. Arthur T is a minority shareholder, alongside other family members who do not hold the same outside-in beliefs. And although these shareholders were rewarded handsomely with dividends, they wanted more.

Market Basket was launched in Massachusetts in 1917, by a Greek immigrant, Athanasios (Arthur) Demoulas. The first small food store opened in 'The Acre' (affectionately known as 'Acre-Acropolis') and catered to the Greek, French and Irish immigrant community in downtown Lowell, Massachusetts. It sold lamb, pork, sausages and fresh vegetables from a farm and slaughterhouse he owned in nearby Dracut.

He sold it for $15,000 to his two sons, Telemachus (Mike) and George, who turned it into a modern chain of 14 stores. In 1971, George passed away, and Mike became the sole head of the DeMoulas supermarkets. He began opening stores under different names, which eventually became the Market Basket chain, and which were controlled entirely by Mike and his family.

After George died, a feud began between the two sides of the family, which came to a head in the mid-1990s. Significant litigation led to a complete redistribution of ownership. George's family was awarded a majority stake (50.5%) and Arthur T, son of Michael, ended up with a minority stake of the holding. Fortunately, he had the support of Rafaela Evans, a family member from the other side and, therefore, the controlling stake. She liked what he was doing, liked the results and said, 'keep going.'

Arthur S's side of the family was unhappy despite receiving generous returns on their stocks. They were receiving large dividends, but they wanted to be paid higher sums more frequently. They wanted Arthur T to spend less money on customer and colleague-friendly initiatives and more on dividends instead. As external forces, they were challenging the outside-in way of doing things at Market Basket. Their fury intensified following two decisions by Arthur T.

First, in 2008, following the financial crash, the company's $500 million pension fund plummeted after investing $46 million in Fanny Mae and Freddie Mac bonds just before the crash. Arthur T atoned for the investment mistake by replacing the loss using company funds.

In early 2014, Arthur T slashed prices across the board by 4%, costing Market Basket an estimated $170 million, around 70% of operating profit. As he told a local newspaper, 'The customer needs the savings more than the company needs the extra profits.'[35] Probably true. But the other family shareholders didn't see it that way.

Arthur T's outside-in beliefs and subsequent decisions were largely protected because of his allegiance with Rafaela, the crucial swing vote in the feuding family. But when her vote switched, everything changed. In June 2013, she decided to support Arthur S, giving him decisive weight in the power struggle. (She has never publicly explained her change of heart.)

On June 23, 2014, three top-level executives – CEO Arthur T, vice president Joseph Rockwell, and operations director William Marsden were fired by Market Basket's board. Market Basket's shareholders were frustrated that Arthur T's outside-in beliefs made him so single-minded about creating such extraordinary benefits for employees and cheap prices for customers. He could charge higher prices for products and still offer good value; he could offer less generous benefits for staff but still provide the best benefits in town. But Arthur T didn't see it this way.

The board members, however, underestimated the support for Arthur T. The following day six high-level managers resigned, and 300 employees held a rally outside Market Basket's Chelsea, Massachusetts flagship store.

A group of anonymous employees created the Save the Market Basket Facebook page. Soon, the movement had its own website, 'We are Market Basket.' Employees flooded it with posts explaining their reasons for supporting their billionaire leader Arthur T.

Both the website and the Facebook page helped the upset groups come together, organising a series of protest rallies with over 5,000 employees and customers singing a protest song:

> Who are we? Market Basket
> Who's our man? Arthur T
> Who do we support? ATD

Eight employees were fired for their roles in organising the protests. Other employees plastered the inside of Market Basket's windows with posters of their CEO saying, 'Reinstate Arthur T.'

Some important suppliers refused to supply, truck drivers refused to deliver, customers stayed away. Politicians got involved. Governors had to intervene because the dispute meant some of their towns had run out of milk. Faithful customers found shelves empty and resorted to higher-priced rivals. In anger, they taped their new, costly grocery receipts to the windows of empty Market Basket stores.

While the specifics of Arthur T's firing relate to a long-running family conflict, to the protesting Market Basket workers and customers it came down to one thing: 'The people aren't as important to the board as the cash is.'[36]

In the end, the employees created a crisis, the customers created a crisis and the family's only way out was to sell their ownership stake to Arthur T.

In the midst of the protests, Arthur T offered to buy the entire company from his cousins, an offer that the board (controlled by Arthur S's family) said it would consider. On August 27, 2014, the shareholders of Market Basket reached a deal to sell the remaining 50.5% shares for $1.5 billion to Arthur T who was supported by a private equity company.

The settlement came at a huge cost. The seven-week-long employee protests emptied the 71 stores of fresh produce, amounting to a collective $583 million in lost sales. Vendors cut ties with the chain, the brand took a huge hit and all the messiness drove many thousands of customers into the aisles of Hannaford, Shaw's, Walmart and Whole Foods.

However, Market Basket's employees rallied to get the retailer back on its feet again. They worked day and night to replenish empty shelves to accomplish a remarkable turnaround. Within a week some 2.3 million cases of beef, poultry and seafood were shipped. An additional 1.65 million cases of non-perishables were processed. On one Friday alone, 88 tractor-trailers full of produce arrived at stores across New England.[37]

'Sales are already at 100 percent of where they were last year,' Arthur T said. 'Everyone just got to it and worked as hard as they could.'[38]

In the wake of his agreement to buy Market Basket, many outsiders have questioned whether the company will be able to maintain the employee profit sharing plan that costs tens of millions of dollars a year. It was one of the sources of contention during the family dispute and hard for some shareholders to stomach. Valuing investment in employees over the long term and securing great service for customers ahead of higher short-term shareholder returns is a clear example of outside-in belief.

Arthur T described his commitment to the plan as 'unwavering.' He recounted a recent retirement party at which all four departing employees left the company with large nest eggs. Two store directors had more than $1 million, a produce supervisor had $800,000, and a truck driver was leaving with more than $700,000. 'We don't anticipate that any of that will change,' he said. 'We're committed to the profit-sharing plan that's been in place now since 1963.'

After the buyout, Arthur T admitted to *The Boston Globe* that the summer-long crisis had created both good and bad attention for the retailer. While it exposed his family's feud, it also illuminated Market Basket's value to employees and customers. He said:

> I think so many people could relate to it because it affects everyone. If everyone in the workplace is equal and treated with dignity, they work with a little extra passion, a little extra dedication. I think that's a wonderful business message to the world.[39]

It's difficult to know how well Market Basket is faring since Arthur T's family took control of the retailer. In 2017, the century-old supermarket chain launched its first ever website. It didn't sell anything, but it told the history of the remarkable business.

And despite Arthur T's determination to fervently protect the outside-in beliefs of Market Basket, the strength of feeling from the board members wanting the retailer to act in a more conventional way was a serious challenge. Even as the chief executive and shareholder, even with the support of his staff, customers and suppliers, external forces ousted Arthur T from his own family business. Now, back at the helm, he will inevitably face more battles ahead.

The challenge of a competing rule changer at Nokia

It's easy to forget that before Steve Jobs walked onto a stage, pulled an Apple iPhone out of his pocket and changed the world in 2007, Nokia was the disruptor. The Finnish mobile phone company became market leader in a rapidly changing industry by delivering and relentlessly improving relevant customer benefits in line with its brand promise, 'connecting people.'

For nearly 20 years, Nokia was consistently customer-led, continually innovating to connect people through mobile telephony. In the 1990s it was a bold, innovative company in broader business terms – more than most people realise. It bravely focused on mobile communications and was an early adopter and driver of 2G technology.

Like many other outside-in companies in this book, Nokia looked beyond the existing boundaries of its industry, spotting opportunities and growth by redefining the market. For example, it was the first mobile company to target a global audience without handsets, looking to reach the 4 billion people still unconnected. And as it grew, Nokia remained in touch with its customers by restructuring the organisation and introducing sophisticated global customer segmentation.

Nokia understood the power of building a strong brand trusted by mobile operators and customers alike. It was the first supplier to sell phones that worked on every major cellular standard. It saw the potential of the mobile handset beyond calls, selling the first examples to have an integrated FM radio, a calendar and with games like Snake (that still has a cult following).

Nokia's iconic designs remained constant. The look and feel of Nokia products were the same everywhere – classic brick phones known by their numbers like the 3310 and 5110, with a swappable coloured fascia. It was among the first to understand that handsets were as much lifestyle as technology products and that consumers highly valued ease of use and beautiful design.

Nokia became a recognised world leader in supply chain management. When booming global sales growth stalled in late 1995, it experienced a rapid inventory build-up. Recognising that the mobile phone industry was as much about logistics as technology, Nokia swiftly reorganised its supply chain and averted a crisis.

In 1999, Nokia supplied more than one out of every four phones in the market.[40] By the end of 2007, half of all smartphones sold in the world were made by Nokia, while Apple's iPhone had a mere 5% share.[41]

Yet, by the first half of 2013, Nokia's market share had plummeted from more than 25% to less than 3% in a sobering reminder that even the strongest companies can fall. Nokia's market capitalisation, which had been close to $250 billion at its peak in 2000, tumbled to around $50 billion in 2010. In the same year, Nokia replaced its CEO. Later, it abandoned software development, and became just a hardware provider, surrendering its position as a leading smartphone competitor. It ultimately exited the industry, selling its mobile business to Microsoft in 2013. So, what went wrong?

Everything changed with the launch of the Apple iPhone. Nokia may have been market leader at this point, but Apple's innovation rewrote the rules of the mobile industry. Apple approached the sector from the outside-in, anticipating that the communications industry would no longer be centred on making phone calls but about facilitating someone's digital life and connecting them with music, photos, retail, each other and more. Apple understood the potential of a rectangle with a screen and data connectivity, enabled by easy-to-use, ubiquitous software, powerful fast processing and data stored in the cloud. With its full touchscreen and app-based operating system, the iPhone changed the definition of what a smartphone could be.

On paper, Nokia should have sailed the choppy waters of competition with ease. It had bountiful economic and intellectual resources and had dominated the mobile industry for years. However, three years after the introduction of Apple's iPhone, Nokia had failed to launch a next-generation smartphone in response. A tech journalist recalls talking to Nokia executives in 2012 and believes that at the root of the company's failure to react robustly was an inability to take risks that grew in proportion to its success. This was compounded by denial in the face of clear and significant warning signs.

> There wasn't a sense of urgency a former Nokia executive told me. When dealing with a machine that pumped out millions of phones, a single mistake or bad call could cost the company billions of dollars. As a result, management was structured around many layers of approval bodies and meetings. The whole structure was built to prevent mistakes.[42]

The lack of urgency is understandable; Nokia's share of both the smartphone and total cellphone markets was in decline, but the drop-off wasn't dramatic. In countless interviews with Nokia executives, they were quick to point to their market leadership as proof they were still in a strong position.[43]

Within the company, Nokia executives were faced with an inconvenient truth – their industry was no longer about churning out devices but something much more. Customers and how they thought about the category had evolved in a different direction to Nokia's executives who were obsessed with managing the machine without screwing up. They'd stopped thinking about their industry from the customer's point of view.

> Our view of our competitors' products' usage was completely distorted ... People didn't know how good Android was, or the iPhone ... It wasn't known throughout the company how good the competitors' products are becoming. The group of people who really knew the pain was way too small.[44]

Another senior strategy consultancy explained that Nokia's middle managers lacked external fear about competition from other firms and were confident that feature phones would prevail over touchscreen phones. Apparently blindsided, they weren't thinking about what the interface was there to do. The iPhone was opening up a whole new world, reshaping the industry while Nokia executives were fighting yesterday's battle.

> Nokians [thought that they] were the best in class. And they didn't even want to hear how you could think about things differently. They just went into their cocoon and patted themselves on the back.[45]

Indeed, many managers within Nokia believed the company was invincible given its market leadership and R&D strength. Between 1992 and 2006, it had made 51,836 patent applications,[46] was estimated to generate more than $600 million in revenue-related patents each year and had invested more than $50 billion in R&D over two decades.[47] Backed by these assets, its growth trajectory seemed secure. In 2005, Nokia sold its billionth phone. Mobile phone subscriptions surpassed 2 billion.[48] And it was from this context of sustained success and leadership for Nokia that the iPhone entered stage left on a platform where the value provided to customers was changing and so were their expectations. According to one upper middle manager:

> The classic smartphones with old-fashioned keyboards sold in such goddam huge numbers that some people questioned why we even should make touchscreen phones – 'We're doing fine as it is.'[49]

This confidence came from the top. For example, after Apple had introduced the iPhone, the CEO said publicly, 'I don't think that what we have seen so far [from Apple] is something that would in any way necessitate us changing our thinking.'[50]

Nokia's decline was reflected in the mobile company's unswerving loyalty to outdated technology. Symbian, the firm's mobile operating system, was simply not up to the job compared to newer operating systems like iOS and later Android. While Samsung chose to adopt Google's Android software for its own devices following this mobile software revolution, Nokia, hoping to ensure sustainable profit, decided to continue improving its own proprietary platform which was Symbian. Yes, it was trying to innovate but without sight of the inevitable future.

So much money, time and resources had been invested in Symbian that even doubters within Nokia were reluctant to suggest the operating system wasn't good enough.

> Our organization had to have faith in it – you must believe in the gun you're holding, because there's nothing else. It takes years to make a new OS. That's why we had to keep the faith with Symbian.[51]

Consumers' responses to Nokia's phones became increasingly negative. A stream of new Nokia smartphones from 2007–2010 failed to impress. In 2007, the N95 had full music features, GPS, internet but no touchscreen.

In 2008, the 5800, its first touch screen smartphone, was a commercial success, but it was about 18 months too late to market because of software glitches. In 2009, the N97 was a failure in terms of user experience. Finally, again a year too late, Nokia launched another 'iPhone killer' – the N8 – to muted reviews. 'Usability is where the Nokia N8 … falls short the most … if you are coming from webOS, iOS, or Android, things are likely to feel kludgy to you.'[52]

Nokia's problems were intensified by its organisational structure. Layers of management were blocking links between the customer and R&D.

> The sales organization had been changed such that the link to the customer was rather unclear … There was a layer between the customer and the units developing the software … This blocked transparency and also motivation.[53]

Similarly, middle managers who were the most likely to challenge existing technology were not encouraged to question managers above them in the hierarchy. There was a climate of fear within the organisation that prevented middle managers from sharing negative opinions with their superiors and peers stifling a sustainable long-term innovation strategy.

> Nokia's TMs [top managers] believed that MMs' [middle managers] narrow internal focus would ensure effective implementation, and therefore they discouraged MMs' external focus … When MMs asked critical questions, the TMs urged them to keep their attention focused on implementing their tasks … the answer typically was that 'this is the direction we have chosen. Don't challenge me but focus on implementation.'[54]

After the crisis and the fall of Nokia, one of these middle managers reflected on how the mobile company's drift into inside-out beliefs had changed his behaviour. He said:

> I should've been much, much more courageous. And I should've made a lot more noise, should've criticized people more directly … I could've made more of an impact. And it would've been breaking the consensus atmosphere … Nobody wanted to rock the boat … I should have been braver about rattling people's cages.[55]

Unfortunately, failure seems inevitable, eventually, for customer-led companies that achieve greatness. While Nokia's early success was a result of being customer-led, the Finnish mobile company found itself gradually losing the boldness and openness characteristic of outside-in beliefs.

Nokia succumbed to a slow, relentless drift from outside-in to inside-out beliefs that became suddenly visible when a competitor changed the rules, disrupting the industry to create value for customers. The problem wasn't created when Apple launched; it started, slowly, several years before, when protecting the 'machine' became more important to Nokia than questioning the way they created customer value.

Nokia was left defending its old model in a new world where it no longer had relevance or understanding of what its customers really wanted. Apple saw what Nokia could no longer see. That the boundaries of the industry were fundamentally shifting. And to return to the analogy of ready meals and Deliveroo – this was not about creating better microwave meals but about understanding consumer value – nice food fast.

Conclusion and recap

Through the rise and fall of four extraordinary companies – O2, Virgin Atlantic, Market Basket and Nokia – we have found examples that underpin our own belief that failure is inevitable for outside-in companies. When a company has transformed itself as a customer-led pioneer, establishing deeply held and widely shared outside-in beliefs, and reaped the rewards, the threat and the pull of inside-out beliefs continues. The effort to hold onto outside-in beliefs must be mindful, proactive and constant.

Unfortunately, when facing pressure from internal forces, external forces or a challenger brand who changes the rules when the missionary zeal has dissipated, it is almost impossible for an outside-in company not to succumb to the inevitable fall back from outside-in to inside-out.

Our final main chapter provides insight, advice and practical guidance for companies that have managed to become outside-in customer-led successes against the odds. We find hope by examining the success stories of those who have managed to succeed, holding onto their outside-in beliefs for multiple generations of management and resisting pressure to operate in normal, conventional ways.

Notes

1   Deutsche Bank. 1 July 2002. *Awaiting Evidence: Re-Initiation of the Mobile Telco Coverage.* London: Deutsche Bank AG European Equity Research, p. 85.

2   Pfeffer, Jeffrey & Christina T. Fong. 2004. 'The business school "business": Some lessons from the US experience.' *Journal of Management Studies*, 41 (8): 1501–1520.

3   O2 senior team member, interview with authors, 9 June 2020.

4   Deb Corless, interview with authors, 9 July 2020.

5   Deb Corless, interview with authors, 9 July 2020.

6   Deb Corless, interview with authors, 9 July 2020.

7   Deb Corless, interview with authors, 9 July 2020.

8   Virgin Atlantic. n.d. 'Our story.' Retrieved from https://corporate.virgina tlantic.com/gb/en/our-story.html

9   Branson, Sir Richard. 21 June 2014. 'Virgin Atlantic: 30 years of fun, flying and competition.' *The Telegraph*. Retrieved from www.telegraph.co.uk/finance/comment/10917094/Virgin-Atlantic-30-years-of-of-fun-flying-and -competition.html

10 Joe Ferry, interview with authors, 12 December 2018.

11 MyCustomer Newsdesk. 15 August 2006. 'Interview: Lyell Strambi, Chief Operating Officer at Virgin Atlantic.' *MyCustomer*. Retrieved from www.m ycustomer.com/marketing/strategy/interview-lyell-strambi-chief-operati ng-officer-at-virgin-atlantic

12 Seawright, Stephen. 10 August 2006. 'Airline industry turbulent since 9/11.' *The Telegraph*. Retrieved from www.telegraph.co.uk/finance/2945214 /Airline-industry-turbulent-since-911.html

13 Seawright, Stephen. 10 August 2006. 'Airline industry turbulent since 9/11.'

14 Joe Ferry, interview with authors, 12 December 2018.

15 Joe Ferry, interview with authors, 12 December 2018.

16 Joe Ferry, interview with authors, 12 December 2018.

17 Civil Aviation Authority and Companies House records for 2003.

18 Joe Ferry, interview with authors, 12 December 2018.

19 Joe Ferry, interview with authors, 12 December 2018.

20 Jeremy Brown, interview with authors, 5 August 2020.

21 Alan Penlington, interview with authors, 28 July 2020.

22 Luke Miles, interview with authors, 4 August 2020.

23 Alan Penlington, interview with authors, 28 July 2020.

24 Alan Penlington, interview with authors, 28 July 2020.

25 Alan Penlington, interview with authors, 28 July 2020.

26 Alan Penlington, interview with authors, 28 July 2020.

27 Alan Penlington, interview with authors, 28 July 2020.

28 Joe Ferry, interview with authors, 12 December 2018.

29 Joe Ferry, interview with authors, 12 December 2018.

30 Grant Welker. 27 July 2014. 'How one woman set off the latest chapter in the Market Basket tale.' Retrieved from www.sentinelandenterprise.com/2014/07/27/how-one-woman-set-off-the-latest-chapter-in-the-market-basket-tale/#ixzz3BShqnYHn

31 Kasperkevic, Jana. 14 August 2014. 'How supermarket chain Market Basket imploded from bad investments.' *The Guardian*. Retrieved from www.theguardian.com/money/2014/aug/14/market-basket-arthur-millions-investing-protests

32 Totally in line with Heskett, J. L., W. E. Sasser, & L. A. Schlesinger. 1997. *The Service Profit Chain: How Leading Companies Link Profit and Growth to Loyalty, Satisfaction, and Value.* New York: The Free Press.

33 Slade, Hollie. 29 September 2014. 'Inside the billionaire family feud that nearly killed Market Basket.' *Forbes*. Retrieved from www.forbes.com/sites/hollieslade/2014/09/10/inside-the-billionaire-family-feud-that-nearly-killed-market-basket/#1370de3642d4

34 Ross, Casey. 12 September 2014. 'Arthur T. Demoulas happy "just being a grocer."' *The Boston Globe*. Retrieved from http://c.oobg.com/business/2014/09/11/after-epic-market-basket-battle-arthur-demoulas-happy-just-being-grocer/Iqd3AyAX6qh36fhldPOyPN/story.html?p1=Article_Related_Box_Article

35 Lannan, Katie. 14 January 2014. 'The customer needs the savings more.' *The Sun*. Retrieved from www.lowellsun.com/business/ci_24907195/customer-needs-savings-more

36 Gittleson, Kim. 1 August 2014. 'Market Basket: Workers risk it all for their boss.' *BBC News*. Retrieved from www.bbc.com/news/business-28580359

37 Ross, Casey. 12 September 2014. 'Arthur T. Demoulas happy "just being a grocer."'

38 Ross, Casey. 12 September 2014. 'Arthur T. Demoulas happy "just being a grocer."'

39 Ross, Casey. 12 September 2014. 'Arthur T. Demoulas happy "just being a grocer."'

40 Lee, David. 3 September 2013. 'Nokia: The rise and fall of a mobile giant.' *BBC News*. Retrieved from www.bbc.co.uk/news/technology-23947212
    Cheng, Roger. 25 April 2014. 'Farewell Nokia: The rise and fall of a mobile pioneer.' *CNET*. Retrieved from www.cnet.com/news/farewell-nokia-the-rise-and-fall-of-a-mobile-pioneer/

41 According to figures from analyst firm Gartner, Nokia's smartphone market share at this time was a dominant 49.4%.

42 Cheng, Roger. 25 April 2014. 'Farewell Nokia: The rise and fall of a mobile pioneer.' *CNET*. Retrieved from www.cnet.com/news/farewell-nokia-the-rise-and-fall-of-a-mobile-pioneer/

43 Cheng, Roger. 25 April 2014. 'Farewell Nokia.'

44 Vuori, Timo O. & Ouy N. Huy. 2015. 'Distributed Attention and Shared Emotions in the Innovation Process: How Nokia Lost the Smartphone Battle.' *Administrative Science Quarterly*. https://doi.org/10.1177/0001839215606951

45 Vuori, Timo O. & Ouy N. Huy. 2015. 'Distributed Attention and Shared Emotions.'

46 Huy, Quy, Timo Vuori, & Lisa Duke. 26 September 2016. 'Nokia: The inside story of the rise and fall of a tech giant.' *INSEAD Publishing*: 7.

47 Talbot, D. 20 June 2012. 'Nokia's mobile patents are its last line of defense.' *MIT Technology Review*. Retrieved from www.technologyreview.com/2012/06/20/185309/nokias-mobile-patents-are-its-last-line-of-defense/

48 Huy, Quy, Timo Vuori, & Lisa Duke. 26 September 2016. 'Nokia: The inside story.'

49 Huy, Quy, Timo Vuori, & Lisa Duke. 26 September 2016. 'Nokia: The inside story.'

50 Constantinescu, Stefan. 3 February 2017. 'Nokia CEO Olli-Pekka Kallasvuo talks about the iPhone.' *intomobile*. Retrieved from www.intomobile.com/2007/02/03/nokia-ceo-olli-pekka-kallasvuo-talks-about-the-iphone/

51 Vuori, Timo O. & Ouy N. Huy. 2015. 'Distributed Attention and Shared Emotions.'

52 Huy, Quy, Timo Vuori, & Lisa Duke. 26 September 2016. 'Nokia: The inside story.'

53 Vuori, Timo O. & Ouy N. Huy. 2015. 'Distributed Attention and Shared Emotions.'

54 Vuori, Timo O. & Ouy N. Huy. 2015. 'Distributed Attention and Shared Emotions.'

55 Vuori, Timo O. & Ouy N. Huy. 2015. 'Distributed Attention and Shared Emotions.'

6

PROTECTING CUSTOMER-LED BELIEFS

One person with a belief is equal to ninety-nine who have only interests.

John Stuart Mill

Handelsbanken: Sustaining outside-in beliefs

Handelsbanken is an extraordinary organisation. It is probably the most successful bank you've never heard of. Founded in 1871, Handelsbanken is one of Sweden's leading banks with over 750 branches in six home markets (Sweden, Denmark, Norway, Finland, the Netherlands and the UK), a presence in the world's most significant economies and nearly 12,000 employees. It has over 200 branches in Britain following its launch in 1982 and a close to £22 billion loan book.[1] For the seven years since 31 December 2012, Handelsbanken generated positive shareholder value of SEK 128 billion (£11.3 billion). Market capitalisation has grown by SEK 53 billion (£4.71 billion), while Handelsbanken has paid out SEK 75 billion (£6.6 billion) in dividends to shareholders.[2]

In 2019, the Swedish bank made post-tax profits of SEK 16,925 million (£1.493 billion) with a return on equity of 11.9% This means that Handelsbanken achieved its corporate goal of a higher return on equity than the average of its competitors for the 48th year running, ever since it was set.[3]

But here's the thing. Handelsbanken is not like other banks. It is low profile and distinctly idiosyncratic. It doesn't do any advertising beyond local promotion. There are no bonuses, no budgets, no sales targets, no call centres. There is not a centralised credit approval process where the computer, or a committee, has the sole authority to say yes or no. Every decision needs local support. Each bank manager of each of Handelsbanken's individual branches takes decisions about local customers – no algorithm, but human judgement instead.

The firm's mantra is that 'the branch is the bank.' Operating with something called the 'church spire principle,' each branch is autonomous and operates in an exclusive geographical area in which all its customers fall – whether an individual, a small business or the headquarters of a multinational, which would then be run from the branch, not from head office. The manager hires staff, decides whether to sign up a new customer, what to charge them, whether to lend to them and the interest rate they would attach.

It sounds like madness when you are conditioned by the way most big banks work. But Handelsbanken has more satisfied customers than the sector average in all its six home markets according to research by the Stockholm School of Economics and the independent research firm SKI/EPSI.[4] Much of its new business comes from referrals – word of mouth from satisfied customers. When was the last time that you were so delighted by your bank that you actually recommended it to a friend? As the Group's recently retired former CEO Anders Bouvin explained.

> Our way of working is based on the concept that there is an absolute connection between customer satisfaction and commercial success. We believe that if we have satisfied customers then product sales will follow. Other banks are sales oriented and believe that in order to sell products you have to set targets. What your brand represents depends on what you do, your actions. You can make up a story but if you don't live by it, it's not going to take off.[5]

Over the last few decades, we have seen some spectacular failures of financial institutions. In the autumn of 1990, a serious crisis emerged in Swedish banking as a result of a deep recession and huge corporate loan losses. During this crisis, Handelsbanken was the only major Swedish bank that was not forced to approach its shareholders or the government for support. Indeed, while other banks had to be nationalised, Handelsbanken came out of the crisis with a net income 50% higher than its pre-crisis record year.[6] It had stuck to its beliefs and its approach, and as a result it continues to produce one of the highest returns on equity in the world.

It suggests, as we've been arguing throughout The Customer Copernicus, that the outside-in beliefs that are clearly good for customers are also good for business. Handelsbanken branch staff serve customers well, think about what helps and cut out what doesn't to increase efficiency, lend prudently when they understand the risks, and the business thrives.

This might have something to do with 'obliquity' – the idea that goals are often best achieved when pursued indirectly or obliquely.[7] According to John Kay, shareholder value or profits are outcomes that indicate success but are unhelpful if pursued directly. Instead, Kay argues, 'the defining purpose of business is to build good businesses.' Kay's idea is that if one builds a good bank, then profits will follow, something demonstrated by Handelsbanken's long run of success.

A good customer-led business is one that has shared and deeply held outside-in beliefs. But we also know that the gravitational pull of inside-out beliefs is relentless. It is often characterised by an attempt to pursue the outcome of higher profits, sales or share price directly. To resist, to keep being 'a good business,' takes bravery.

One crucial element of the Handelsbanken model is the very flat hierarchy – just three layers consisting of the branches, the regions and the headquarters. Showing they are not afraid to make difficult decisions if components of this outside-in model are challenged, the previous chief executive Frank Vang-Jensen parted ways with the bank after a mere 18 months in the job, reputedly for trying to introduce a fourth layer of decision-making. The Financial Times reported insiders as saying Vang-Jensen was seeking to centralise power. Explaining what elsewhere would certainly be seen as an unusual reason for ousting a chief executive, chairman

Pär Boman underlined the important role of leadership in supporting the decentralised model:

> When you take important decisions strategically, you must do it in a way that gives your decentralised managers the tools to implement them and not just tell them what to do.[8]

Bouvin explains:

> What happened might in other organisations have raised one eyebrow. But that is the sense of ownership here – everyone feels it very strongly. It was enough for the board for them to say, 'we don't want to risk spreading the seeds of doubt about who we are and what we stand for.'[9]

It wasn't an administrative disagreement; it was a threat to the firm's belief system.

The difficulty in sustaining outside-in beliefs

Handelsbanken's parting of ways with its chief executive is a stark illustration of the lengths to which a serious outside-in business will go to protect its beliefs.

We have seen how even great customer-led successes have eventually failed. But a few, including this extraordinary Swedish bank, have remained outside-in for a long time, across successive generations of managers. This chapter is about the ingredients behind their success. There are very particular conditions that are needed for a business to turn from a natural inside-out belief system to the far more unusual outside-in. And having got there, we have seen how inside-out gravity, in its relentless way, brings even an exceptional organisation crashing back to earth. However much history there is, however tough the journey, however convincing the story and however deeply rooted the conviction in the formative years, could it be that an unnatural outside-in belief system is impossible to successfully pass on?

While we can't find examples of everlasting organisations of any kind, we can find a few that have maintained outside-in beliefs well beyond a single generation of managers. Handelsbanken is one. And later in this chapter, we'll be analysing the success of four other companies with unusual outside-in sets of beliefs – The John Lewis Partnership, W.L. Gore, LEGO and Hilti. How have they done it?

Handelsbanken's story from the beginning: How does it work?

Handelsbanken began its life in 1871, and to all intents and purposes, it was a conventional bank until we join its story. Following a succession of crises around lending, an acquisition and foreign exchange transactions that contravened regulations, the managing director and several other senior managers were forced to leave the bank in 1969. It was a major crisis that also impacted profits and results. Something had to change to save the bank.

A remarkable academic economist called Jan Wallander joined Handelsbanken in 1970, ambitious to work on the turnaround. He had already made a success of a small lending bank in northern Sweden based on unusually devolved principles, and he was persuaded to become Handelsbanken's CEO by being given the freedom to make it work in the same way.

This burningness from the pain of Handelsbanken's crisis combined with Wallander's ambition to apply his principles to a larger organisation created the perfect environment for change when only bold, decisive action would make enough of a difference to succeed.

Wallander brought his radically decentralised way of running a banking business with him based on a belief that this resulted in a customer-led organisation set up to succeed over the long term. To replicate the model he knew, a 70-branch bank, he divided Handelsbanken into eight units of 70 branches and over the course of a difficult few years pushed hard to devolve most of the head office's decision-making down to the branch level. As Wallander explains:

> It is reasonable to presume – even though it may initially seem extremely improbable to us directors – that the local staff can help to solve the problems we are faced with. It is actually conceivable that people in small towns all over the Scandinavian countryside can produce better solutions than those we at the head office at Stockholm have managed to find.[10]

What this decentralised approach means for customers is that they can go into their local Handelsbanken branch, hand in a loan application for $5,000 and the man or woman behind the counter will normally be able to say yes or no according to their own judgement. Before Wallander's changes, a credit decision took on average two months of deliberation ahead of the customer getting a yes or a no. In 1968, over 2,400 loan applications had to be decided by the management board or board of directors.[11]

At a more conventional bank, getting a loan can sometimes be straightforward if the customer is lucky enough to fit a 'normal' profile. However, for anything mildly out of the ordinary, or anything beyond the bank's tight credit policy, it's a completely different experience. During the meeting, it will dawn on the customer that this is going to take longer than they thought, and probably require far more documentation. Once this is all in place, the branch-based advisor will fill in the details, but the decision will then be referred to a specialist team, often based centrally either onshore or offshore. If they're lucky, the specialists might be available on the phone there and then. If not, it might take a day or two to review the application and documentation, before a final decision is given to the anxious customer.

Hopefully, the decision is a yes. Often, it will be a 'computer says no,' disappointing the customer while providing no real insight into why the application has been declined. Cue disappointment, frustration and anger for both the customer and the branch-based advisor having to break the news to them.

The bureaucratic nature of the banking industry, despite the widely accepted need for checks, balances and controls, is much maligned by frustrated customers around the world and is the subject of more than one insightful reflection by frustrated executives.[12]

Jan Wallander was one such executive, and he described it taking around five years for the bank to reach the goal of decentralisation. 'Decentralising is like pulling a rubber band. You have to hold the ends firmly, otherwise it will snap back in your face and you'll have to start all over again,' he said.[13] He was describing the journey from inside-out beliefs to outside-in, and the need for patience as people's beliefs only change as they see the new and unconventional approach working for real.

He described this journey in detail. When Wallander joined the bank in 1970 there was much to do. In his own words, it was first necessary to 'stop the train.' Head office departments were banned from sending out any more memos to the branch offices. All activities connected with setting up or following up budgets were closed down. In head office, 110 committees and working groups were told to stop their work at once with secretaries asked to submit a one-page report outlining their results so far. Work was stopped on a new data system. The long-term planning and strategy department was told to down tools. The marketing department's work was stopped. At the time, Handelsbanken was one of Sweden's largest advertisers. The number of employees in that department fell from forty people to one.

Finally, all 100th anniversary celebrations were cancelled. As Wallander recalled:

> Like nothing else the calling off of the anniversary celebrations created a crisis mentality that was a great advantage when we set to work to drastically change the organisation and its direction. That is how the work of the head office was brought to a close. The mighty train came to a halt with screaming brakes ...[14]

Wallander stripped everything down to basics. There is no picture of the organisation's roles and responsibilities beyond the internal telephone directory. There is just one very simple goal – to try all the time to have a greater profitability, measured by return on equity, than competitors, achieved by having more satisfied customers and lower costs.

In the new organisation, there were just three levels of decision-making – the branch offices, the regional banks and the central board. The overwhelming majority of credit decisions were made at the branch level.

As we've already observed the company has a saying. 'The branch is the bank.' And those branches are comprised of people who are given the power to make choices about how they do business. They set their own goals, they hire their own staff, they are free to choose which customers they sign up and, most importantly, they make their own lending decisions. Back at home in Sweden, 70% of decisions are taken solely at branch level and a mere 2% go to the central board. They seem pretty conservative in their judgements – a mere 0.04% of loans are non-performing.

To avoid conflict between branches, each bank can serve customers only from its own local area, with no overlap between branches. Handelsbanken calls this 'the church spire principle' and it's another method of ensuring that branches know their borrowers well.

There's an analogy within the bank that neatly explains this premise. If you're lending to a baker in Inverness and you're in Inverness, then you can see whether there's smoke coming out of their chimney or not, and you know whether the bakers are baking; in other words, you know whether it's a good business or not. You can't do that from London by just looking at numbers. It's about making grounded decisions.

And since 2001, local office managers also decide how many employees the branch should have and how much they should be paid. This is all testament to the trust and strongly held shared beliefs between management and employees at Handelsbanken.

Unlike the usual short tenure of a bank employee, Handelsbanken people tend to be lifers and benefit from the bank's profit-sharing foundation Oktogonen, which is similar to a group pension scheme, whereby it is paid out to them as individuals on retirement. There are currently 24,600 members of the scheme, more than double the number of Handelsbanken employees. In March 2019, 2,197 colleagues took full or partial distributions from the scheme. After working for 30 years at Handelsbanken, an employee could withdraw around SEK 7 million ($750,000).

Today, the Oktogonen Foundation looks after around SEK 23 billion, and 90% of the capital is invested in Handelsbanken shares, creating a joint staff ownership of just over 10% of the bank's shares. This makes the Foundation (and thereby the staff) the largest shareholder, alongside another very long-term investor, Industrivärden, a patient asset manager and active owner in listed Nordic companies.

How to sustain an outside-in belief system:
Three critical elements

Handelsbanken is extraordinary because it has maintained an outside-in belief system for nearly 50 years, a phenomenal achievement. Our study of this Swedish bank and other companies that have maintained outside-in beliefs suggests that they do three things that, together, resist the lethal pull of inside-out:

1. Knowing that something as unusual as a shared set of beliefs really matters and paying close conscious attention to the prevailing belief system as THE critical success factor in the business.

2. Ensuring a continual flow of Moments of Belief, like continual small rocket boosts to maintain orbit despite the gravitational pull of inside-out forces. They can be small and local or larger and more widely visible, but each one is counterintuitive when viewed through a conventional inside-out lens.

3. The third is being boldest when most challenged and when it matters most. In other words, when a competitor, or a new disruptor providing an alternative, creates a new and better way of solving a customer's problems or getting them to the outcomes they want, then the response is to change the business model at considerable pain, cost and risk, acting like a challenger, not to defend like an incumbent whose instincts are to protect the existing business model.

Examples large and small across these three points are easy to find at Handelsbanken.

Knowing that shared beliefs really matter

Bernie Charles, head of HR UK, Handelsbanken, says that the recruitment process isn't just testing technical competence and skills but an affinity with the bank's values as well. 'We're not for everybody,' he says, a phrase that is echoed by many other Handelsbanken people. 'We spend a lot of time explaining our culture, values and what decentralisation means in practice. We need people who are comfortable taking decisions and responsibility within our framework.'[15] Hannah Pearce, who joined the bank in 2014 straight from university, reflected on the recruitment process:

> You were actually speaking to someone. With the others, it was all through computers and you had to pass tests. Handelsbanken wanted to know you as a person. Trying to see if you were the right kind of person for the bank. Not just mental arithmetic tests![16]

Handelsbanken has a pamphlet, 'Our Way,' outlining the organisation's philosophy, which is handed out during the induction process, central to training and often referred to during meetings and decision-making. 'We refer to "Our Way" in everything we do,' says Pernille Sahl Taylor, chief communications officer, Handelsbanken. 'It's ingrained in everything.'[17]

Figure 6.1 The Arrow: Handelsbanken's organisational chart. (Source: Handelsbanken briefing document, September 2017)

Handelsbanken is a flat structure, and this is described by 'the arrow' (see Figure 6.1) – a horizontal organisational chart that shows the customer as the most important element. Emphasis is placed on collaboration as a team rather than a star culture. 'It is quite flat – maybe that doesn't suit everyone. We don't talk about being further up or down in the organisation,' says Sahl Taylor.

As Charles explains:

> Everything in our operating model reinforces the culture. A key part of our leadership criteria is to live the culture. We have a number of factors we look to in salary reviews and being a cultural ambassador is one of those.[18]

A story they like to tell as an example of the Handelsbanken way involves one of their customers racing to the train station to attend meetings in London. When he got there, he realised he'd forgotten his wallet. He couldn't get through to his wife, so he called his Handelsbanken manager who ran to the station and, just trusting him because he knew him, gave him £100 cash so he could catch his train and make his meeting on time.

A continual flow of Moments of Belief

Ownership of Handelsbanken's beliefs is felt strongly throughout the organisation. If you attempt to mess with the philosophy, then retribution can be swift. As referred to earlier, Frank Vang-Jensen lasted a mere 18 months in the job having reputedly started down the track of adding a new layer of management to the operating structure, which would have meant that the lean three layers became four.

As UK CEO Mikael Sørensen described it, there is no absolute reason that three layers works, and four layers cannot. But if four, then next year why not five, then six? He was describing precisely the creeping effect of gravity at work, of inside-out beliefs with their apparently sensible thinking and by-degrees way of pulling you back to Earth. The firing was a huge Moment of Belief, a signal to every person in the organisation that some beliefs are not to be messed with.

Sørensen also described a much smaller, more everyday Moment of Belief. It came from the recent introduction of a new credit card. A well-meaning younger team member had started to record how many were being applied for each month by each branch's customers. Mikael asked him to stop. He explained that although no one has a target for sales of any kind, including the credit card, human nature is such that if anyone from a branch saw the numbers, they would compare them with other branches.

> It would be natural to wonder if others had higher figures, that perhaps there were ways to learn from them and 'do better.' But at this point, we would become a volume bank, not a customer bank, and we are a customer bank. A customer bank only cares about its customers and what they want – if they want the credit card, they will ask for it; if they don't, we will withdraw it and do something else more useful.[19]

Moments of Belief can come from going against fashion. 'We are always taking the outside-in view,' Anders Bouvin said in an interview with the *Financial Times*. 'When call centres were in vogue we always looked at this from a customer's point of view and said this won't add value for our customers.'[20] Because it is going against the conventional wisdom, employees take particular interest in it, rationalise it, process the rationale and in this sense-making process they reinforce their beliefs and their understanding about 'how (and why) we do things around here.'

Moments of Belief can perhaps be best described by people who are on the receiving end of them. Charles has a story from 2013 when he was part of the bank's only acquisition in the UK to date, a small wealth and investment management company. He recalls:

> Very soon afterwards we were visited by the Group CEO – he came to the UK once a year, and we put a lot of effort into our presentation on integration and how we would offer our services to Handelsbanken customers. His words were, 'Let's do it properly. Don't rush it; we want to be here in 100 years. You're a good business with solid foundations,

now let's do this in a measured safe way rather than chasing dead-lines and targets.' It was really clear. We'd heard similar sentiments all the way through the process, but here was the Group CEO affirming everything. It was incredibly powerful. We let out a collective sigh of relief. And it's not that the pressure was off. The pressure was on to do a really good job.[21]

Summing all this up, Mikael Sørensen had his own way of describing the gravitational battle:

Decentralisation is like a cork in a bottle of water. You press it in, but when you leave it, very slowly, it starts to come out again. Every now and again you have to press it down to keep it in, and in this organisa-tion, it is the main part of my job.[22]

It is part of every manager's job. Managers at each of the bank's few levels continually assert that decentralisation means empowerment. That can take some getting used to for new joiners. Jonathan Croney, a career banker, arrived from Credit Agricole and before that was with Barclays. He found the difference in culture at Handelsbanken to be extreme and in contrast-ing these experiences pointed to the sense of ownership and empower-ment that came from decentralisation:

I was asking my manager what to do and he passed it straight back, asking me what I thought. You soon start to realise 'this is completely on me.' You can't pass the buck. Saying yes or saying no – it's our call. I didn't expect that, and I can see the difference it makes to customer service and trust.[23]

The beliefs affect everything. Measurement and targets for example are notably different and the serve as everyday Moments of Belief. Sarah Hanson, a regional area manager described the effect:

People are driven but calm. People are judged by how productive they are – satisfaction from customers and work/life balance are equally important. Each branch has its own yearly business plan with goals and actions on how it can improve its cost/income ratio. You get monthly MI [management information] on perfor-mance growing income for the branch. The branch manager is MD [managing director] of their own business, so it's up to them what they spend their money on and how they control their costs and drive income.[24]

Being boldest when most challenged and when it matters most

In the UK, one of Handelsbanken's most challenging times has come as they engage with regulators around their unusual customer-led model. And true to form, the Swedish bank rose to the challenge as it took a step to set up a UK subsidiary in 2018. This saw Handelsbanken move from existing as a branch of a Swedish bank, regulated by Swedish law, to becoming a standalone UK-licensed bank, under UK regulations. This change was no mean feat and involved a new banking license, new structure, new board as well as a huge investment and a lot of work. Georgina Silvester, chief operating officer, Handelsbanken UK, explains:

> With the uncertainty of Brexit, we very quickly engaged with the regulators. We wanted to take control of the situation and find a pathway forward. Others are sitting back and creating contingency plans but not invoking action.[25]

The process saw the Swedish bank spend a lot of time, energy and resources explaining its decentralised model to UK regulators in order to receive a UK banking licence. As Silvester elaborated:

> One really interesting challenge was articulating our business model. We live and breathe it every day but writing it down and thinking how you express it to external stakeholders was a challenge. How to encapsulate what's in our DNA? Until you write it down, it's not something you think about. Then the regulators came back with questions, and it became clear we didn't fit the mould, didn't tick the box, so had to work harder and explain why it works for customers.[26]

Unlike other banks, Handelsbanken's business model isn't a centralised process based mainly on quantitative evidence and analysis; instead, it is about empowering local branches to use their judgement to make decisions that weigh the risks as they see them, including their knowledge of the

customer relationships. Hence, questions from regulators around risk management have been tough to prove purely in terms of process, even though
their track record is industry leading. According to Silvester:

> Risk management is embedded into the way we work. There's not a
> centralised model where restrictions are put in place and the com-
> puter says no. So, a lot of our work has been about formalising what
> we already do.[27]

This is an important point. The regulators' role is to look out for customers, but if they adopt models that reflect inside-out beliefs, then they force
the market to adopt behaviour that fits, and they also reinforce the kind of
'common sense' but unhelpful beliefs in this case that centralised control is
safer than devolving decisions to branches that sit behind them.

Handelsbanken has prevailed. It now has a UK banking licence and from
December 2018 has operated as Handelsbanken plc in the UK. The plc is a
fully owned subsidiary of Handelsbanken group. Silvester says:

> Many other organisations would have waited to see how things played
> out until they were at the point when they were forced to take action.
> For us, this is the next natural step. It's a huge investment.[28]

We'll now investigate each of these three critical elements for sustaining
an outside-in belief system in more detail drawing on examples from the
John Lewis Partnership, W.L. Gore, Hilti and LEGO. Like Handelsbanken,
these companies have maintained outside-in beliefs well beyond a single
generation of managers. There is much to be learned from the ways they
have sustained them.

Knowing a belief system really matters at John Lewis Partnership and W.L. Gore

An outside-in belief system is not natural. It means finding ways to stand
in the shoes of customers, seeing the bigger picture of their real problem
and all the possible solutions well beyond your market. And then it means
being utterly determined to find new and better answers, unlimited by preconceptions of a market and the competition. We believe it matters because

it produces innovation that makes things work better for customers, it is rewarding for employees and it can deliver spectacular commercial results.

John Lewis

John Spedan Lewis was a founder's son with an instinctive understanding of what worked best for customers and colleagues, and a visionary eye for how to organise in support of it. Broadly, he was convinced that his father's retail business would be more successful if workers participated in decision-making and shared more equally and transparently in the financial success.

Spedan's father was John Lewis, who opened his first department store in Oxford Street, London in 1864. It became a long-lived British retail success story, an employee-owned partnership spanning high-end department stores under the John Lewis brand and the premium supermarket chain Waitrose. John Lewis has traded under the slogan, 'never knowingly undersold' since 1925, and in 2017/18, the Partnership generated sales of £11.5 billion in a challenging, fast-paced environment.

When Spedan Lewis first joined his father's business, he felt it was old-fashioned and unfair to workers. While he, his father and brother earned £26,000 divided between the three of them, John Lewis's employees shared earnings of £16,000 between 300 − £8,667 compared to £53.33. Spedan felt this was not fair, so he made a change.

Exchanging his stake in the Oxford Street store for total control over Peter Jones in Sloane Square, London, he increased wages, improved conditions and provided an extra week's holiday for workers. Within five years, the greater engagement, trust and motivation was being recognised by customers and in the store's takings. The store turned an annual loss of £8,000 into a profit of £20,000, awarding a bonus amounting to seven weeks' pay to its workers.

This became a huge Moment of Belief in the journey of the business from inside-out to outside-in.

It came from some unusual outside-in beliefs from Spedan Lewis – that it is 'all wrong to have millionaires before you have ceased to have slums'; that 'the dividends paid to some shareholders' for doing essentially nothing were obscene when 'workers earn hardly more than a bare living'; and that co-ownership and partnership, rather than exploitative employment, might be 'the new source of working energy of which our country is in such grave need.'[29]

When his father died, Spedan took over the Oxford Street store, applying similar principles and again finding they worked, another big Moment of Belief for all those involved.

Spedan certainly practiced what he preached, and in a further pivotal Moment of Belief, he signed away his personal ownership of the retailer to allow future generations of employees to take forward this approach. In 1929 and 1950, through two settlements of the Trust, he established the John Lewis Partnership, owned for the benefit of its members who are referred to as Partners from the day they join.

Spedan's beliefs about employee engagement are clear – that giving the employees a say and a stake motivates behaviour that is greatly beneficial to customers and that results in commercial success.

These shared beliefs have shaped its unique ownership and governance model. The Trust's directors, appointed by the Partnership council, safe-guard the company's constitution, which states that the ultimate purpose of the Partnership is 'the happiness of all its members' recognising that such happiness depends on having a satisfying job in a successful business. 'It establishes the "rights and responsibilities" which places on all Partners the obligation to work for the improvement of our business in the knowledge that they share in the rewards.'[30]

The organisation has remained faithful to this belief system, which is central to the retailer's whole way of working. Partners share profits and have a say in the business. There is an annual meeting with the ceremonial opening of an envelope revealing the percentage profit share for each and every one of the Partners, and a structure that encourages open question-ing of senior management by all employees. Like Spedan Lewis, the senior leaders see their job as handing over the Partnership to the next generation in better shape than when they joined.

These democratic principles mean a lot of thought is put into making sure the most important issues in the business are recognised and tackled. The elected council meets four times a year with the chairman and senior executives to discuss strategy. Specific roles have been created within the organisation to represent the voice of the Partners – Partnership registrars who represent their views to the board and the board's views to the Partners.

There are other elements in play that pay conscious attention to these shared beliefs. For example, when they're not working, John Lewis Partners can stay in one of the five holiday centres the Partnership owns and runs for the benefit of its employees. These include a 16th-century castle with private beach on Brownsea Island in Poole Harbour, a Victorian hotel on the shores of Lake Windermere, a 24-room hotel, spa and activity centre at Lake Bala in North Wales, and a country house hotel on 4,000 rolling acres in Hampshire. The bed and breakfast costs just £20.25 per person per night and the three-course dinner is just £11.25. And there are no locks on the doors.[31] There's also a surf club, a photography club, a gliding club …

Patrick Lewis, a senior executive related to Spedan, described to us how maintaining these shared beliefs doesn't happen by accident:

> This is like the design of a particular kind of building where, although conversations happen between people in random ways, the architecture makes sure you bump into the issues that matter …[32]

Co-ownership means employees 'make that extra effort. And because you're all Partners, there's no backstabbing. Motivation's different,' Beth Smith, from the floor-coverings and furnishings department in the Cardiff store, told The Guardian newspaper. As she explained:

> The thinking's long-term. It's not about making a quick profit at the expense of bigger values. The Partners' voices really do carry weight. It's not just window-dressing: we decided we didn't want to work on Boxing Day, and we didn't.[33]

When the Cardiff store opened in 2015, there were 9,000 applicants for 750 jobs. And while half the Cardiff employees had no retail experience, the John Lewis Partnership was recruiting for behaviour, mirroring Handelsbanken's approach. 'You can train anyone to do things,' said Beth Smith. 'But nobody can teach someone how to be.' At John Lewis it's known as having 'green blood.'[34]

Today, The John Lewis Partnership is facing an existential challenge. What does it take for a department store to thrive in a changing world with a declining high street, where digital competition shows no sign of abating? At the end of 2018, the retail Partnership – which includes Waitrose supermarkets as well as John Lewis department stores – confirmed that Partners would receive a 3% bonus, the lowest since 1953, when workers got no bonus at all. Profits at the Partnership sank by more than 45% to £160 million with poor home sales, discounting, higher IT charges and the cost of opening two new stores accounting for the drop. John Lewis famously promises that it is 'never knowingly undersold,' meaning it matches its high street rivals' prices, but the Partnership said 'near constant discounting' from rivals hit profits, particularly in its department store shops.

The retailer has always faced challenges by holding onto its belief system with the instinctive understanding that what matters most to customers and Partners will, in the long term, also work best for the John Lewis Partnership. The firm is currently working on what this means, exploring a move from retailing into services as one new and better way to solve its customers' problems. It will take a number of years to see whether this can work for all involved.

W.L. Gore

W.L. Gore, a global materials science company, stands out from its peers because of the way the entire organisation has been designed around a set of shared beliefs that encourage innovation. It is a $3 billion global company that spans many industries, including medicine, textiles, cables and music by manipulating a form of PTFE, a plastic with some unusual properties.

The company is most famous for Gore-Tex, a waterproof, breathable fabric used in outdoor wear. In 1981, the spacesuits worn by NASA astronauts on the space shuttle Columbia 1 used Gore-Tex. But it is just one part of a diverse portfolio that includes dental floss, guitar strings and medical devices to treat heart defects. By 2011, Gore held more than 2,000 patents worldwide.

The company was born from the frustrated energy of Bill Gore, a DuPont engineer who had spent 17 years investigating the potential of PTFE under the brand name of Teflon. He was deep in the challenge of manipulating the material. How to maintain the intensity and connection of molecules when you pull them apart? What stretching process, what optimum temperatures would result in a stronger compound? But Dupont wanted him to move on to other more 'useful' projects at work, so he was forced to continue innovating in the basement of his home instead.

Gore was convinced this slick, waxy material had more commercial use beyond thermoplastics. But DuPont wanted to focus on its roots as a raw material supplier. Denied the chance to invent and explore the potential of PTFE further, Gore left DuPont. And, in 1958, Gore and his wife Genevieve (Vieve) invested their life savings to open W.L. Gore Associates in the basement of their home in Newark, Delaware.

Gore was angry with DuPont's way of managing innovation, and he was ambitious too. He could see the potential of this material. This created the burningness he needed to launch a new company with a pure, single-minded focus on innovation.

He felt there was tremendous value to be realised in applying the high energy and innovation from DuPont's small R&D teams more widely across a business at scale. He asked:

> Could you build a company with no hierarchy – where everyone was free to talk with everyone else? How about a company where there were no bosses, no supervisors, and no vice presidents? Could you let people choose what they wanted to work on, rather than assigning them tasks? Could you create a company with no core business, where people would put as much energy into finding the next big thing as they did into milking the last big thing? And could you do all of this while still delivering consistent growth and profitability?[35]

What Gore put in place in terms of company structure and culture demonstrates a very particular set of shared beliefs focused on encouraging innovation. This vision has created a very unusual company that has reaped rewards for paying conscious attention to a set of beliefs.

There are no management layers, no organisation charts, no job titles. Everyone is called an associate, and specific roles are negotiated within teams. Everyone has the same level of company car.

Newcomers are not given roles or responsibilities. Instead they must forge their own path, join a group of people and find a way to contribute. At Gore, a premium is placed on the quality of ideas.

The Gore culture highly values employee involvement, keeping its facilities small to enable employees to influence decisions and actions. Typically, when a facility (which usually combines sales, R&D and manufacturing) reaches 300 associates, it is split in two. Gore believes that once you reach 300 people on a site you lose personal connections.

There is some structure – a CEO, four divisions (fabric, medical, industrial and electronic products), a number of product-focused business units and business support functions each with a recognised leader. Terri Kelly, Gore's CEO from 2005–2018 explains, 'We resist titles, it puts you in a position that you have assumed authority that you can command over an organisation.'[36]

Instead, the peer-based organisation recognises leaders through their ability to attract followers. Kelly explained, 'The voice of the organisation determines who will be a leader based on who will follow them.'[37]

It's a place where everyone is your boss. Associates' contributions are evaluated by their peers – the people who see them every day and know what they've done. An associate is typically evaluated by 20–30 peers, and this information is developed into an overall ranking by a sub-committee. Compensation is based upon the company's success that fiscal year alongside the associate's ranking. Kelly elaborates:

> We don't tell our associates what criteria to use; we simply ask them to base their ranking on who's making the greatest contribution to the success of the enterprise. You don't evaluate people solely on the basis of what they're doing within their team, but in terms of the broader impact they may be having across the company. And then beyond their contributions, are they behaving in ways that are collaborative? Are they living the values? Sometimes someone will get great results but at great expense to the organization. These are the issues associates think about when they're putting together their rankings.[38]

This peer-based ranking pays proper attention to Gore's founding beliefs. Back to Kelly:

> You get a lot of negative behaviour when you have narrow metrics that really don't represent the complexity of the business. Instead, we ask our associates to view performance holistically, in terms of someone's total impact, versus focusing on a few specific variables.[39]

And the cultural idea that 'we're all in the same boat' is reinforced by the ownership of the company, just like The John Lewis Partnership. All associates are part owners of the business through the associate stock plan, sharing risks and rewards. Gore believed this made employees more committed to a long-term view and willing to take action that was in the best interests of the enterprise.

Today, the business-to-business (B2B) company has offices in more than 25 countries. And while some markets have adapted to inevitable local cultural issues, the fundamental beliefs of Gore are held sacred. For example, in South Korea, associates have business cards with clearly labelled titles, but internally, they know that these titles count for nothing compared to the respect of their colleagues.[40]

Box 6.1 GORE'S GUIDING PRINCIPLES

Instead of using a detailed policy book, the firm relies on four guiding principles originally articulated by Bill Gore to help guide associates:

1. **Freedom**: We encourage each other to grow in knowledge, skill, scope of responsibility and range of activities. We believe that Associates will exceed expectations when given the freedom to do so.
2. **Fairness**: Everyone at Gore sincerely tries to be fair with each other, our suppliers, our customers and anyone else with whom we do business.
3. **Commitment**: We are not assigned tasks; rather, we each make our own commitments and keep them.
4. **Waterline**: Everyone at Gore consults with other knowledgeable Associates before taking actions that might be 'below the waterline,' causing serious damage to the enterprise.

(Source: Company website. Retrieved from www.gore. com/about/our-beliefs-and-principles)

This metaphor about the waterline helps manage risk. If you make one bad decision and that makes a hole in the ship above the waterline, the ship may be damaged, but it will survive. You can learn from the experience and move on. But if you make a hole below the waterline, the ship could sink.

Like many other outside-in companies profiled in this book, Gore takes a long-term view, focused on making life better for customers, finding new and better solutions to their problems.

Gore's dental floss began life back in 1971, when Bill Gore used a Gore-Tex fabric ribbon to floss his teeth. But for 20 years, the company wasn't able to persuade healthcare companies or local pharmacies to stock it. In 1991, they decided to promote it as a medical technology product instead of a consumer-facing one, giving free samples to dentists who were impressed with the way the floss held together. In time, this built a strong army of fans among dental hygienists. By 2003, when Gore sold its floss business to Procter & Gamble, it had reached dental floss sales of over $45 million in the US market.

From the beginning, W.L. Gore has placed a very particular set of beliefs at the centre of the company, paying close attention to them in terms of structure, remuneration and stories. This outside-in belief system began with Bill Gore's clear-eyed, big picture determination that PTFE could solve so many more real customer problems than the coating on a saucepan. Everything came back to the purity of finding new and better answers, breaking conventions, creating new ways of innovating, a new kind of company – that all delivered spectacular commercial results.

A continual flow of Moments of Belief at Hilti

In the customer-led companies we examined, Moments of Belief are not one-offs; they are normal, they are decisions and behaviours that are explained by a shared and (eventually) unquestioned belief that creating customer value in new and better ways is, in fact, the top priority and the strategy. While normal in customer-led companies, this continual flow of Moments of Belief is critically important in keeping the shared belief system strong, in sharing it with newcomers and keeping in perspective the legitimate and natural forces that would otherwise pull management inward. Hilti provides a helpful illustration.

Hilti, famous for the red drills used by construction workers around the globe, is a privately owned business that develops, manufactures and markets premium products and solutions for use by professionals in the construction, building maintenance, energy, extraction and manufacturing industries. In 2018, its nearly 30,000 employees generated revenues of just over €5 billion from its activities in 120 countries. The words of founder Martin Hilti continue to resonate throughout the organisation, 'Markets are more important than factories.' His first-hand observations of users informed product design, organisational design and later leadership behaviour. Market immersion simply became, and remains, the norm for leadership and decision making at Hilti. It provides the outside-in perspective that defines being customer-led. It also is the source of opportunities to create customer value in new and better ways as this flow over time of Moments of Belief at Hilti illustrates.

1996 – Challenging conventional wisdom

In 1996, France country manager Alain Baumann uncovered the large and highly attractive – but for Hilti, underserved – market of tradesmen working as sole traders or in small companies. To reach them, he intended to create a new route to market dedicated to professionals. This was completely outside of the norms of Hilti's existing, longstanding and unique-to-the-industry business model, which relied on a huge team of sales and service engineers (7,500 globally at the time) to sell directly to customers. Customers saw Hilti's expensive route to market model as an integral part of the Hilti offer. They valued the expertise offered by the sales team.

Baumann's plan truly challenged the company's executive board. While there were considerable known costs (putting a highly qualified Hilti sales engineer in store for all opening hours) and significant risks (the success or otherwise of the new retailer brand and its strategy including the eventual product range offered would reflect on Hilti; the territories of the existing Hilti sales engineers would most probably be cannibalised), the true potential of the move could not be properly assessed. After some considerable hesitancy, the executive board supported the move. It was the right thing to do. It was consistent with the kinds of customer-led innovation it wanted to see; moreover, some customers that highly valued Hilti were poorly served by the existing model. The support was well placed. Within a year it became clear that the model was viable, scalable and highly appreciated by the target segment customers, offering them considerably more convenience – an issue of enormous economic significance especially to sole or small traders. As the retailer grew, Hilti

France grew with it, achieving coverage levels that would be impossible with the existing route to market approach. For Hilti colleagues around the world, it had been another Moment of Belief, another big decision demonstrating the company's customer-led priorities. The shared beliefs were stronger as a result and led others, most notably Hilti US, to pursue similar approaches.

2000 – Mining: The outside-in approach to building a better future

Hilti's move into mining was bold. It meant that an organisation dedicated to the construction and building industry was going to enter an unfamiliar domain. The insight came from a Hilti sales representative who served one of the largest mining companies in South Africa. Being an expert on Hilti capabilities and solutions and being immersed in the client's world, he realised the difference a Hilti tool could make.

He believed Hilti could apply its technical drilling know-how to make the work of miners operating at the 'stope' (the face of the mine where rock is broken) safer and reduce the damaging noise that traditional drills produce.

New equipment would need to be developed, a different sales process required and mining unions would need to be considered as the solution envisaged would lead to fewer equipment operators being required for the mineral extraction.

The crucial moment came when executive board member Ewald Hoelker made the trip to South Africa, descended to the face of one of the world's deepest mines and saw the conditions the front-line miners worked in. He immediately saw the opportunity for Hilti to significantly improve the efficiency, effectiveness and safety of the process. And so Hilti set out on a long and ultimately successful development process. Today the business is stable, successful and established, creating customer value in new and better ways. The commitment to mining was an important Moment of Belief because it reiterated the importance of customer-led innovation to the whole organisation, something achieved by thinking broadly about the challenges of customers throughout their business systems. It reminded everyone of Hilti's priorities and beliefs.

2001 – Evolving the business model: Moving from products to services

One of the most important developments in the company's history was its decision to launch 'Hilti Fleet Management,' which like a car lease agreement allows customers to use (but not own) equipment for a fixed monthly fee. The fee includes the cost of service and repairs. In 2018, a little over ten years after its launch, more than one million tools were under contract with 100,000 customers. It is an important revenue and profit driver and success was neither obvious nor immediate. Indeed, it might never have happened if Marco Meyrat, head of the Swiss market, had not been pressured by one of his larger clients.

Whilst Meyrat understood the customer's need, he also knew his organisation did not have the capabilities to deliver the service well and at scale. Embracing the opportunity would require building new capabilities, especially in contracting. Even Hilti's core competence of direct selling would need to be adapted. Sales would take longer, with a different decision process involving different stakeholders. Further, questions arose such as how salespeople should be compensated, given they had previously been rewarded for the sale of specific equipment.

Yet, with the backing of the executive board that Meyrat is now part of, the company took a leap of faith. By asking for this service, customers had shown immense trust in the Hilti brand. Customers typically had tens of thousands (and sometimes hundreds of thousands) of Swiss francs tied up financing all on-site equipment. All of this was at risk every day from theft, poor handling and sub-optimal working and storing conditions. In the same way that office managers realised they didn't need to be in the business of owning and maintaining expensive and temperamental printing equipment, construction companies realised they didn't need to own much of their equipment on open sites. As they looked for a partner to take these risks on their behalf, who they could rely on for the best, most up-to-date technology, they turned to Hilti, a company and brand they had come to trust.

The executive board realised the implications, the set-up costs involved and the risks if they did not manage roll-out successfully. What they could not predict was the level of demand or indeed the reaction of other customers and their own salesforce. They took a brave step away from their core, but it worked, leading eventually to the company expanding the fleet business to cover non-Hilti assets.

These Moments of Beliefs have ensured Hilti maintains its outside-in shared beliefs, continually re-asserting that the business succeeds by being customer-led. Not only did these Moments of Belief create value for customers in new and better ways, they also led to profitable new revenue streams and business models. In so doing, they showed the organisation that outside-in thinking is the way things are done around here. They ensure Hilti maintains its outside-in orbit despite the relentless gravitational pull of inside-out forces, a pull strengthened by challenges to trading coming from the economic cycle and sharper shocks such as the global economic crisis and extreme currency movements.

Being boldest when challenged most: LEGO

Our third and final element to sustain an outside-in belief system over many years is being boldest when challenged most. When the chips are down, outside-in companies are brave. We've seen how Sky launched NOW TV, a pay-as-you-go offering to appeal to millennials, as viewers flocked to disruptive competitors like Netflix. And how Handelsbanken faced up to the UK regulators in order to hold onto its outside-in business model when launching a subsidiary. Meanwhile, in 2004, in a rapidly changing world where children's' attention was increasingly dominated by technology, LEGO, the Danish family-owned toy company, returned to its roots of creative play.

LEGO operates in a tough environment competing against toy companies like Mattel and Hasbro, as well as tech companies like Microsoft and Sony. Since its launch as a wooden toy company in 1932, LEGO has always taken a long-term view, seeking to create customer value in new and better ways, whether that means creating plastic bricks when wood was in scarce supply after World War Two or creating the LEGO movie in 2014.

Today, there are more than 3,700 types of basic components, from mini figures to tubes and accessories such as wheels and swords. More than 900 million building combinations are possible with just six bricks of the same colour.[41] LEGO mini figures outnumber real people.[42]

We are interested in the story of LEGO because it has clearly demonstrated a willingness to be boldest when facing a crisis, with numerous examples of this behaviour throughout its long history.

In the aftermath of the Wall Street crash in 1929, Ole Kirk Kristiansen's carpentry workshop was suffering. Many of Kristiansen's farmer customers were unable to commission work. Kristiansen laid staff off and focused on what he was best at – stepladders, ironing boards and his personal passion – toys. As his toy orders picked up, he focused on this product line, renamed his company LEGO in 1934 and invested DKK 3,000 in the company's first milling machine. This was a huge leap of faith at the time when you consider that a house would have cost between DKK 4,000 and 5,000. But this was about quality, and the milling machine enabled Kristiansen to make safer toys with rounded edges at scale.

In 1942, disaster struck. A devastating fire razed the woodworking factory to the ground, destroying Kristiansen's life work. Without insurance coverage to rebuild the factory, Kristiansen nearly gave it all up. In his memoirs he wrote, 'I have tried to find another site – but there doesn't seem to be anywhere suitable ... Our aim is to do a really good and solid and pleasing piece of work so that people will know that LEGO products are quality.' In the end, Kristiansen took out a sizeable bank loan to build a dedicated toy factory, securing the jobs of his 15 employees. The following year, he was employing 40 people.[43]

Wood was scarce and expensive after World War II, so Kristiansen needed to rethink. In 1947, he imported an expensive injection-moulding machine, and by 1949, he had developed the company's first plastic interlocking bricks – Automatic Binding Bricks, 31.8mm long by 15.8mm wide, with eight studs in two rows of four, marketed in sets for kids to build whatever their imagination desired.

Ole Kirk Kristiansen's sons saw plastic production as ruinous for the business. They decided to persuade their father to switch back exclusively to wood products. Ole Kirk Kristiansen's response: 'Have you no faith? Can't you see? If we get this right, we can sell these bricks all over the world!'[44]

Quality remained essential for LEGO's founder, but he had found a new and better way to create value for his customers through plastic bricks, a way to create an even more engaging toy. Staying with wood would have been about protecting an existing business model, acting like an incumbent. Moving to high-quality plastic bricks was a bold, outside-in move that created new value for LEGO customers. It was about being boldest when it mattered most.

After decades of growth, LEGO had become synonymous with children's play. With three or more generations across the Western world knowing the unmistakable LEGO bricks, brand awareness and understanding was almost total. Engagement and advocacy were enviable.

But by the late 1990s, under price pressure from large retailers and with growth slowing, LEGO faced a crisis in confidence. Sales of electronic games were storming ahead, changing customers' expectations. Executives tortured themselves: how could LEGO remain relevant in this dramatically changing world?

The business went in many directions at once. It chased after the girls' market with new ranges, even jewellery. It expanded its theme park business. It introduced a line of kids' clothes and watches. And it made a concerted attempt to develop LEGO-themed video games. In 2003, LEGO's sales dropped by almost a third (versus 2002) and the company reported a loss of DKK 935 million. Sales continued to fall in 2004 and with a restructuring in full swing, losses that year mounted to almost DKK 2 billion.

This was a decisive moment, and LEGO's response – to be true to its outside-in beliefs or to continue to chase sales – was going to be pivotal. Nokia's response to a similar crisis when Apple invented the iPhone was to continue to try holding back the tide.

By contrast, LEGO's CEO at the time, Jørgen Vig Knudstorp, led a bold response, returning the toy company to its roots. 'What we realised is that the more we're true to ourselves, the better we are,' he said, quoting TS Eliot's 'Little Gidding. 'The end of all our exploring will be to arrive where we started and know the place for the first time.'[45]

Mads Nipper led LEGO's marketing and product development during this period and was also responsible for tackling complacency among employees. The root of the problem was that LEGO had lost touch with its core customers – boys (mostly) and girls aged 5 to 11.

Nipper challenged soothsaying strategists weary of the 'now' generation demanding easier more immediate solutions; they believed kids would not spend the time to create and build what was in their imagination. To him the evolution of LEGO's classic fire truck told an important story. By 2001, the once iconic fire truck was futuristic, replete with bubble cockpit and oversized tyres. And in response to the trend that kids wanted everything now, the construction process had been simplified so the end result could be built more rapidly.

LEGO had lost touch, focusing on retailers and parents because that's where the money came from, not kids, which is where the value was truly created. Kids that loved LEGO loved the process of construction. Making the end result easier to achieve gave them *less* value, not more. The toy had fallen between two stools all because an important insight had been lost – kids aren't obsessed with the outcome at the cost of the process; the fun was in the challenge.[46]

Nipper reimagined the design process, drastically reducing the total number of parts used across the range. Rather than rubber-stamping each request, he let all the designers vote on proposed new parts. LEGO observer Jaap Grolleman notes:

> Gone were the days when designers could (follow) wherever their imagination would take them. When LEGO confined its designers, it ran the risk of diminishing its competitive advantage. Except it didn't. Gone were the complex components and the fire truck looked like a fire truck. It allowed kids to build their own creations again – instead of being left with components that were already identified.[47]

Nipper was determined to bring kids at play back into the centre. He insisted the development teams systematically involve kids in the product design and development process. Just watching and listening to kids tell you what you need to know. 'Children and drunks are the last honest people left on the face of the earth,' he said.[48]

By March 2004, Knudstorp's dramatic turnaround sold every part of the business that wasn't core to the product; this included property in the US, South Korea and Australia, four theme parks and a videogames development division. He let go of 1,000 employees and outsourced many processes, reducing the headcount again by 3,500. LEGO reduced the number of parts it used from nearly 7,000 to 3,000, and it injected a sense of urgency into the design and production process, halving the time it took to develop a concept from idea to box from two years to 12 months.[49] By 2005, the company was again making money – it turned a profit of DKK 505 million (which it tripled in 2006).

Throughout its history, LEGO has understood the importance of being boldest when it matters most. At times when the toy company is challenged hardest, it reacts in an outside-in way. From investing in an expensive plastic moulding machine when wood was scarce after World War Two and using that move to create a better, more engaging toys, to having the courage to return to its roots and help kids play creatively when the rest of the toy industry was chasing technology. It is this bravery that has enabled LEGO to sustain an outside-in belief system successfully over many years.

While LEGO's dramatic turnaround led to a decade of growth for the toy company, nothing lasts forever. By early 2018, LEGO admitted that it had stretched itself too thin, revealing an 18% slide in pre-tax profits to DKK 10.4 billion in 2017. Chairman Knudstorp realised that once again adding complexity to the company had made it harder for the toymaker to grow further, so the firm pressed 'the reset button' with the aim of building 'a smaller and less complex organisation.'[50] The work of an outside-in company is never done, and once again LEGO had to be boldest when it mattered most.

Conclusion and recap

The companies we've written about in this chapter vary dramatically in terms of industry and business challenge. However, what they all have in common is a deep awareness and respect for the power of their shared beliefs.

In particular, they have chosen and actively support a system of customer-led outside-in beliefs.

From Handelsbanken's determination to hold onto its values no matter what, to Michael Hilti's significant investment in nurturing its values, to LEGO's bravery in being boldest when it matters most and returning the toy company to its roots in 2004, they have all invested personal reputation, bravery, conviction as well as time, money and attention to hold onto their belief systems.

They each accept that outside-in beliefs are unnatural, so their belief systems need constant attention. They need to know where they're at, creating some kind of architecture that means people bump into and question the shared beliefs of themselves and their colleagues continually.

They ensure there is a continual stream of Moments of Belief, small and sizeable, and by these inconvenient choices being visible, explicit and effective, their shared outside-in beliefs are reinforced.

At really big turning points, from a failing business model to a global financial crisis, they go back to their core beliefs and find a bold response that reflects them, changing the business model to find a genuinely new and better way to meet customers' needs.

To do this, these companies need to be able to tap into considerable mental resources of belief and conviction because they will always aim to go their own way not to follow the herd. Handelsbanken's Jan Wallander shows how deeply he had thought about the choices he, and they, were making:

> By our philosophy I mean the principle and the outlook on human nature that forms the foundation of the organisation we have built up. How we act in certain situations is then the logical consequence of this central idea and basic sets of values. To these must be added our practical experience and the attitude we have to the management of various issues. This attitude may be characterised by phrases such as 'down to earth', 'pragmatic' and 'little respect for what experts say.' The issues are judged according to their merits and without any side-long glances at what is in fashion just at that moment. We go our own way and feel secure in what we do.[51]

So now we understand the constant attention, commitment and grit required for outside-in companies to stay in orbit and resist gravity. It's not impossible to hold onto outside-in beliefs for generations, as the stories of Handelsbanken, The John Lewis Partnership, Hilti, W.L. Gore and LEGO demonstrate. But it's not easy either.

As we've shown, holding onto the three critical elements – recognising that a shared set of beliefs really matters, sustaining outside-in beliefs with a continual flow of Moments of Belief and being boldest when challenged most and when it matters most – together make the difference and make this feat possible.

Now, in our concluding remarks, we will explore why Moments of Belief are the best way to address the saying/doing gap we see in so many organisations hoping to become customer-led. This is the power of believing in better.

Notes

1   Figures retrieved from https://vp292.alertir.com/afw/files/press/handelsb
    anken/202002135859-1.pdf

2   ibid.

3   ibid.

4   ibid.

5   Saunders, Andrew. 28 June 2017. 'Handelsbanken: A beacon of better
    banking.' *Management Today.* Retrieved from www.managementtoday.
    co.uk/handelsbanken-beacon-better-banking/reputation-matters/article/1
    437348

6   Kroner, Niels. 2011. *A Blueprint for Better Banking: Svenska Handelsbanken
    and a Proven Model for More Stable and Profitable Banking.* Petersfield:
    Harriman House, p. 5.

7   Kay, John. 30 October 2014. 'The Future of Purpose-Driven Business.'
    A Blueprint for Better Business conference proceedings. Retrieved from
    www.blueprintforbusiness.org/wp-content/uploads/2015/04/John-Kay-
    transcript.pdf

8   Milne, Richard. 16 August 2016. 'Handelsbanken fires chief executive
    Frank Vang-Jensen.' *Financial Times.* Retrieved from www.ft.com/content
    /3b90c532-6378-11e6-8310-ecfobddad227

9   Saunders, Andrew. 28 June 2017. 'Handelsbanken.'

10 Wallander, Jan. 1 April 2003. *Decentralisation – Why and How to Make it
    Work: The Handelsbanken Way.* Stockholm: SNS Förlag, p. 38.

11 Wallander, Jan. 1 April 2003. *Decentralisation,* pp. 33–37.

12 One such memoir from October 2017 is provided by Mansfield, Graham.
    9 October 2017. 'Banks' technology teams are a bureaucratic nightmare.'
    eFinancialCareers. Retrieved from https://news.efinancialcareers.com/ch
    -en/297894/banking-technology-problems

13 Wallander, Jan. 1 April 2003. *Decentralisation,* p 125.

14 Wallander, Jan. 1 April 2003. *Decentralisation,* p. 50.

15 Interview with authors, 17 October 2018.

16 Interview with authors, 11 November 2019.

17 Interview with authors, 17 October 2018.

18 Interview with authors, 17 October 2018.

19 Interview with authors, 28 September 2017.

20   Milne, Richard. 19 March 2015. 'Handelsbanken is intent on getting bank-ing back to the future.' *Financial Times*. Retrieved from www.ft.com/cont ent/85640c38-ad2a-11e4-a5c1-00144feab7de

21   Interview with authors, 17 October 2018.

22   Interview with authors, 28 September 2017.

23   Interview with authors, 13 January 2020.

24   Interview with authors, 26 November 2019.

25   Interview with authors, 19 October 2018.

26   Interview with authors, 19 October 2018.

27   Interview with authors, 19 October 2018.

28   Interview with authors, 19 October 2018.

29   Henley, John. 16 March 2010. 'Is John Lewis the best company in Britain to work for?' *The Guardian*. Retrieved from www.theguardian.com/business /2010/mar/16/john-lewis

30   John Lewis Partnership. n.d. 'The John Lewis Partnership Constitution.' Retrieved from www.johnlewispartnership.co.uk/content/dam/cws/pdfs/ Juniper/jlp-constitution-feb-2020.pdf

31   Henley, John. 16 March 2010. 'Is John Lewis the best company in Britain to work for?'

32   Interview with authors, 15 October 2015.

33   Henley, John. 16 March 2010. 'Is John Lewis the best company in Britain to work for?'

34   Henley, John. 16 March 2010. 'Is John Lewis the best company in Britain to work for?'

35   Hamel, Gary with Bill Breen. 2007. *The Future of Management*. Boston, MA: Harvard Business School Press, p. 86.

36   Epiphany Admin (YouTube channel). 11 February 2015. 'Team Building Terri Kelly' (Video). Retrieved from www.youtube.com/watch?v= -50Zh9lQhyk

37   Epiphany Admin (YouTube channel). 11 February 2015. 'Team Building Terri Kelly'.

38   Hamel, Gary. 2 April 2010. 'W.L. Gore: Lessons from a Management Revolutionary, Part 2.' *Wall Street Journal*. Retrieved from http://blogs.wsj .com/management/2010/04/02/wl-gore-lessons-from-a-management-rev olutionary-part-2/

39   Hamel, Gary. 2 April 2010. 'W.L. Gore.'

40 Kelly, Terri. 9 December 2008. 'Nurturing a Vibrant Culture to Drive Innovation.' *MIT World*. Retrieved from https://techtv.mit.edu/videos/16462-nurturing-a-vibrant-culture-to-drive-innovation

41 Handley, Lucy. 27 April 2018. 'How marketing built Lego into the world's favorite toy brand.' *CNBC*. Retrieved from www.cnbc.com/2018/04/27/lego-marketing-strategy-made-it-world-favorite-toy-brand.html

42 Delingpole, James. 18 December 2009. 'When Lego lost its head – and how this toy story got its happy ending.' *Daily Mail*. Retrieved from www.dailymail.co.uk/home/moslive/article-1234465/When-Lego-lost-head--toy-story-got-happy-ending.html

43 LEGO. n.d. 'Disaster strikes.' LEGO website. Retrieved from www.lego.com/en-us/lego-history/disaster-strikes-b19dce5285564b368bd48342f70b4c23

44 LEGO. n.d. 'Entering the age of plastics.' LEGO website. Retrieved from www.lego.com/en-us/lego-history/entering-the-age-of-plastics-cef6607f3856452d920b728b982ce947

45 Delingpole, James. 18 December 2009. 'When Lego lost its head.'

46 Nipper, Mads. 9 September 2011. 'The Central Role of Customer Insights: How LEGO Group Leverages Consumer Insight and Engagement to Feed its Innovation Process.' IMD CMO Roundtable, IMD Lausanne, Switzerland.

47 Grolleman, Jaap. 10 August 2010. 'Rebuilding the Brick: LEGO Case Study.' Jaap Grolleman blog. Retrieved from https://jaapgrolleman.com/2010/08/10/6/

48 Jenkins, William. 6 June 2015. 'Lego: Entrepreneurship Education for Kids.' *EduTech Stories*. Retrieved from http://edutechstories.blogspot.com/2015/06/lego-entrepreneurship-education-for-kids.html

49 Delingpole, James. 18 December 2009. 'When Lego lost its head.'

50 *BBC*. 6 March 2018. 'Lego admits it made too many bricks.' *BBC News*. Retrieved from www.bbc.co.uk/news/business-43298897

51 Wallander, Jan. 1 April 2003. *Decentralisation*, p. 50.

CONCLUSION

BELIEVE IN BETTER

Man is what he believes.

Anton Chekhov

Not long into his tenure as CEO of Unilever, Paul Polman introduced his 'sustainable living plan' motivated in part by customers wanting more ethically sourced products produced in a sustainable manner using less water, energy and packaging. It wasn't clear they would pay more for these qualities though. But the argument ran that if it could be done economically and, therefore, innovatively, then it would be good for the planet and good for customers, and if it was good for them, it would be good for Unilever's brands, employees and shareholders. With the company's shares lagging competitors and the market, Polman offered analysts covering the company this logic but not a business case.

Since his appointment as CEO of one of the world's best-recognised, most widely traded 'large cap' companies, Polman had been unusually strident. In February 2009, on his first day in office, he abolished quarterly earnings guidance saying that the company did not want to attract an investor base that wanted purely short-term financial results steadily rising across rigid timeframes. (He reasoned years later in telling the story that the day on which he was least likely to be fired was his first, so he got the news out then.)

Polman was clear what was required, was ahead of the market and knew his plan would need time to work. Although colleagues and investors didn't have a business case to dissect, it was clear there would be pain before gain. In abandoning earnings guidance, he also appeared to drop previously announced margin targets and Unilever's shares lost 5.8% of their value.

Over the subsequent 10 years, shareholders who bought into the plan were not disappointed. Bloomberg put Unilever's return at 282% compared to 182% for Nestlé shareholders and 131% for investors in the FTSE index over the same period.[1]

Polman's response to critics arguing he could have achieved even higher shareholder returns is characteristically clear:

> We prefer to focus on serving the billions and not the few billionaires. Reaching over 600 million more people with health and well-being, teaching 400 million children handwashing, giving 100 million people access to clean water, providing 5 million more jobs for smallholder farmers, driving gender equality through our value chain or building 25 million toilets is indeed something we are proud of especially as it also has resulted in good returns for our shareholders. Sure, we could have had even higher returns, but then what about all the other stakeholders who help us be successful or what about our desire to be around for hundreds more years?[2]

Polman describes success as serving customers, and he has achieved success by starting with customers and making the business model work to achieve good enough returns for all involved, a truly customer-led approach.

This is returning Unilever to its original purpose. William Hesketh Lever would approve. In the 1890s, the founder of Lever Brothers wrote down his ideas for Sunlight Soap, a revolutionary new product that helped to popularise cleanliness and hygiene in the Victorian slums. He wrote that he wanted to 'make cleanliness commonplace; to lessen work for women, to foster health and contribute to personal attractiveness, that life may be more enjoyable and rewarding for the people who use our products.'[3]

This book describes the critical role of Moments of Belief in bringing a customer-led strategy to life, Moments of Belief such as Paul Polman's abandonment of quarterly earnings guidance and subsequent strong performance, and Arthur T Demoulas' refusal to change his business model so his family shareholders would enjoy higher returns at the expense of Market Basket's customers. Moments of Belief such as Carolyn McCall's challenge to easyJet's discount operating model with allocated seating and Tesco's investment in the unproven One-In-Front initiative. And Moments of Belief such as Hilti's breaking with their commitment to their direct distribution model to widen access, and Martin Glen and Walkers continually improving the quality of their crisps with foil instead of plastic and then nitrogen in place of air inside their packs, or Handelsbanken's Par Bowman and his board's decision to fire the centralising CEO Frank Vang-Jensen.

Moments of Belief are needed most of all by colleagues. They address more than anything else the saying/doing gap we exposed at the outset. They show 'this is for real, and have faith, it works.' In fact, they are doing, not saying.

When a first Moment of Belief is followed by others – a flow of material acts, decisions and choices that starts with what customers value – they become recognised as significant and authentic, not one-offs.

This, we believe, is the only way to establish shared beliefs that are uncommon and that are outside-in. They help everyone understand 'how we work, how we compete, how we succeed, how we create value.' They show 'we are not the same as everyone else.'

Collectively Moments of Belief serve as the backbone of customer-led success. While this is lucrative it remains unusual because despite appearing attractive and obvious from a distance, when everything's working, being customer-led is completely unnatural in practice. So how does this unlikely journey take place?

The move from inside-out to outside-in means a body of people going ahead with initiatives that have definite and immediate costs, with benefits that are probable at best, and in the future, once customers have experienced the improvements, appreciated them and chosen to change their behaviour. For a business, this literally takes conviction and belief that the move will pay off, as we've demonstrated with Unilever's journey under Polman's leadership.

We have seen that businesses only start on this journey when the people involved feel burningness – that the current situation and the current model is on fire, and conventional action untenable if the business is to succeed. Burningness has three possible causes: pain, fear or ambition, and that is in descending order of effectiveness. Pain is most commonly good at creating these conditions because things are going wrong, visibly, viscerally, now. No one can argue with the conclusion that bold action must be taken. Handelsbanken started with pain – a crisis that led to Jan Wallander being recruited and given license to do things his way. easyJet started with pain – a business in need of a turnaround. Later as these businesses gained confidence, they both moved on to ambition.

Fear is a step less convincing because things are fine now; it's just that they are clearly going to get worse at some point in the future. In this situation, the leaders can wait, and often they do. When an established industry sees disruption coming, the first actions only add cost or reduce revenue against a threat that is not completely understood – think about Kodak and digital photography, the music industry and new digital alternatives, the oil industry facing drops in profits as 'easy oil' runs out and environmental pressure heightens, or the automotive industry grappling with transformative change as sales shift and environmental regulations tighten. How quickly and boldly can you tear up your business model given the likely reactions of shareholders, colleagues and the like?

DBS Bank's fear was prompted by seeing first-hand how Chinese disruptors extended their digital messaging, entertainment and commerce platforms into financial services. AO was propelled by fear that in white goods ecommerce, anything other than a decisive customer advantage would see the business crushed by established players. Again, as these organisations progressed further into their journeys, ambition became a driving force, as they continued innovating to improve customers' lives.

Ambition is the least likely cause of burningness to work. This is not because it is weak – far from it. But because it has to come entirely from within. There is no crisis on the horizon. Instead the leader or the leading team has a burning desire to reach somewhere further on, somewhere seriously stretching. We call it burningness because this belief is held so strongly it makes all of the conventional, safe, predictable alternatives unacceptable, leaving only the bold, the mad, the options that are impossible to fully, logically justify. Burning ambition must come entirely from the leaders themselves, not from the external environment. Tesco's leaders were motivated by ambition to beat Sainsbury's, while Bill Gore's frustration with DuPont's way of managing research and development led to his ambition to create W.L. Gore, a company with a single-minded focus on innovation. Sky's desire to 'believe in better' could be applied to all of the outside-in organisations we've profiled. For example, easyJet travelled from turnaround into a purposeful mission to make discount air travel easy as well as affordable.

This explains why the transition from inside-out to outside-in is so rare.

But we have another observation that explains why staying outside-in for generations is even rarer.

We described how an outside-in belief system is only sustained by a continual flow of Moments of Belief, the actions that have clear customer value but uncertain value to the business. We also described how the biggest tests need to be met by the boldest responses, protecting the principle of creating customer value in new and even better ways than the innovative challengers.

But when a business has achieved success through its journey to becoming outside-in in the first place, where can the burningness come from?

Not pain, because things are going well. Not fear, unless it is manufactured and amplified somehow. Only ambition remains. The least effective of the trio.

To stay outside-in, leadership team members must find fire in their bellies, a sense of purpose that means they truly believe in the customer-led mission. It requires them to keep on challenging conventional wisdom, common practice, regulators and even customers who grow to expect what they have always had. It requires them to be willing to teach, explain, illustrate and coach so the unnatural feels natural and customer-led beliefs continue to be widely shared despite the pull of common sense and the easier life of operating inside-out.

When Jeff Bezos talks about retaining the vitality of Day 1 and fending off Day 2, he means outside-in and inside-out. His famous 2016 letter to shareholders[4] is as good a summary of what it takes to stay outside-in as we have seen anywhere.

> Jeff, what does Day 2 look like?
> That's a question I just got at our most recent all-hands meeting.
> I've been reminding people that it's Day 1 for a couple of decades. I

work in an Amazon building named Day 1, and when I moved build-
ings, I took the name with me. I spend time thinking about this
topic.

Day 2 is stasis. Followed by irrelevance. Followed by excruciating,
painful decline. Followed by death. And that is why it is always Day 1.[5]

Even despite this, he knows that the battle is insurmountable. Eventually
inside-out – Day 2 – will win.

Jeff Bezos: Companies have short life spans Charlie. And Amazon will be disrupted one day.

Charlie Rose: And you worry about that?

Jeff Bezos: I don't worry about it 'cause I know it's inevitable. Companies come
and go. And the companies that are, you know, the shiniest and most
important of any era, you wait a few decades and they're gone.

Charlie Rose: And your job is to make sure that you delay that date?

Jeff Bezos: I would love for it to be after I'm dead.[6]

To end *The Customer Copernicus*, we want to focus on the 'saying/doing' gap we
observed at the outset – people say they are customer-led, but they lack the
belief and commitment to do it for real.

While 62% of businesses claim being customer-led is one of the main drivers of success of their business, our data suggest only 24% behave accordingly.
We've explained what being customer-led looks and feels like and emphasised
what is required for the belief in being customer-led to be widely shared and
maintained. We've provided ample evidence that this is good business.

We hope to inspire leaders to have the courage and desire to build truly
customer-led organisations, businesses that create customer value in new
and better ways, and to keep on doing so into the future.

This is business with its original purpose – to do something valued by
customers, to create a customer in Peter Drucker's words.

Every story we've told across many different industries and markets has
one thing in common.

From Hilti's desire to improve working conditions for miners to
Virgin Atlantic's injection of glamour and joy into long-haul flights, and
Handelsbanken's forensic and decentralised approach to customer service
in banking, they all share Sky's desire to 'believe in better.'

By creating and sustaining Moments of Belief, for a finite period of time, our outside-in companies believe in better – for their customers, for themselves, for their industries and for the world at large.

Notes

1   Abboud, Lelia. 29 November 2018. 'High-flying Dutchman Polman divided opinion but leaves positive legacy.' *Financial Times*. Retrieved from www.ft.com/content/565399e4-f3f9-11e8-9623-d7f9881e729f

2   Skapinker, Michael. 11 December 2018. 'Unilever's Paul Polman was a standout CEO of the past decade.' *Financial Times*. Retrieved from www.ft.com/content/e7040df4-fa19-11e8-8b7c-6fa24bd5409c

3   Unilever. 2020. 'Our history: Making sustainable living commonplace.' Unilever website. Retrieved from www.unilever.co.uk/about/who-we-are/our-history/

4   Amazon. 17 April 2017. '2016 Letter to Shareholders.' The Amazon blog. Retrieved from https://blog.aboutamazon.com/company-news/2016-letter-to-shareholders

5   Amazon. 17 April 2017. '2016 Letter to Shareholders.'

6   CBS. 1 December 2013. 'Amazon's Jeff Bezos Looks to the Future.' Interviewed by Charlie Rose, *60 Minutes* (Transcript). Retrieved from www.cbsnews.com/news/amazons-jeff-bezos-looks-to-the-future/

INDEX

Aadhaar card 123
AEG 145
Aggreko 63
airline industry 9, 51, 52, 104–7,
    110, 113, 115, 117–19, 137, 150,
    151, 153–57
Air Zimbabwe 111, 119
Aldi 16, 17, 26, 27
Alibaba 121
Allen, James 3, 11
allocated seating 105–7, 114–16, 119,
    132, 208
Amazon 1, 8, 72, 83, 87, 92, 96, 99, 211
Amazon Prime 83
American Airlines 151, 154
AMP 90
Amstrad 67
Android 164–66
Ansett 151
AO 119, 123–27, 131, 132, 209
Apple 61, 139, 140, 146, 162, 163, 165,
    167, 199
Aristotle 104
Asda 28
ASOS 92
Atom Bank 121
Audi 113
average revenue per user (ARPU) 87
Axe 50

Ballard, Kyle 6
Bank Danamon 121
Barclays 183
Baumann, Alain 194
BCG 155
beliefs 3–16, 18–25, 27–33, 40, 41, 44,
    46–48, 60, 61, 63, 69–76, 78–82, 84–
    94, 96–99, 107–10, 115, 116, 118, 119,
    122, 123, 125–29, 131, 132, 137–40,
    142–46, 149, 151, 152, 155–59, 161,
    162, 164–67, 172–77, 179–83, 185–93,
    195, 197, 199, 201, 202, 207–12
Berlin Wall 76
Bezos, Jeff 1, 72, 87, 210, 211
Big Brother 141
biometrics 123
Blackley, Neil 80
boarding cards 105, 106, 115, 116
Boman, Pär 175, 208
bonuses 7, 89, 158, 173, 186, 189
Booth, Mark 80
Boots 124
BOSS (bums on selected seats) 106
Bouvin, Anders 173, 175, 182
Branson, Richard 150
Brexit 184
British Airways (BA) 151, 152, 155
British Broadcasting Corporation (BBC) 67,
    68, 77, 85, 86

British Satellite Broadcasting (BSB) 76, 77
British Telecom (BT) 35, 80, 88, 136, 140, 141
broadband 79–83, 147
Brown, Darren 6
Brown, Jeremy 154
BSkyB 66–69, 78, 80, 81, 87
burningness 13, 17, 19, 23, 31, 87, 89, 92, 107–9, 111, 114, 116, 119–25, 128, 131, 132, 138, 141–43, 155, 156, 176, 190, 208–10
business class 151
business roundtable 4
business-to-business (B2B) 192

Caddy, Andy 110, 113
Campbell, Neil 56
Campbell-Gray, Gordon 96
Candover 2
Capita 148
Carlton 80
Carphone Warehouse 80, 140, 143
Cathay Pacific 51
Caunce, Steve 126
Cellnet 140, 141
Charles, Bernie 180–82
Cheetos 37
Chekhov, Anton 206
cheques 92, 94, 123, 127
Chisholm, Sam 67, 77
church spire principle 173, 178
Clarke, Philip 27
Clipper teas 116
CNN 76
Coe, Sebastian 68
Cohen, Jack 20
Comcast 88
Comet 124
Commonwealth Bank (CBA) 90
computer says no 177, 185
Computers for Schools scheme (Tesco) 48
co-ownership 186, 188
Copernicus, Nicolaus 5
Corless, Deb 144, 145, 148
Cornell, Brian 62, 63
Credit Agricole 183
Croney, Jonathan 183
customers 1–6, 8, 10–14, 16–22, 24–33, 37, 38, 40, 41, 45, 46, 48–53, 55–58, 61–63, 68, 69, 75, 79, 81–84, 86–89, 91–99, 105, 107, 110, 111, 113, 116–18, 120, 122, 123, 125–27, 129, 130, 136–38, 140–48, 150–52, 154, 155, 157, 159, 162, 166, 167, 173, 177, 181–83, 185, 193–95, 197, 209–11
customer-centricity 7, 14, 142, 148
customer-led 1–6, 8–14, 16, 18–20, 22–26, 28, 29, 31–33, 36–41, 46–49, 51, 53–58, 63, 66, 68–70, 72, 74, 78, 82, 94, 95, 99, 104–7, 110, 114, 117–19, 123, 125–28, 130, 132, 136–42, 146, 149, 151, 156, 162, 167, 172, 174–76, 184, 193–95, 197, 201, 202, 207, 208, 210, 211

Dames, Filip 92–95
Darroch, Jeremy 84, 85
Davis, Peter 55
DBS Bank 33, 119–23, 131, 132, 209; Digibank India 122
decentralisation 20, 175–77, 180, 183, 184, 211
Deliveroo 8, 39, 41, 119, 127–32, 167
Delta Airlines 151, 154
Demoulas, Arthur S. 157, 159
Demoulas, Arthur T. 60, 157, 208
Demoulas, Athanasios 158
Demoulas, George 158
Demoulas, Telemachus 158
Demoulas supermarkets 158
dental floss 189, 193
digital 53, 78–81, 88, 113, 117, 122, 131, 132, 143, 154, 163, 188, 209; photography 120, 209; satellite 80; television 78, 80; video 81
discounts 6, 16, 26, 93, 105, 110, 113–15, 117, 141, 189, 208, 210
discourse 9, 12, 25, 32, 70, 72, 73, 86, 97, 98, 100, 112
Discovery 78
Disney 78, 97
disruption 51, 79, 104, 127, 131, 162, 167, 180, 197, 209, 211
Doritos 37, 39, 43, 44, 46, 51, 52, 54–57
Dove 51
Drucker, Peter 4, 16, 20, 211
Duffy, Peter 106, 107, 113, 116–19
Dunant, Henri 108
DuPont 189, 190, 210
Dyke, Greg 67

easyJet 9, 33, 104–7, 110–20, 131, 132, 156, 208–10; Flight Club 117
Easynet 81

Econsultancy 19
Edison, Thomas 66
electric cars 61
Ereaut, Gill 73, 97
Erskine, Peter 146
Eurosport 76
Evans, Rafaela 159
Expert Logistics 125

Fanny Mae 159
Ferrari 49, 50
Ferry, Joe 150–54, 156
Fever Tree 116
financial crashes 137, 139, 147, 159, 198
fintechs 121–23, 132
football 47, 48, 67–69, 79, 85
Ford 99
Ford, Henry 41
Formula 1 106, 132, 151
Foucault, Michel 72
France Telecom 80, 141
Freddie Mac 159
Free Books for Schools programme 48
Fresh & Easy 26, 27
Frito-Lay 37

Gatwick Airport 107, 111, 152
Genchi Genbutsu 63, 72
General Electric (GE) 29, 52
Gentles, Anthony 53
giffgaff 146
Gledhill, Dave 120
Glenn, Martin 37, 40, 43, 44, 46–48,
    56–58, 62, 208
Godin, Seth 36
Google 140, 165
Gordon, Erik 91
Gore, Bill 189, 190, 193
Gore, Genevieve 190
Gore-Tex 189, 193
gotcha pricing 115
Granada 80
Grandstand 68
Green, Nick 83–86
Green Shield Stamps 20
Greiner, Larry 35
Grolleman, Jaap 200
group pension scheme 179
growth 3, 5, 11, 13, 16, 18, 21, 26, 28, 33,
    35, 36, 38, 39, 42, 46, 48–50, 56, 78,
    79, 82, 85, 87, 92–94, 105, 119, 121,
    122, 124, 129, 131, 140, 141, 147,

148, 152, 156, 162, 163, 165, 190,
    199, 201
Guardian Media Group 112
Gupta, Piyush 120–23

Haji-Ioannou, Stelios 110
Hamilton-Fisher, Gouy 6
Handelsbanken 29, 32, 33, 172–85, 188,
    197, 201, 202, 208, 209, 211
Hannaford 161
Hanson, Sarah 183
Harrison, Andrew 110, 113
Healthy Living range (Tesco) 22
Heathrow Airport 76, 87, 152, 153
Hendricks gin 116
Henry VIII 108
Hill, David 67
Hilti 176, 185, 193–97, 201, 202, 208, 211
Hilti, Martin 194
Hilti Fleet Management 196
Hoelker, Ewald 195
Hubbard, Sid 8
Human-Centered Design Lab 122
Humby, Clive 21
Hutchison 141, 149

IBM 19
IKEA 96
Industrivärden 179
International Air Transport Association
    (IATA) 151
iPhone 99, 139, 146, 162–66, 199
iPlayer (BBC) 85
ITV 67, 77, 86

Jensen, Michael C. 3, 34
Jobs, Steve 162
John Lewis 176, 185–89, 192, 202
Johnson, Mark 90
joint ventures (JVs) 24, 140, 145, 154

Kamprad, Ingvar 96
Kaplan, Robert S. 24
Kasisto 123
Kay, John 71, 174
Keers, Cath 142
Kelly, Terri 191
Kettle Foods 43, 45
Key, Matthew 142, 143, 146
key performance indicators (KPIs) 24, 56
King, Mark 52
King, Martin Luther 109, 110

Knudstorp, Jørgen Vig 199–201
Kodak 120, 209
Kreeger, Craig 154, 155
Kristiansen, Ole Kirk 198

Leahy, Terry 17, 21–23, 26, 27, 32, 57, 61, 114
Lego 176, 185, 197–202
Leicester City Football Club 48
Leighton, Janet 8
Lever, William Hesketh 207
Lever Brothers 207
Lewis, John Spedan 186–88
Lewis, Patrick 188
Lidl 16, 26, 27
Lieberman, Matthew 73
Lineker, Gary 47
Linguistic Landscapes 73, 97
Link, The 146
loyalty schemes 20–22, 50, 51, 60, 114, 117, 150, 157, 158
Lynx 50

MacLaurin, Ian 20, 21, 23
Macquarie 90
MacTaggart Lecture 77
managerial capitalism 3
Mandela, Nelson 76
Market Basket 29, 59, 60, 137, 139, 149, 157–62, 167, 208
Marketing Science Institute 34
Marks & Spencer 20
Marsden, William 159
Martin, Roger 4
Mason, Tim 21, 23, 26, 61
McCall, Carolyn 105–7, 110–15, 118, 208
McLaren 106
McLaurin, Ian 61
Meckling, William H. 3
Meller, Craig 90
Melvin, Andy 67
mergers and acquisitions 77, 91, 121, 149
Merrill Lynch 80
Meyrat, Marco 196
Microsoft 81, 154, 163, 197
Miles, Luke 154
Mill, John Stuart 172
millennium celebrations 145
Millennium Dome 137, 145
Millett, James 113
mining 195, 211

mmO2 136
Moments of Belief 5–7, 11–13, 18, 19, 21–23, 25, 28, 30–33, 41, 47, 78–80, 83–85, 89, 92–94, 96, 98, 99, 107–10, 115, 116, 119, 123, 125–27, 129, 131–33, 137, 140, 143, 145, 151, 156, 180–83, 186, 187, 193–95, 197, 202, 207, 208, 210, 212
Montezemolo, Luca di 50
Montgomery bus boycott 108, 109, 131
Moore, Paul 113
Morgan Stanley 26
Movistar 146
Mugabe, Robert 111
Murdoch, Elizabeth 80
Murdoch, James 81–83
Murdoch, Rupert 66–68, 76, 77, 87, 88
MVNO (Mobile Virtual Network Operator) 145

NAACP 109
Nando's 131
NASA 189
National Australia Bank (NAB) 90
National Geographic 78
nationalisation 140, 174
Neil, Andrew 76
Nespresso 51, 59
Nestlé 59, 207
Netflix 79, 83, 84, 197
News International 48, 77
New Zealand Banking Group (ANZ) 90
Nike 94
Nipper, Mads 199, 200
Nokia 29, 137, 139, 149, 162–67
Nordstrom 3
Northwest Airlines 151
Norton, David P. 24
Now Tv 79, 83–85, 197
ntl 81

O'Brien, Justin 90
O'Leary, Michael 118
O2 9, 24, 29, 51, 56, 136, 137, 139, 140–149, 167
obliquity 174
Office of Fair Trading (OFT) 116
Oktogonen Foundation 179
ONdigital 80
OneAldwych 96
One-In-Front initiative 17, 18, 25, 32, 75, 208

One-to-One 140
online shopping 23, 95, 158
Operation Checkout 20
Orange 80, 96, 140, 141, 149
organisational culture 71
outside-in 3, 5, 6, 9, 11–13, 18, 19,
    23–25, 28–33, 35, 38–41, 45, 46, 48,
    49, 56, 58, 60, 61, 63, 69, 70, 74–76,
    78, 82, 83, 85–89, 92, 94–99, 104,
    107–10, 113, 116, 117, 119, 120,
    122, 123, 126–28, 130–32, 136–39,
    146, 147, 149, 157–59, 161–63,
    167, 174–77, 179, 182, 185, 186,
    193, 194, 197, 199, 201, 202, 208,
    210, 212
Oval tube station, London 53, 54

Pagano, Camillo 59
Parks, Rosa 108–10, 131
partnership 185–89
pay-per-view 78
Pearce, Hannah 180
Penlington, Alan 154
PepsiCo 33, 36, 37, 42, 45, 47, 52, 54,
    55, 57
Peter Jones 186
Petter, John 35
Phileas Fogg 37
Phones4U 140, 143
Polman, Paul 206–8
Pratt & Whitney 52
Premier Inn 114
Premier League 48, 67–69, 78, 79, 88
Pret A Manger 39
Procter & Gamble 85, 193
Prostate Cancer UK 97
PTFE 189, 190, 193
purpose 25–27, 71, 97, 105, 113, 114, 119,
    126, 130, 174, 187, 207, 210, 211

queuing 17, 18, 24, 32, 75, 106, 122, 152

recruitment 7, 21, 180
Ridgway, Steve 150, 152
Ritter, Rubin 95
Roberts, John 123–27
Rockwell, Joseph 159
Rolls-Royce 51, 52
Rolls-Royce Aero Engines 51
Rose, Charlie 211
Rose, Stuart 60
Royal Bank of Scotland 24

Royal College of Art 150
Royal Lancaster Hotel 67
Ruffles 37
Russian Revolution 108
Rutherford, Greg 136
Ryanair 104, 111, 118

Sabena 151
Sahl Taylor, Pernille 180, 181
Sainsbury's 16, 17, 20, 28, 31, 55, 58, 124,
    125, 131, 143, 209
Salancik, Gerald R. 138
sales targets 2, 5, 7, 25, 74, 75, 89, 91,
    92, 173
Samsung 165
Schein, Ed 71
Securicor 140, 141
Segafredo 116
Sensations 37–39, 43–46, 51–53, 55
shareholder value capitalism 3
Shaw's 161
Sheringham, Teddy 68
Shu, Will 128–31
Silvester, Georgina 184, 185
Singapore Airlines 150, 151, 154
SKI/EPSI 173
Sky 8, 33, 66–70, 76–88, 98, 147, 197, 210,
    211; Sky+ 79, 82; Sky Deutschland 87
Sky Go 79, 85; Sky Italia 87; Sky Movies 76;
    Sky News 76; Sky One 76; SkyQ 79, 85;
    Sky Sports 67–69, 79
smartphones 122, 123, 163–66
Smith, Beth 188
Snook, Hans 96
Soames, Rupert 63
Soho House 153
Sony 197
Southern, Julie 152
Southwest Airlines 104
stakeholders 4, 10, 12, 15, 19, 20, 97, 151,
    184, 196, 207
Stansfeld, Mark 142
steadicam 69
Stockholm School of Economics 173
Strambi, Lyell 152, 168
structural equation models (SEM) 15
Stumpf, John 1, 91
Sugar, Alan 67
Sutherland, Glen 53
Swissair 151
Symbian 165
Sørensen, Mikael 181–83

Taoism 53
Tata Group 55
Taylor, Kathleen 73
Teflon 189
Telefonica 137, 139, 140, 146, 148, 149
Tendulkar, Sachin 123
Tesco 9, 11, 16–18, 20–29, 31–34, 38, 47,
    48, 55–58, 61, 69, 75, 88, 114, 128,
    136, 143, 145, 208, 209; tesco.com 21,
    23; Clubcard 21–24, 27, 32, 57; Tesco
    Mobile 24, 145; Tesco Personal Finance 24
Tesla 61, 99
thought for the day 53, 54
Three 148, 149
Timpson 2, 3, 5–8
Timpson, James 6
Timpson, John 2, 3, 6, 8
T-Mobile 140, 149
TotalCare 51, 52
touchscreen phones 163–65
Toyota 63, 72; Toyota Way 63, 72, 100
Transport for London (TfL) 53

Uber Eats 39
ultra-slow-motion 69
Umbro 48
Unilever 50, 206–8
United Airlines 151
US Airways 151

Vang-Jensen, Frank 174, 181, 208
Virgin 29, 81, 113, 137–39, 149–56,
    167, 211; Virgin Atlantic 29, 137–39,
    149–56, 167, 211; Virgin Mobile 81
Vodafone 81, 140

W.L. Gore 32, 33, 53, 176, 185, 189–93,
    202, 210
Waitrose 21, 186, 188
Wakeling, Vic 67, 69
Walker, Henry 42
Walkers 33, 36–54, 56–58, 62, 69, 208
Wallander, Jan 176–78, 202, 209
Wall Street Crash 198
Walmart 61, 161
Welch, Jack 29
Wells Fargo 1, 19, 25, 75, 90, 91
Westpac (WBC) 90
Westwood, Vivienne 154
Whole Foods 161
Wilkinson, David 125, 134
Wilson, Bob 68
World Foods range (Tesco) 22
World War Two 197, 201

Zalando 92–96, 98; Zalando-Lounge 92
Zappos 92
Zook, Chris 3, 11
Zweifel 40

Printed in Great Britain
by Amazon

36909162R00130